D1372055

Future-Proof Web Design

STAM
TK
5105.888
.D3947
2012

Future-Proof Web Design

A Survival Guide

Alexander Dawson

A John Wiley and Sons, Ltd, Publication

STAM
TK
5105.888
.D3947
2012

This edition first published 2012

© 2012 John Wiley & Sons, Ltd

Registered office

John Wiley & Sons Ltd, The Atrium, Southern Gate, Chichester, West Sussex, PO19 8SQ, United Kingdom

For details of our global editorial offices, for customer services and for information about how to apply for permission to reuse the copyright material in this book, please see our Web site at www.wiley.com.

The right of the author to be identified as the author of this work has been asserted in accordance with the Copyright, Designs and Patents Act 1988.

All rights reserved. No part of this publication may be reproduced, stored in a retrieval system, or transmitted, in any form or by any means, electronic, mechanical, photocopying, recording or otherwise, except as permitted by the UK Copyright, Designs and Patents Act 1988, without the prior permission of the publisher.

Wiley also publishes its books in a variety of electronic formats. Some content that appears in print may not be available in electronic books.

DESIGNATIONS USED BY COMPANIES TO DISTINGUISH THEIR PRODUCTS ARE OFTEN CLAIMED AS TRADE-MARKS. ALL BRAND NAMES AND PRODUCT NAMES USED IN THIS BOOK ARE TRADE NAMES, SERVICE MARKS, TRADEMARKS OR REGISTERED TRADEMARKS OF THEIR RESPECTIVE OWNERS. THE PUBLISHER IS NOT ASSO-CIATED WITH ANY PRODUCT OR VENDOR MENTIONED IN THIS BOOK. THIS PUBLICATION IS DESIGNED TO PROVIDE ACCURATE AND AUTHORITATIVE INFORMATION IN REGARD TO THE SUBJECT MATTER COVERED. IT IS SOLD ON THE UNDERSTANDING THAT THE PUBLISHER IS NOT ENGAGED IN RENDERING PROFESSIONAL SERVICES. IF PROFESSIONAL ADVICE OR OTHER EXPERT ASSISTANCE IS REQUIRED, THE SERVICES OF A COM-PETENT PROFESSIONAL SHOULD BE SOUGHT.

978-1-119-97877-0

A catalogue record for this book is available from the British Library.

Set in 10/14 Chaparral Pro by Wiley Composition Services

Printed in Italy by Trento

About the Author

ALEXANDER DAWSON (@AlexDawsonUK) is an award-winning, self-taught, freelance web professional, writer, published author, and recreational software developer from Brighton (UK). With more than 10 years of industry experience, he spends his days running his consultancy firm HiTechy (www.hitechy.com), writing professionally about web design and giving his free time to assist others in the field.

In recent years, Alexander has become an established web writer, providing articles for some of the industry's most respected sites including *Smashing Magazine* and *Six Revisions*. In addition, as a member of the Guild of Accessible Web Designers, he actively promotes and advocates the benefits of a good user experience and web standards. When Alexander isn't coding or writing about design and development, he enjoys a game of tennis or chess and watching movies.

Credits

Some of the people who helped bring this book to market include the following:

Editorial and Production:

VP Consumer and Technology Publishing
Director: Michelle Leete

Associate Director- Book Content
Management: Martin Tribe

Associate Publisher: Chris Webb

Publishing Assistant: Ellie Scott

Development Editor: Colleen Totz
Diamond

Technical Editor: Kayla Knight

Copy Editor: Melba Hopper

Editorial Manager: Jodi Jensen

Senior Project Editor: Sara Shlaer

Editorial Assistant: Leslie Saxman

Marketing:

Senior Marketing Manager: Louise
Breinholt

Marketing Executive: Kate Parrett

Composition Services:

Compositor: Jennifer Mayberry

Proof Reader: Melissa D. Buddendeck

Indexer: Potomac Indexing, LLC

For the long-suffering professionals who work tirelessly to make the web a better place, and those individuals who continue to strive for a more accessible, standards-compliant Internet.

Author's Acknowledgments

Writing a book is always a challenge and this title, in particular, had more ahead of it than many; but with a fantastic group of people behind you, anything becomes possible. As always, my thanks firstly have to go out to the entire team at Wiley (including Chris Webb and Ellie Scott in particular) whose hard work and effort in getting this unusual idea out of my head and into print shouldn't go unsung. Without such an understanding group of individuals who've worked tirelessly at every level (behind the scenes) to ensure the quality of this book and its content, it likely wouldn't have succeeded!

Next, there are three further individuals who deserve an incredible amount of credit. Firstly, I need to give a shout out to my copy editor (Melba) who has done an exceptional job at helping me craft my occasionally mind-boggling prose into something legible! Also, there's my great technical editor (Kayla Knight) who kept my facts in check and offered lots of useful advice to improve the reading experience, making this title all the better for you. Finally, my gratitude has to go out to my editor (Colleen Diamond) who undertook a superhero-like performance, despite the universe attempting to disrupt our efforts.

Next, I would like to thank all of the people who have supported me throughout the writing process: from my friends and followers on social networks, IRC, instant messenger, and the websites where I've written, to the amazing and inspiring individuals who I've met at conferences or just chat to on a daily basis (you know who you are!). Ending this, the biggest thanks of all go out to you, the reader. By purchasing this title, you are supporting months of hard work, and if this book can help you craft flexible, future-proofed layouts that withstand the test of time, accounting for the many variables at work in a site, all of that effort I've put into writing this reference guide will have been worthwhile.

Contents

Introduction

The Web is wondrous. From its humble beginnings as a text-only interface, to its modern incarnation as an interactive, immersive experience, it has suffered many highs and lows (like the move toward web standards or the past obtrusiveness of scripting). Throughout the Web's development, designers have been forced to innovate, endure, and push through limitations to ensure that their sites retain stability and flexibility. By making sites usable in a wide range of situations (future-proofed against changing usage), we can ensure that sites may be enjoyed by the next generation of Internet users, no matter how they use the Web.

Forget dogs. Man's new best friend is the Internet. In a short period of time, the Web has grown from being accessible solely upon a desktop or laptop with one or two browsers to being experienced on netbooks (using one of many configurations), smartphones, and a range of other devices like TV sets! It has become a vital means of communication for the world as well as a port for those seeking knowledge, entertainment, or a place to voice opinions. Also: It can be used practically anywhere and is only limited by our imagination.

With each change and improvement the Web has encountered comes an increasing range and number of tools to help you build more engaging interfaces. However, with the sweet comes the sour. This fast-paced, increasingly diverse medium provides web designers with more challenges than ever to overcome and so many variables to account for. Making our layouts continue to work with old (compatibility quirks in devices) and new situations (future-proofing to withstand the test of time) is an investment to ensure long-term success.

What's This Book About?

If you regularly build web sites, you've probably noticed that your content is consumed in increasingly unique ways. Back in the '90s, you could assume that users accessed your site using a desktop computer, with one or two base resolutions and either Internet Explorer or Netscape Navigator. Today, just trying to guesstimate how much screen real estate a user has is like chasing a pot of gold at the end of a rainbow. You'll either get lucky or end up targeting what doesn't exist (except in legend or mythology), such as the "average user."

During the browser wars (the time of Internet Explorer versus Netscape), web designers focused heavily on ensuring that interfaces worked in specific situations, building rigid, inflexible layouts (because of a lack of situations where diverse layouts would make a real difference). Some designers still build fixed layouts and have failed to notice how the Web's landscape is changing. Variables that used to be considered a safe default no longer apply, attitudes are altering, and the designer's challenge is to understand the scenarios visitors may encounter, determine whether these users require a specific solution, and then account for these factors within his or her site (to encourage visitors to keep visiting the site).

More and more, devices are gaining the "web enablement" treatment. Unique hardware products have gained online support. Software is playing a more active role in how layouts render. New standards and web languages are gaining traction. Even users are changing and adapting their behavior to match new technologies. To stay ahead of the curve, you must ensure that your site functions with what a user has, while also accounting for future variables that may spring up and become popular (as they gain mainstream adoption).

Your work isn't just affected by code and browsers. You need to split apart the various layers of the Web (such as devices, hardware, software, standards, and consumers) to uncover the wealth of factors that can affect your site's stability and users' experiences. Accounting for each layer involves considering what can impact how users interact with your site (such as the operating system or browsers in the case of the software layer), and making sure that your layouts can withstand any changes that may occur as a result of a user's environment.

No Artificial Flavorings

Now that you understand that the Web is evolving, allow me to introduce myself. My name is Alexander Dawson, and I'm a web designer who's been building and improving sites for more than ten years (in addition to writing on the subject). If you're the type of person who relishes any opportunity for trial and error, enjoys learning from the perspective of users, and has a passion for straightforward advice, fantastic! You've got the right book. For those of you who prefer detailed step-by-step instructions, this book may present more of a challenge.

It's worth cutting to the chase and saying that this isn't going to be a progressive tutorial to help you build some mobile layout (or an explicit design for any other type of device, for that matter). Because every situation you design for will be different, my philosophy is that the space in this book is better served by giving you the tools you need to make practical decisions, instead of providing you with a template (or "color by numbers" guide), which really serves its purpose only in a generic environment aimed at a non-existent audience.

This book is not made up of tips and techniques for creating that perfect layout, and it's not a book of inspiration, reeling from the wonderful work of others (though I do encourage design by inspiration). What you will find within these pages is a wealth of information regarding the variables that can affect your sites or render them differently, occasionally causing issues. If the Web were a living, breathing entity, it's *possible* that this book would be considered a guide to its ever-diverse biology and how to ensure its long term health!

My motivation for writing this book is straightforward. As is often the case with designers, I noticed the recent upsurge in new technologies that demanded additional testing, restrictive design considerations, or a more flexible method of serving data. So, my goal within these pages is to break down the misconceptions regarding what makes user experiences unique and to highlight some lesser-appreciated factors in the designer's workflow. By examining the variables listed within this book, you can adapt your sites to meet the needs of each user.

Conventions Within This Book

Many enjoy the free content that gives some extra insight into movies they watch. When it comes to books, I like to think the same is also true. Of course, only so much information will fit within a set number of pages we have to explore this subject, so to give you more for your money, I have planted some useful "extras" within the pages of this book where possible, all with the aim of giving you some food for thought, useful links, and important details to keep you better informed. Keep an eye out for these extras as they appear.

Below are the conventions, with details about their purpose and function:

> **Tips and Notes:** Throughout the book, I provide tips and tricks to give you ideas, words of caution, and important, relevant details that can help you on your quest.

> **Resources:** Don't just take my word for it. Throughout the book I include useful links that expand upon the variables to help you design in various situations.

> **Checklists:** Marking your progress can be helpful and fun. The lists at the end of a variable set goals to help you ensure a site will be as stable as possible.

If you are new to the web design world, you probably should work through this book in order (accounting for each variable as you read about it), but if you are a veteran, you may want to use the book as a quick reference guide, jumping to sections you want to know more about. This will allow you to account for the many cool new technologies on the horizon that will soon become "required reading" and keep up-to-date with the subjects that require our attention to ensure that our work continues to function on legacy devices.

Your Marauders Map

Keeping up-to-date with the latest trends and innovations is tough, especially in the field of web design. Within this book, you'll explore the variables in that environment, learn, or see how designers are trying to maximize performance between platforms, and gain basic advice to help you when venturing into the unknown.

Chapter 1 has one goal in mind: Survival. Because the Web is still evolving at a rapid pace, from time to time new variables appear that must be catered to. They could literally be anything making its first appearance into your workflow; don't you just love surprises! Perhaps it'll be one of the predictions made by this book, or something totally obscure. As such, it seems only fitting that you are prepared for whatever may happen, and this chapter acts as a training session before you start engaging in the battle for site stability that's ahead.

Chapter 2 builds on the work of the first chapter, showcasing the methodologies that many designers are using to build increasingly flexible layouts. However you build your sites, accounting for as many variables as possible is important. Getting used to the concepts provided will help you better meet an audience's needs. Because each variable has its own requirements and considerations, applying these useful tricks requires some imagination and clever coding, but this goal is entirely possible to achieve if you put in the hard work.

Finally, you find the variables themselves, the true substance of this book, in a wealth of useful chapters (denoted in the following bulleted list by the category each chapter falls into). Each layer has several chapters, and each chapter has several variables that affect a layout!

Here are the various layers (or factors) of the Web, as covered in this book:

> **Devices:** Desktops, handhelds, entertainment, and appliances (Chapters 3-6)

> **Hardware:** Input and output tools plus environmental factors (Chapters 7-9)

> **Software:** OSs, web editors, browsers, plug-ins, and more (Chapters 10-14)

> **Standards:** Code, third parties, design, and innovations (Chapters 15-18)

> **Consumers:** Robotic influences and human-based factors (Chapters 19-20)

Addressing problems with every variable goes beyond the scope of this book, as there are far too many considerations to account for. If you think about a keyboard, users may have faulty keys, be slow typists, and have access to backlighting or more! This book aims to give you a few pointers in the right direction and actually showcase how complex and intricate the web machine actually is; by doing so, you should be able to consider the tips and tricks that are provided and build better personas and solutions accounting for these variables.

This journey will serve as a landmark for your future design and development projects as you come to appreciate how delicate our sites are against the veritable storm of the under-lying processes involved. By coming to terms with the variables mentioned (and any yet to make themselves known) and changing your way of thinking, you can become a better designer! While this subject may seem overly theoretical, it needs to be explored and the truth is, when we start asking the right questions, good decisions follow.

Building a site is a challenge, and it's one that will only increase in complexity as the Web evolves. We've gone from a world in which desktops ruled like dinosaurs to a landscape filled with many creatures with their own unique characteristics. The thing to remember is that visitors remain firmly in the driver's seat, dictating how they'll engage with your sites. Mobile devices, 3D, new browsers, CSS3, social networks, and more have their unique place in this scenario. As a designer of the next generation of sites, you need to be prepared.

Future-Proof Survival Techniques

Tools for tomorrow's Web

WEB DESIGN PROJECTS contain four essential components. First, you must know your environment. Then you need to plan ahead, learn to adapt, and finish the process by resolving compatibility issues as they arise. Meeting these objectives is challenging, but the work is necessary if you are to successfully future-proof your site. This chapter describes each of these components and illustrates the importance of being flexible to change your way of thinking about your design methodology, now and in the future.

Understanding the Environment

When you design a site, understanding the environment where it will exist is critical. You need to know what factors increase or decrease the chances of your site being noticed, and you need to be familiar with the tools visitors will have at their disposal when interacting with your site. Understanding what makes up the Web's current incarnation is important, as is learning what is and isn't possible (or useful) when designing for it. Before you can access any of that information, however, a number of untruths need to be dispelled.

The truth behind terminology

Throughout the Web's history, designers have become adept at assigning names to things, even if the names aren't required or deserved. Names have been assigned to specific technologies, techniques, and events that occurred long ago, and abbreviations have been created that try to encompass entire technologies. Although some of these terms (for example, HTML and CSS) do a great job at identifying an important technology, an unfortunate slew of buzzwords has been forged, leading to confusion among designers.

Here are three of the biggest offenders:

> AJAX

> Web 1.0, Web 2.0, and Web 3.0

> the Mobile Web

Although forged from the technologies it employs, AJAX (asynchronous JavaScript and XML) didn't need a shorthand name because developers were already employing these techniques in their work. The mechanism behind AJAX is a sound one, in that you can avoid page refreshes by pulling or pushing data from the server to a user's device in the background, but as far as the stability of your site is concerned, the mechanism can be fraught with problems, such as the unavailability of scripting.

Ubiquitous and future-friendly layouts cannot be obtained by jumping onboard with every new technique or technology as it arrives (as AJAX shows). No matter how popular these buzzwords become, the name of the technique is never important; what matters is the problem that the technology aims to solve and whether it, in fact, solves it. A great example of this is the Web 1.0 to 3.0 movement. The terms themselves have little meaning except to try to "mark" the Web's evolutionary progress. Yet, for all of its public appeal, it solves nothing.

Note

What makes buzzwords extra confusing is that some of them have different connotations, so they can mean different things to different people or in different situations. Web 2.0, for example, isn't just a defining era of the Web; it's also a highly recognized design trend.

Terms like *Web 2.0* have come to mean different things to different people, and often just stereotype sites as meeting a list of criteria that keeps them current. The trouble is that not all users will demand the same things and not all devices or browsers will be capable of reliably implementing the proposed features, which, as such terms imply, are critical to the evolution of the Web. In essence, not all sites require AJAX or collaboration features, and including them could damage a user's experience on your site.

I've established that AJAX can be problem for certain users and that Web 2.0 doesn't offer a firm solution to help create or maintain a stable and usable site, so the next step is to investigate what's been dubbed *the Mobile Web*. This term appeared when the use of handheld, non-desktop, web-enabled devices increased, which put pressure on designers to make their sites mobile friendly. Unlike Web 2.0, this term makes some practical sense, but the trouble begins when you try to define what actually constitutes a "mobile" device, and trying to define mobile variables just creates more questions, including these:

> If mobile just equates to a small screen, aren't laptops mobile?

> If mobile is about not being "desktop," are 100-inch TVs mobile?

> If mobile is focused on the new wave of technology, what about PDAs?

> Perhaps mobile equates to data speed, so what about dialup users?

If your aim is to make a flexible and usable layout, all that matters is that users of such devices can take advantage of your site. To achieve this goal, avoid stereotyping users' needs and situations and build real-world solutions that are flexible and durable enough to accommodate every environment, whether it's a handheld device with a touch screen attached or a desktop computer with a large display, mouse, and keyboard.

Mythology and folklore in design

In the following sections, I confront a few common myths in web design. The information in these sections will help you look beyond the old one-size-fits-all environment and begin to understand the need for layouts that flex to your users' demands. The critical thing to take away is that no silver bullets or shortcuts can ensure a stable site that'll last into the future. Instead, future-proofing your site includes balancing the needs of users with the tools you can provide.

Myth #1: Layouts can be made to appear pixel-perfect

Web designers try to make the sites they design look and feel as consistent as possible in various environments, but the idea of being pixel-perfect is flawed. By making something *pixel-perfect,* I mean trying to enforce strict viewing guidelines akin to those in the print industry, thereby making everything look the same in every situation. Because so many variables play a role in a site's rendering, situations will continue to exist where users experience some kind of limitation. Perhaps they're missing speakers for sound, or they navigate using a dodgy browser. Not all experiences are created equal.

Note   For older devices, pixel-perfect layouts were impossible from the outset. Desktops could handle feature-rich HTML and CSS layouts with plenty of complex interactive features, but traditional featurephones could handle only WML code devoid of the stylistic beauty and script-powered behavior that desktops were afforded for years.

The truth is, user experiences don't have to be identical for your site to work. You may actually want to design so that user experiences differ among platforms and make your site more usable. You might offer separate, altered experiences based on the capabilities of the different devices. (Note that a unique WML layout was compelling for older hand-held devices.) As long as your content remains visible and users are willing, within reason, to adapt their navigation techniques to interact with your site in a way that matches the requirements of their devices, you don't need to worry about precision design.

Myth #2: Designs can be considered "complete"

I'm a big believer in continued improvement, and because standards and use of sites will always be changing, based in large part on users' activities and preferences, sticking with one layout and declaring to the world "I'm finished" is . . . well, surely said in jest. Your goal as a designer is to make sure your site continues to gauge the interests of users, and although you don't want to redesign a site every week, it makes sense to iterate and improve your services regularly (as shown in Figure 1-1). As technologies and best practices change, new methods to help your visitors will appear.

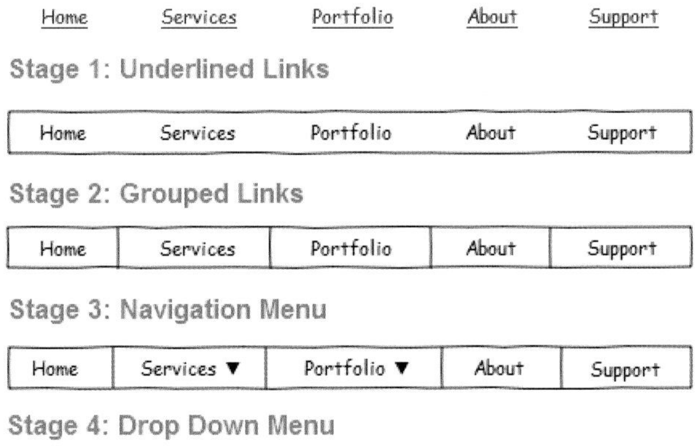

Home   Services   Portfolio   About   Support

Stage 1: Underlined Links

| Home | Services | Portfolio | About | Support |

Stage 2: Grouped Links

| Home | Services | Portfolio | About | Support |

Stage 3: Navigation Menu

| Home | Services ▼ | Portfolio ▼ | About | Support |

Stage 4: Drop Down Menu

FIGURE 1-1: Iteration allows designers to continually improve their work.

The idea behind a *completed site* is that nothing can be done to make it better, which doesn't add up. Improvements can always be made and new features can always be added. Also, be sure to maintain and update the content on your site to encourage visitors to return. If you own the site that you're building, you can set it up so that iteration can occur naturally. When you're building for clients, suggest that they establish maintenance schedules and frequently improve the content of their site.

Myth #3: A design can be totally bulletproof or future-proof

Although this book's goal is to help you maintain stability in a layout and make your site as future-proof as possible, ultimately no design is immune from all that the Web can throw at it. When a site is said to be *bulletproof,* it means that the site won't fall apart under any circumstance. That a site can be bulletproof is an idealistic and unattainable notion. When a site is said to be *future-proof,* the implication is that the site will work successfully forever, across new devices and emerging platforms, all while maintaining compatibility with previous browsers and devices. In this book, I do my best to help you head toward that goal, but as much as I'd like to guarantee that goal, I can't, because the Web is far too unpredictable.

By considering the variables in this book, you can better address the concerns that designers of today's sites deal with. Keep in mind that those variables will play an important role in the Web's future landscape. But who knows what's on the horizon? In ten years, the Web may change so drastically that designers will once again find themselves building sites in new, unconventional ways. Perhaps a whole new range of variables will exist. Ultimately, all you can do is use the information you have and make the most of it.

Myth #4: Validation ensures quality and compatibility

Many Web designers make the mistake of taking validation of code as a guarantee of standards, which is why you see so many of those "Valid" buttons embedded within so many sites (see Figure 1-2). However, as you probably already know, you can have some of the best-formed code and still see quirks and inconsistencies in how a site will render among browsers and devices. This isn't to say that validation is useless because, for example, knowing how to spot bugs that could lead to quirks is important. They just aren't a silver bullet for ensuring the stability of websites.

FIGURE 1-2: Validation buttons don't guarantee the quality of code or impress average visitors.

Validation is a useful tool that can help identify common flaws and mistakes that designers make when coding. Including validation in your workflow is useful, but it's just a tool. Don't consider validation programs as an alternative to or replacement for testing your work properly, and don't assume that all validation programs work equally well. Accessibility validators are notoriously bad at uncovering major failings in accessibility; manual testing is the only safe option.

Myth #5: The newer, the better — the more, the merrier

Designers often get carried away in their bid to be creative, and more importantly, they can be overly zealous about how much of a good thing their visitors will enjoy. In an effort to stay current, some designers revamp their sites regularly, when redesigning is clearly unnecessary; or they add too much information, media, or imagery to their pages thinking that substance in great quantity encourages more interaction. Of course, keeping your design and content updated is necessary; just be rational about when and how to do so.

Note Be sure to remove clutter from your interfaces. Often, pages become stagnant and bloated as a result of mismanagement or residual features such as animation effects that you think look great but offer no real benefit to users. Overuse of design or content is a common problem, so try to keep your designs tasteful.

Incorporating the latest and greatest features can be an improvement if your goal is to improve users' experiences. If you use these features mainly to compensate for poor-quality content, you could create a real problem for visitors to your site. For each new redesign you create, just remember that your visitors' learning curves will increase because they must readapt to the new interface. The same goes for bundling more features and content on a page. Simplicity is often better than complexity. Keep in mind that adding features and too many choices may be a burden for some visitors.

Myth #6: You profile the average user or device

Design is rarely an objective art form, and as much as designers want to base their decisions on the needs of users, designers' personal biases and skewed perspectives can influence their work. For example, when designers think of a visitor, they often visualize an idealized visitor rather than one based on reality. Moreover, when designers try to profile the type of environment visitors will be using, those profiles may fail to take into account the differences between different users' experiences. The idea that an "average" user (Figure 1-3) or browsing environment exists is unrealistic.

FIGURE 1-3: Designers often use personas to group variables together, forming a browsing scenario.

The differences among the environments where your site must function can be substantial — for example, whether Flash or JavaScript are supported. The differences among users are important, too. Some users may encounter accessibility issues, and others may simply be more selective in the features they've enabled. Designing for ubiquity requires looking beyond stereotypes; instead, you need to be open and adaptable in terms of your audience. Promote equality and be flexible with whatever your site needs to function. By doing so you'll end up with a stable and usable layout.

Keeping up with the Joneses

Designing for next-generation devices poses a real challenge. After all, how can you be expected to design for something that doesn't exist or, if it does exist, hasn't gained widespread adoption? Consider how the Web works on cellphones and tablets. In a few years, the Web may work on all sorts of other unique devices, such as televisions. When you think about it, gadgets like the iPod Nano have the potential for web enablement, and it's only the size of a wristwatch, so imagine how diverse web experiences may become!

Hardware is becoming less expensive to produce, and infrastructure for web connectivity is gaining adoption worldwide (even in hard-to-reach places like Mount Everest). This situation fosters the perfect environment for ubiquity because reduced cost and low-barrier entry encourages more people to go online using devices they have handy, be it in their homes, offices, or on the move. As the number and variety of devices used on the Web increases, you have two options: Patch as new devices appear, or be generic, yet flexible, regarding usage.

When a new device gains popularity, many designers immediately patch their sites to support it, target the device for a special independent site that caters to the platform, or just ignore it. These don't seem like good options because they require you to choose what you will support and provide constant patches to the ever-growing technologies that arrive online. In some situations, but not all, a separate site might be helpful.

Reference

The debate over separate versus internal sites has been brewing for a while, leading to the idea of "One Web." Some individuals believe this principle can achieve discrimination-free usability; others believe in the stricter definition of eliminating all proprietary, single-case solutions (which means demands ensuring that everything works for everyone). Check out Opera's view of the "One Web" debate at this site: http://www.opera.com/business/oneweb/.

A better approach is to examine the symptoms, make a diagnosis, and find suitable solutions to treat the condition. It isn't the brand or model that makes a device; the components make the device. The inside of an iPhone and the code it supports (such as HTML) differ significantly from what you find in a Nokia 6610i (which supports only WML, as shown in Figure 1-4). The issue boils down to two independently built renderers doing what they can.

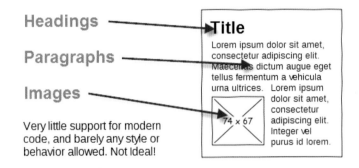

FIGURE 1-4: When compared to today's rich and engaging HTML and CSS, WML is a real ugly character.

Ultimately, the choice to keep up with the trends or retain support for only a select few of your audience's situations is entirely up to you. It may be impractical to produce a site that is so flexible that it supports every type of product and situation without issue, and if you know what your audience requires, there's no need to go over the top, covering all possible bases. However, unless you have a good reason to do otherwise, ensuring that your site caters to as many situations as you can eliminates the need to patch your site's code in the future.

The browser wars proved that creating sites that depended on everything rendering in one way was problematic. Designers have since adopted more stringent measures for testing workflows. Currently, designers are struggling with the fact that devices and platforms force you to rethink how you present and organize content. In the future, perhaps your next tussle will be over dependency on frameworks, the continued support for deprecated code, or something else entirely. I do enjoy a good mystery—don't you?

Planning for a Successful Website

Understanding the environment you're designing for is critical when building a site, and knowing the needs of your audience is critical to a successful design. After all, recognizing potential situations beforehand allows you to make more informed, practical choices. With information about a user's environment, you can avoid making potentially costly mistakes that could reduce a site's usability, and by planning ahead, you can direct your attention to specific aspects of a design that may be more open to implementation quirks than others.

Determining project requirements

When developing for the Web, you must be able to determine the requirements and needs of a project. Often, for service providers, the demands of a project include the additional features, functionality, and layout choices that users may find helpful. For situations in which you produce work for clients, the ability to look beyond just the scope of a site and into the future needs of their businesses will help ensure that the design works for the specific audiences the clients are targeting. Because every site will be different, catering to niches is important.

The initial requirements that influence your tactics are those laid down by the users of the site. Happy visitors often result in customer loyalty, so, whenever you can, put users first. Ensuring that your users have access to sites and services regardless of the platform or device they use (which equals ubiquity) means that you can more easily get them to choose you over a competitor — and choice is a powerful motivator.

Here are some features that make for happy users:

> Consistency in a site's design

> Accessible and easy-to-use layouts

> Aesthetically pleasing designs

> Goal-oriented, useful layouts

Remember, the benefits of a ubiquitous interface extend beyond what the user sees and the devices the user uses to access your site. The number of social networks, search engines, and third-party tools connecting to your site is increasing, and it's likely that the more demanding and restrictive methods they use to view and utilize your content will become increasingly important. Just think about software like Instapaper or an RSS reader, and you'll understand how your site can be interpreted by a machine, not a human being; any errors affecting it will certainly reflect in the output.

Here are some features that make for happy robots:

> Search engines may struggle with proprietary code.

> Social networks require meaningful, contextual data.

> Browsers demand well-formed code to render pages.

If you're working for a client, you can't just plan around the needs of your users and the specific devices they use or the automated solutions that exist; you must also plan around the business or client. Clients may have certain niche requirements — if they are making an intranet, for example — or perhaps they want the added usefulness of platform-explicit applications (such as those in Android's marketplace or Apple's App Store). These days, sites encompass many more options than they used to, and every site's require-ments will be different.

Note

Consider the client-user scenario as an adaptation of the "three laws" from Isaac Asimov's *I, Robot*. Sites cannot harm a user, must obey clients' orders (unless it violates the first law), and must do the same for designers (unless it violates the previous two). With this idealistic balance, the designer's priorities should be set.

The needs of a site depend on the factors described in this section. You'll probably spend as much time researching what is needed on an interface as you do building it. In a design-er's ideal world, people would conform to stereotypes, devices would be standardized, and clients would jump for joy at the thought of accessibility. Unfortunately, you don't live in an ideal world, and it'll be many years before widespread compatibility and ubiquity will exist (if it comes to exist) because meeting expectations can be fraught with hurdles. Changing dogmas or perceptions takes time.

Setting goals while dodging holes

As the Web has evolved, designers have found themselves playing a superhero-like role, which you'll understand if you're a fan of fantasy and shows such as *Buffy the Vampire Slayer*. Buffy worked her way through demons, taking on increasingly dangerous and deadly foes (you can relate to this if you've coded for Internet Explorer 6), and ended up in a final showdown with the "big bad." In the show, overcoming each challenge on the path to winning the war wasn't a matter of luck or charging in blindly; it involved careful planning and research.

Because each user and situation is different depending on the type of site being built, you must carefully consider any implementation that enhances or degrades a user's experience. You need to establish primary goals to ensure that decisions are made for the right reasons. Perhaps your site will require visitors to enter some log-in details, but remember that input mechanisms can vary among web devices. Maybe a visitor will browse while on the move. These kinds of situations can trigger and affect the many variables you must consider.

The following situations affect specific factors or variables:

> HD video is affected by bandwidth and connection speeds.

> Color is eliminated if a visitor has a monochrome display.

> Mouse precision and accuracy are affected by click regions.

During the brainstorming stage, establishing where and how a site might be used is a great idea. Sites that compare prices of products are likely to be in heavy demand while visitors are on the move — for example, traveling on primary business streets and in shopping malls. The use of sites like the Internet Movie Database require specific consideration because they may be used in collaboration with cinemas, rental shops, and media retailers. Creating scenarios or profiles of these actions help you gauge targeted markets, although, of course, users browse in other kinds of situations, too.

The trick is to determine which influences and variables will affect your users; what those effects will be; how you can ensure that the interface will cater to your specific audience without negatively affecting others; and how to implement required changes in the most suitable way. Making these determinations requires a fundamental understanding of how human-computer interactions work and of the subtleties of users' devices. For example, a smartphone may be subjected to data caps and roaming charges, and an old desktop computer may have a slow or low-quality connection (see Figure 1-5). Goals must always be identified within the context of acceptable methods of interaction.

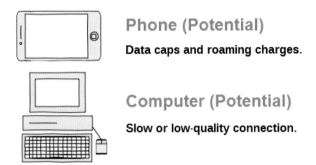

Phone (Potential)

Data caps and roaming charges.

Computer (Potential)

Slow or low-quality connection.

FIGURE 1-5: Certain situations may require you to consider how data-heavy your sites and pages are.

Dodging some of the major pitfalls in design can be tricky, especially if you've become comfortable that what you have "works." Ultimately, for any plan involving the longevity of a site, you need to observe changes in patterns of use, determine methods for improvement, and identify potential causes of concern. However, keep in mind that because the Web is constantly evolving, new standards will make providing flexibility increasingly convenient (as is the case with CSS media queries), and, as a result, your solutions can be better implemented.

Planning for implementation

Planning for the implementation of a ubiquitous site can be challenging. All too often, you'll find yourself asking a variety of questions about your audience that have, in turn, a variety of answers. For example, what screen resolutions do they use? What browsers do they use? Do they visit the site on cellphones? Does your site please or somehow irritate them? You have many design and development tools available, and with tweaks, they'll aid your ubiquity goals.

Planning ahead makes building a successful site more feasible. When envisioning your site, plan for code and a design that are well formed and as uncomplicated as possible. Set clear objectives and be willing to compromise for the sake of your users. While planning, identify where you can make implementations more accessible to and useful for your site's users, as well as related variables they will interact with. Remember to set realistic goals; otherwise, your site may fail users in some way.

Note

Treating how users will access and use your site as an afterthought is very risky. Every site relies on content and functionality; nevertheless, the basic design of the layout should always make users the top priority.

Ideally, the process of determining site-specific goals begins with competitor analysis and user testing. Next, you use wireframes, prototypes, mockups, concept sketches, and other tools to discover the specific needs of the project. If you think users may want something, don't shy away from considering it. Planning can become second nature, once you get into the swing of things. Moreover, if you determine the needs of clients or of visitors to a site, you can implement suitable outcomes, right from the start. At its heart, web design involves inspiration, iteration, formulation, and publication (see Figure 1-6).

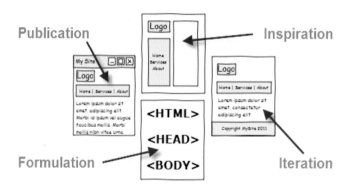

FIGURE 1-6: Inspiration, iteration, formulation, and publication are critical elements of web design.

Consider the issue of whether to offer a secondary mobile-oriented site. If you provide a separate site for visitors who are using less-capable devices, those visitors might avoid optimized environments entirely. Therefore, it's important to give them the option of returning to the "full site" (if, for example, the optimized version is slimmed down, offering users less content). Remember, having choices empowers users.

When you empower users, you give them a sense of control, enabling them to feel as though they aren't just at the mercy of a site's demands. Perhaps you deem CSS or JS a necessity. That would be fine if it couldn't be turned off, disabled, or unavailable. The best approach is to plan for the worst and hope for the best. If you make your content available to even the weakest link in the chain and, at the same time, enhance the experiences in more unique situations, you'll ensure the maximum visibility of your content.

Learning to Adapt or Evolve

You know what's going on, and you have a clever plan to provide a service that will be the envy of your competitors. Fantastic! Next on the agenda is deciding how to adapt your best-laid plans to particular environments. If you get dropped into a jungle, you don't act like you landed in Siberia. Likewise, online, you'll need a box of tricks to cope with the many different requirements a site may throw at you. Every site is different, as is its audience. Your job is to be prepared to find the answers to the difficult questions that environments can present.

Taking advantage of new technologies

Although you don't want to use every new technology just for the sake of keeping up appearances, you also don't want to let your concern over compatibility get the better of you. In an effort to appease the "old ones" (for example, Internet Explorer 6), many web designers have failed to take advantage of CSS3 (for example) purely because it creates inconsistencies with a browser's older counterpart. Although I'm all for compatibility, as I said earlier in this chapter, trying to be pixel-perfect is neither worth the effort nor possible.

Compatibility should always be possible because of the following:

> If everything is disabled, content is the one thing that remains visible.

> Many technologies, when unsupported, can have an appropriate alternative.

> Targeting specific variables allows you to offer independent fallbacks.

Going beyond the bare necessities with your code is, of course, entirely possible. If you want to provide a particular piece of functionality, make sure you have a *fallback* (alternative) for users who are less fortunate. Such functionality can work against making a site ubiquitous, but that will occur only if you fail to update the site as new and better solutions arise. Ideally, rather than restrict yourself to a limited layout, train code around issues as they appear (see Figure 1-7).

As a web designer, you have a responsibility to your clients and customers. Failings on your site raise the risk of losing visitors, even if the failings are just small, but annoying, quirks. Knowing how to write code for a site helps you understand in advance where experiences can falter, provided that you take steps to ensure that your work flows and responds appropriately to user interaction and the environment in which it's consumed. If you ignore the signs, however, issues are likely to occur and reoccur.

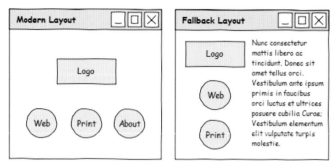

CSS3 and jQuery content
"on-demand" navigation.

Compatible CSS 2.1 and
traditional "flexible" layout.

FIGURE 1-7: There's no shame in providing Internet Explorer 6 users with a very usable and satisfying experience.

As the use of tablets increased in popularity, web designers on the cutting edge began to investigate how this unique input method could affect interactions on sites. At first, it seemed strange that people might not be using a mouse or keyboard. Continued study is the best route to understanding any device or design variable.

You want to make your site as unique and easy to use as possible—and give users a memorable experience (don't go over the top). Designers have come to look fondly on trends (see Figure 1-8), conventions, and patterns for this very reason. Part of adaptation is moving with the times, working with your surroundings, and recognizing when views of how the Web should operate alter over the years. Maintaining a high level of awareness and staying ahead of the curve makes sense.

FIGURE 1-8: Following trends isn't a bad thing, especially because they're usually based on established solutions.

Sometimes *cutting edge* or *bleeding edge* is used in reference to designers or developers who use tools that aren't yet supported by the mainstream. Although both the cutting and bleeding edge may appear as unsuitable candidates for crafting a stable site, using one or a mixture of both can be done in such a way that those who have access to the supporting tools benefit and those who don't have access have something just as fitting to use in its place.

If your competitors are going to provide support for a tool, and you look around to find that you could be the last person standing in the traditional-techniques circle, it may be time to investigate whether moving on can benefit your audience. Often, new technologies provide designers with appealing solutions that otherwise wouldn't be possible (for example, CSS sprite rollover menus). Many designers keep an eye on sites that use cutting-edge work, looking for inspiration and creative ways to polish their own skills.

Adapting your site to account for the many existing variables gives you insight into the habits of users and how they embrace technology, and it gives you the opportunity to offer them more user-centered designs. You will see an increase in the use of small screens and the removal of the barriers of fixed-width design. Also, you'll see how reducing the requirement for inputting text helps users without quick access to a normal keyboard. Creating future-proof sites is about molding platforms around experiences that can benefit every user.

Solutions for a successful layout

This section covers techniques for producing first-rate, scalable layouts. Before you can understand design variables in their entirety, you must first be conversant with the methods designers use to make layouts as flexible and future-proof as possible. This information includes making decisions about which methods you will use, why using a particular technique will benefit your audience, and which of the many layout techniques will sustain the highest levels of ubiquity.

Consideration #1: Need versus none

At first glance, it may appear a bit silly to ask, "Do I really need a flexible site?" For the purpose of this discussion, the aim isn't to question whether having a flexible site is a good thing, because clearly it is. Also, if you design flexible layouts from the outset, you will reduce the chances that users will face problems with your site later on. However,

understanding the needs of your audience can tell you a lot about their specific requirements or about non-issues that may influence decisions to build or postpone the implementation (see Figure 1-9).

It's not a desktop computer, so flexibility is required!

FIGURE 1-9: If a site primarily attracts users of desktop browsers, you could postpone the flexible
upgrade.

If you were to produce a site purely for consumers of Apple products, you would probably
question the need for a stress-testing spree to try out the site with as many emulators,
browsers, and devices as possible. On the other hand, making your site as flexible as possible is important, but there isn't really much point in spending the next year and three
months scaling your site to be in line with every potential variable. Let your users and
their needs determine the level of flexibility and whether you can afford to cut corners.

Consideration #2: Rigid versus fluid

You can lay out content in different ways. In one camp, you have the grounded, rigid units
of measurement that can cause unpleasant horizontal scrolling when the available space
doesn't match the demands of the interface (think fixed designs using pixel widths). In
the other camp, you have fluid designs that are pleasing, until there's too much or too
little assigned space (causing occasional spillages or overflow from scrolling). In both
cases, entire layouts can break if the equations don't add up.

Reference

An article I have written shows how the formats of layouts are changing. Not too long ago, you had only fixed, fluid, and elastic to contend with. Today, you have no less than ten choices! They range from units aimed at print or default preferences to complex mathematically instigated alternatives. For details on how each could affect a design's flexibility, visit this site: http://sixrevisions.com/web_design/a-guide-on-layout-types-in-web-design.

You can choose units of measurement based on compatibility (units aren't treated equally online), on a design method (such as responsive design), and even on a hybrid of one or more techniques. Making the right decision about the mechanism of layouts can play a critical role in how variables interact with a layout and, more importantly, how a page will respond when under stress. You want to base such needs primarily on the requirements of the content and then on the space required for functionality on the web page.

Consideration #3: Dynamic versus static

Dynamic and static layouts also play a part in the construction of sites. *Static designs* are those with little to no interaction, are comprised entirely of text or images, and are more focused on a read-only approach. *Dynamic designs,* on the other hand, usually include scripts, changeable content, features, and perhaps some clever code in order to boost the site's core flexibility (as shown in Figure 1-10). Both of these design types have advantages and disadvantages, and both affect a layout's core stability.

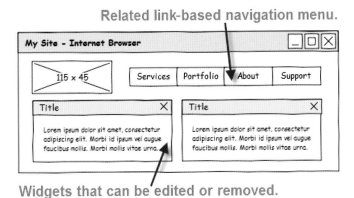

FIGURE 1-10: You may be able to improve the flexibility of dynamic sites by structuring them around visitors' preferences.

Static sites have little going on under the hood. What you see is really what you get. The benefits of this traditional form of layout are that once you've ensured the content scales appropriately, little else beyond the visual arrangement can go wrong. With dynamic sites, you may find that if scripting becomes unavailable or interaction requires additional user involvement, trouble can occur. However, even with such concerns, dynamic sites can offer a greater level of individually oriented flexibility than static sites can, so the payoff might be worth the effort.

Consideration #4: Internal versus external

This consideration relates to how to handle alternative device requirements. Sometimes, designers choose a "one site rules all" approach and account for variables by using scripts or stylistic fallbacks. Tools such as browser-detection scripts, frameworks, and media queries allow the layout's appearance to change based on a user's needs. Although this is the best choice (requiring little added maintenance), the major catch is that it forces you to rethink a site's mechanics, based on assumed scenarios of use. Figure 1-11 illustrates the concept of a script working as a robot to "build" a site around you.

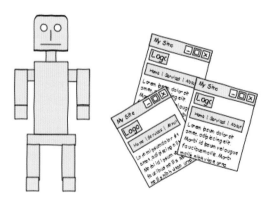

FIGURE 1-11: Scripts act like little robots, reporting on what will or won't work.

If the work of designing for the lowest common denominator isn't your cup of tea, a quick-and-dirty solution is to provide an external site that does the job, similar to what you may have seen in mobile-specific sites. In these optimized layouts, however, you'll often find that content is either "dumbed down" to reduce the pressure of the layout or condensed to make things more lightweight. These layouts, however, beg the question, "If it's not needed on a mobile site, why would you want it on the desktop?"

Consideration #5: Redesign versus realign

If you choose to accommodate various browsing environments, such as the use of specific devices or products by creating separate layouts, you must determine whether to build a new layout entirely from scratch or to realign an existing site's design (if one exists) to consider the more diverse uses being asked of it. Ultimately, situations will exist when a new and separate layout may be beneficial (perhaps for a mobile-only service that's not available for desktops), but in the vast majority of cases, keeping sites together requires less work.

Calculating whether to redesign or realign may be easy, depending on the state of the site in question. For example, if the layout is falling apart, cannot match the needs of the content, or is simply unattractive, redesign it! After all, revitalizing the layout can't make it look, work, or feel any worse to your visitors than it does in the state it's in now, right?

If you choose to redesign a site from the ground up, all your previous work may be wasted. In addition, you'll have to go through various iterations to regain the previous layout's level of flexibility before the total revamp (which means more testing and, perhaps, some secret sauce). Just realigning can be tricky, too, because you may encounter various barriers hiding under the hood, waiting for their moment to break the site or its underlying system.

Consideration #6: App versus online site

This final consideration is a quick one, and it rounds off the fundamental considerations involved in planning a site. First, my question: Should you provide your site in the form of a native, downloadable app or within the wrapper of a well-crafted, browser-based site? As with the previous issue, no one answer will work for everyone. Apps have the advantage for offline use, guaranteed rendering, and more, but because they require no compiling per device, sites require less work, if the variables are accounted for.

Note The divide between services and applications is getting thinner by the day. You can, in many ways, rightfully claim that most apps can be built using modern web browsers, but compatibility remains a constant issue because you'll attract all sorts of platforms.

In the apps versus online debate, I have my own biases and preferences. Desktop apps are suited for situations in which access to a device's native hardware is essential. Also, desktop apps are ideally suited if you want to build a single app for a specific platform (such as iOS). In my opinion, however, beyond those exceptions, web apps are the better option: You ensure that users have the most recent version, you can build for every platform equally, and in most cases, web apps can be made to perform offline.

Beyond design: An essential business guide

Because building sites is a business for many (if you're reading this book in an attempt to improve your own quality control, this includes you), I need to offer some cautionary words about how striving to survive the Web's future may affect the way you craft or maintain interfaces, and how you bill for doing so.

First, the all-important consideration: money. Budgeting for the work you will do to bring an older, less flexible site into the "here and now" is a complex calculation. At one time, you could design sites so that they were cross-compatible by writing well-formed code (which designers often failed to do). Justifying it as cost-effective wasn't difficult because you could literally see bandwidth bills drop (moving on from messy and inaccessible table-based layouts). Now it's a different story with fewer immediate gains or losses involved (see Figure 1-12).

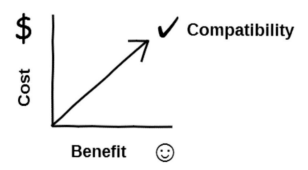

FIGURE 1-12: The extra costs of ensuring flexibility can result in a bigger audience.

Building a mobile-friendly site demands regular testing, and not on the same level as in the old days. Testing on large numbers of browsers, both desktop and handheld, can adversely affect billable hours, and testing on physical devices could potentially be very costly if you want to guarantee device-specific support. Because of the overwhelming array of possible combinations of browsers and devices, testing on all of them will be impossible, so you need to find ways around this issue in order to test as economically and accurately as possible.

Also, you must consider the increased time it could take to build such a scalable site. If a site was originally built with flexibility in mind, updating it with newer variables probably will not take as much time as it would to bring an older, less flexible site up to modern standards. Be sure to account for how long you'll assign to the test phase, which types of tests you'll run, and if you want to consider only a baseline set of commonplace variables in your package, providing less common ones as "billable extras."

Tip   If you're like me, you probably find checking off your progress helpful. By determining a set range of variables you're willing to test against and estimating how long you believe each test will take, you can plan a release cycle fairly accurately.

Furthermore, part of the process of running a business relates to how well you understand your client's niche, users, and community. Considering variables that will not affect a site's audience could be deemed wasteful. However, forgetting about or not adding support as it's needed could just as easily be deemed neglectful! It's a tightrope that you'll need to walk, so know who you'll be coding for—a flexible site is more important than ever in accurate designing!

Finally, there is the educational side of things, which could potentially create a few issues. As a designer, you know that it's good to remain vigilant and keep up with the ever-changing environment. Factoring in the effort it takes to retrain yourself (if needed) to a particular technique and making sure you have the tools required to test against variables is critical. Ideally, you'll spend as much time learning as you do coding.

Here are some ways to stay up-to-date:

> Read books, magazines, and blogs on what interests you.

> Attend web-design conferences and network with others.

> Listen to podcasts and do training via video tutorials.

> Examine the design code of others, and gain inspiration!

Running a business has all sorts of practical considerations, and it's only natural that you evaluate the need or your ability to consider everything in this book. Focusing your attention on what matters to your visitors is part of what makes a great designer. It takes a good amount of common sense and experimentation to organize your workflow in a way that benefits those who'll be affected by it.

Resolving Issues of Compatibility

There is one final, essential survival skill that all designers must have if they want to overcome the challenges of achieving compatibility. By understanding an environment, you can identify the core issues you need to address; by planning ahead, you can reduce the chances for errors; and by remaining open to adaptation, you can implement satisfactory outcomes. But every now and then, you will encounter quirks that trip you up and solutions that fall short of meeting your layouts' requirements. Knowing what to do when things go wrong will help you survive and maintain ubiquity.

Debugging for durable devices

Comprehending the complexities of the Web involves knowing how to spot errors, determining the cause of the problem, and finding a nice, clean, and workable solution. Ideally, all your sites will look and feel amazing on every medium and in every environment, but of course, things often don't work out that way. By ensuring that your sites work well for your many users, you provide a perception of professionalism and competence.

To the average person, the Web may be a bit of a mystery. People don't understand its origins and complexity (Figure 1-13), but they marvel at how it can be experienced and utilized through many mediums. Your responsibility to produce durable, bug-free experiences for users is much an extension of this. Because the Web seems so mysterious, part of its appeal is simply that it works. However, if compatibility on the Web falls apart, any illusion is lost, the failings of a site are exposed, and its elegance and beauty evaporate.

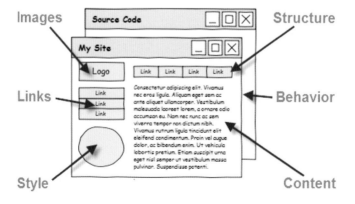

FIGURE 1-13: The average website contains many variables.

In the past, bugs in browsers have caused a number of problems for designers. However, because of the limited array of devices and circumstances in which sites were regularly viewed, issues related to a damaged experience had a minimal impact (you could fix a problem by throwing hacks at it, often resolving early browser bugs). So, the problems of maintaining a stable and ubiquitous site have always existed; it's just that the method of interaction and content absorption has dramatically changed in the visitor's favor.

Many site issues could be labeled as critical (severe), moderate, and mild, but I'm not one to place labels on quirks because what may appear as an inconsequential error to one individual may well be a catastrophic, game-changing bug for another! An essential part of designing your sites to be durable on many different devices (and within many different situations) is that you really focus on identifying flaws and solving them. Often, designers get so caught up in the debate about best practices and ideals that they may lose sight of the bigger picture.

When a problem occurs, don't conclude that you must attack it in a "nuclear-warhead" fashion. Actually, it's rare for a site to be in such a poor state that users' online experiences become totally inaccessible. Often, the quirks and issues are mild enough to simply cause irritation or confusion. On the other hand, don't put off implementing a flexible design just because it seems trivial to you, even if the fix for that quirk could have a similar effect!

You can debug code in many different ways. You have concurrent debugging that effectively involves checking and retesting your work as you progress through a series of stages. There's elimination debugging, where you find a problem and begin crippling bits of code in order to eliminate potential causes from the list (what Sherlock Homes would do if he were a programmer). Finally, there's proactive testing in which you uncover quirks or issues (plus the effectiveness of fixes) by getting users to report faults (Figure 1-14).

FIGURE 1-14: Proactive testing can consist of structured usability studies or simple verification tests.

Uncovering problems can involve as much investigation as any detective novel does. Throwing a site into all sorts of unique situations can also help you understand what users may be seeing on their screens and in the case of really old technology, that view can turn a classic detective novel into a horror franchise. Methods of testing vary among developers, and you probably have your own style. Just remember that you'll probably need to spend a good deal of time proactively trialing out use cases.

Cultivating customer service

If you don't have visitors to your site, it will, of course, fail. If your site isn't accessible or usable in its current form, you will lose visitors. The Web is a beacon of ubiquity and universal access, and as its facilitator and representative, your job is to help ensure that this beacon remains a reliable one over time. By empowering users with the tools they need to engage with your site, you're likely to see an increase in user activity. Also, if more people can access and use your services effectively, they're more likely to pass the link on to their friends.

All of this discussion centers on the importance of understanding your users and their needs. Also, it centers on looking beyond how individual pages or page elements appear to you and considering what such features will look like to different users, whether they're using popular tools or ones with little recognition. Your selection of features to implement will depend on necessity, so calculating your options may involve working out a "cost versus reward" ratio, prioritizing upgrade release cycles, and keeping visitors informed while engaging them in this process.

Note

An example of testing by necessity includes, for example, the justification for ensuring that a site works in older versions of Internet Explorer. Although we'd happily like to see them evaporate from the earth's atmosphere, they often stick around for a long time!

Involving your clients in the design process has never been more important. Because their satisfaction is central to achieving popularity and widespread use of the site, you'll want to take every opportunity you can to obtain meaningful feedback, useful assistance, and potentially groundbreaking ideas. The key to gaining useful feedback is trust. Be ready with open ears and mind and be honest and transparent with your processes. It also pays to thank users when they get in touch with you, even if it's uncomplimentary.

Don't be afraid to ask a community for help in testing your work or letting you know what things they'd like to see in future versions of your site. Feedback of a negative nature may seem like a miserable way to spend a day of inbox catching-up, but it's often the less-flattering stuff that has the biggest impact. If everyone says that your work is perfect, be suspicious; if some send hate mail, don't take it personally — see it as a chance to improve. Users matter in the design process, so don't neglect this mighty resource.

Here are some ways you can initiate communication with your visitors:

> Direct methods like e-mail, instant messaging, and chat rooms.

> Indirect methods like forums, feedback systems, or bug trackers.

> External solutions like social networks and review websites.

Of the different ways that you can gauge this feedback, your two primary sources of useful data will come from *quantitative* (numbers and statistics) and *qualitative* (descriptive and opinionated) research. Measuring this data is a challenge, but the benefits that they bring include faster identification of flaws and ideas to help you make your site more flexible. If users want 3D video, for example, you can implement it.

Ultimately, as with any type of community involvement, there will be disputes, and not everyone will agree on every action. Just know that, as you test to ensure compatibility and durability, you'll encounter a few bumps along the way. Finding a happy medium is something many designers do in their daily jobs with clients, users, and each other. Because going for broke and leaving users to their own devices aren't acceptable options, compromising (that is, going for adequate rather than optimal solutions) is a satisfactory alternative.

The Web: Survival of the fittest

The modern Web presents many challenges. With competitors breathing down your neck, a layout that fails to work on a range of devices and hardware, such as the simple ones of the laptop shown in Figure 1-15, represents a missed opportunity. Sites are like children, needing lots of care and attention. Nurturing unique devices will encourage return visits, and providing enough education to ensure users can react appropriately in current situations helps, too. In this ever-demanding environment, you want to think in terms of taking small steps toward achieving long-term goals.

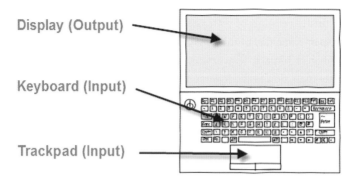

FIGURE 1-15: Devices contain input and output hardware, and your layout must work with both.

Design based on the experiences of users is an expanding area of interest, particularly with the new ideas that are pushing us toward a more sociable and useful Web. Survival isn't just a matter of ensuring that your site looks great via Internet Explorer, Firefox, Chrome, Safari, and Opera. Being future-proof depends on the devices, hardware, software, standards, and consumer variables explored in greater detail throughout this book. So, whatever you do, be sure to stay up with the times with updated and feature-rich layouts.

The Five Principles of Ubiquity

Methods and approaches to the flexible Web

OVER THE YEARS, two forces have offered a highly compatible environment for users. In one corner, you have graceful degradation, which uses numerous fallbacks. In the other corner, you have progressive enhancement, which layers nonessential features as optional extras. With features, or variables, fighting for users' attention online, selecting the best method to implement a flexible layout is critical. This chapter examines the five available options and shows how you can account for such variables and build a flexible design.

Websites Are like Onions

In the movie *Shrek,* it's said that ogres are like onions because they have layers. The same is true of the Web, which is represented as a collection of layers that comprise its finished form. These layers include the content, structure, style, and behavior of your sites.

When you consider the layers of your sites, you must account for the variables that affect users' environments and understand the fragility of these factors. These variables and their fragility play an active role in the rendered layout. Having this understanding allows you to determine whether your site will survive in the future.

Targeting specific variables is a tough job because browsers generally provide little means of detecting a user's environment. Occasionally, you might strike it lucky by using JavaScript or other tools like CSS media queries, HTTP header feedback, or conditional comments, but these detectable events are the exceptions to the rule, and even when they appear to work, they aren't always reliable. Because variables intertwine and can affect multiple features of a site, you need to think outside the box to ensure that you have considered and accounted for every angle.

As an example, consider the variable of screen real estate. Many factors affect this variable:

> The resolution within the OS

> Changes to DPI or text size

> Artificial zoom functionality

> The orientation of the window

> Open toolbars and sidebars

> The browser's UI requirements

> Whether the window is maximized

> The use of frames in a window

> The size of the screen itself

Every issue you examine builds a profile of factors that can influence the environment in which your site functions. You shouldn't rest on your laurels or assume that one solution will be perfect. For example, your visitors may browse in portrait mode, or they may view your site in landscape mode (see Figure 2-1). Consider that your CSS background images may look great now, but what happens when the user cripples his CSS? What if your visitors use a text browser like Lynx? What if they use a custom stylesheet to aid their reading? What if they use a craggy old browser that doesn't support CSS3? These are the factors you must consider.

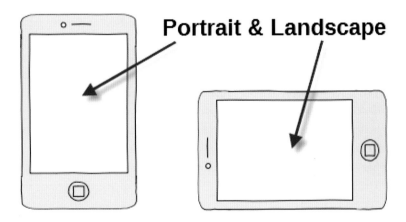

FIGURE 2-1: Whether your visitors browse in portrait versus landscape mode is an important consideration.

When you build layouts and consider variables, you need to look at the direct implications of what you produce and its side effects. Consider the big picture and how variables will interact with one another. The more questions and situations you pose and account for, the more stable and flexible your site will be. When you design a site, establish particular usage scenarios, environments, and events that could affect your visitors. By building this audience profile, you can account for their unique needs and situations.

Level 1: Graceful Design

When web development first came on the scene, web designers had few variables meddling with their pages, and the average user really did equate to something measurable. During the browser wars, however, users required more flexibility. This is when the philosophy behind graceful degradation was born. This philosophy purports that offering patches and quick fixes, once the optimum experience has been designed, allows designers to stop restricting their sites' potential, all while keeping acceptable alternatives for visitors.

Beginning graceful degradation

Fault tolerance is something that has existed in the computing and electronics industry for many years, so the concept of gracefully degrading code is nothing new. When you build layouts, you must be prepared for those times when things go wrong, or when a browser or device simply can't keep up with the technology. The idea behind this methodology is as simple as you could hope for: You build for the best and most capable, fixing sites for less-fortunate users.

When you build a gracefully degrading layout, you first forge whatever design you want (use whatever tools you like, as you address issues and their resolutions post-process). Then you identify situations in which your own scenario might differ from a user's scenario and build an alternative solution to ensure that the content remains useful (see Figure 2-2). For example, if users had images disabled, they could rely on `alt` attributes. If the user has IE6, you could offer a less complex or patch-supported layout.

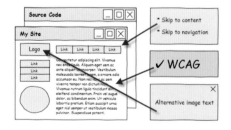

FIGURE 2-2: The fault tolerance mechanics aren't hard to grasp; it's all about offering a safety net.

This style of thinking has led to all sorts of innovative solutions in design regarding "what happens when something breaks." This methodology only works (of course) if the solution you offer provides a useful alternative to the original feature. Empty `alt` attributes, for example, don't help anyone who suffers broken images. However, you shouldn't feel ashamed in offering an alternative experience for less-capable environments, especially as the visitor is more likely to appreciate a site that works well as opposed to a site that doesn't.

Important

Offering alternatives is important. In today's accessibility-regulated world, if you don't ensure that your work flexes and catches disabled users effectively, you could face a lawsuit. Gracefully degrading code isn't always pretty, but it at least offers users something!

In the past, graceful degradation was predominantly used as a workaround method for ensuring that every user saw the same thing (as often as possible), such as the hacking that went on to make print layouts work across browsers. Since then, many designers have taken to the use of detection scripts, and others have focused on offering in-page safety features, instead of simply offering layers of patches or hacks.

The use of detection scripts in such cases has caused quite a debate, but with the arrival of frameworks it's undeniable that their use has become easier and more widespread. Many designers are also using conditional comments, a perfect example of targeting code in a non-destructive way, to implement browser-specific fixes (for Internet Explorer). Beyond code targeting to avoid degraded experiences, you can use skip links and alternative text to resolve feature dependency. Your aim is to offer fail-safe mechanisms to stave off disaster.

Some further examples of degrading code include the following:

> Video or audio transcripts for when the media isn't available

> An alternative layout for when Flash isn't installed or usable

> Print stylesheets to make using the device less ink wasteful

The modern philosophy toward producing gracefully degrading code has altered slightly in its overall goal. When an experience degrades, it must do so gracefully and continue to aid users, providing tools to achieve certain tasks. Modern incarnations of the technique focus less on cheap, hacky workarounds, which ensure a consistent experience between every browser (which, let's face it, is next to impossible these days), and instead focus on the idea that a graceful solution could involve something completely different to the ideal one.

Justification for applying graceful degradation

Many practical routes provide a gracefully degrading layout, some of which showcase its inherent benefits more than others. However, there are three prime examples that offer some ideal situations in which to apply the gracefully degrading methodology.

The three ideal situations in which to apply the gracefully degrading methodology are

> Audits (to make your site more disabled friendly)

> Retrofitted web designs (such as for intranets)

> Web apps

Post-production issues in complicated layouts are also a popular occasion to invoke the graceful mentality.

The success of any site depends on the central point of your layout: its content. Without content being available or visible, users are left with a "hollow shell" filled with nothing but eye candy, which doesn't sustain them.

In order to maintain the content's visibility and readability, your site must be accessible. Without your content maintaining this ubiquity, it may as well not exist for less-fortunate users. Graceful degradation helps designers who struggle to make their sites accessible.

Reference

Making a layout accessible can be tricky if you're not used to considering such needs. However, the W3C provides you with a useful specification (known to many as WCAG), that provides a good starting point. Ultimately, there will always be a certain number of users who, because of unique circumstances, will have issues accessing your site, but it's your job to help as many of them as you can. Here is the link for the W3C website with information on WCAG: http://www.w3.org/TR/WCAG20/.

When you attempt to make a site accessible, it's likely that you'll recognize a few common practices and implement them into your code as you go. Specifications like WCAG (mentioned in the preceding Reference paragraph) do help to underline these ideas, but you may find yourself considering the implications of what you produce after you build it. Auditing is pretty commonplace on the Web, and if you're a fan of this particular way of improvement, you'll use graceful degradation as you're literally offering a fail-safe mechanism to cope with additional specialist needs which an audit would identify.

And just when you thought wow, that's a lot to consider — accessibility involves much more than WCAG:

> Country-specific laws like the Disability Discrimination Act

> Testing with accessibility software

> WAI-ARIA and other best practices

Beyond auditing and tweaking, the same need to adjust a design for certain situations exists for retrofitting existing layouts. Because of the costs and time involved, it's unrealistic to demand that an entire design be rebuilt from scratch to account for the variables that a user may struggle with (unless the site is so poorly built that the only viable option is to totally demolish it). When dealing with post-production or technical redesigns, degrading makes sense as it also avoids wasting the old design, and reduces the learning curve for visitors.

The beauty of graceful degradation is that it mostly avoids the need to consider variables until you have a solid backbone for the layout you've established. This is a good philosophy if you are servicing an existing design, but it's arguably not the cleanest method to dodge future quirks and issues in a new site. Yet there is one situation that could potentially require the use of a layout that is graceful from the outset, and that's web apps (see Figure 2-3), as they often rely on JavaScript and demand compromise if the user doesn't have it enabled.

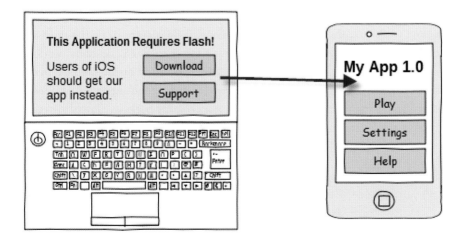

FIGURE 2-3: If you feel that a web app is going to struggle under flexible requirements, go native instead.

You may have justifiable reasons for using a technology that isn't as cross-compatible as you might like. Rare occasions exist when you must demand a feature be enabled (remember, regular sites should never be in this situation). If a user doesn't have what you need at the client side, you can, as a graceful fail safe, attempt it at the server side. If you need users to view a video, for example, you can link to the file, and if all else fails, you should inform them of any requirements and how to meet demands.

Considerations of compatibility: Graceful design

Because of the methodology it takes, graceful degradation can become quite the logistical nightmare in terms of ensuring that all your bases are covered. I'm not saying that it's better to go without than to employ it, but you'll find that the graceful methodology isn't exactly the friendliest method for users or designers. The ideal environment for using this technique is situations where small glitches occur, in post-production, and when you need a situational patch or fix. In all other situations, use the ever-durable progressive enhancement.

The first and most obvious compatibility issue that can occur from graceful degradation is that it tends to discriminate against the "lesser beings" that fail to meet the layout's own primary requirements. If you don't have JavaScript and the site wants the technology, the graceful approach might allow you to still browse around the site, but you could find major pieces of functionality out of action. As with individuals who build separate mobile layouts, there has been a nasty trend of leaving outsiders with an unnecessarily lesser-quality experience.

It's worth stating at this point that all techniques and technologies can be used for good or evil, and while graceful degradation isn't alone, it does seem to be the most regular offender in the past and present of design. In an effort to avoid additional work, many designers dumb down their layouts to the point of absurdity in the premise that basic accessibility and the ability to just browse a site (barely) is good enough. Alas, if we want to ensure a stable foundation that will keep visitors coming back, we should give them an equally enjoyable experience.

Note The aim of graceful degradation isn't to create a site that looks the same for every user (or if that fails, falls back into something primitive); it's to offer the next best option that can be taken advantage of under the circumstances. Life isn't perfect, and nor is a site, but we can try to aim for equality by degrading experiences to an acceptable quality level.

One effect of graceful degradation that causes the most concern is the flaw of backward compatibility, which in basic terms highlights that we should only patch on the basis of "as it's needed on a one-to-one basis." Users who aren't as likely to come forward and declare issues are unlikely to see their devices or environments get the support they desire. In most cases, graceful degradation doesn't consider the effect that future situations may have because the truth is that designers are too busy dealing with current situations.

Over the lifespan of a site, you may find that a great deal of redundancy occurs in your gracefully built code. Often, when designers write a bunch of purpose-built hacks for a particular browser and it falls out of use, they are unlikely to weed out the dead code. This causes pages to bloat, and maintenance demands to increase. Separating your structure, style, and behavior makes code easier to maintain, yet few designers consistently optimize their code to take advantage of doing so. Being graceful often comes at the cost of being clean.

While things may appear pretty grim for designers using gracefully degrading techniques such as patches and fail safes, never fear. Ultimately, as with any technique, it really comes down to how you choose to implement and maintain your code that has the biggest overall impact upon your users. Patching can be a good thing, if you control your workflow and maintain your code regularly, and offering fail safes can be fantastic, but you'll need to put the time into testing the tripwires to ensure you don't leave any users out in the cold.

Level 2: Progressive Design

While graceful degradation has gained popularity for its highly unconstrained attitude toward hoping for the best but planning for the worst, it has proven less popular with designers who are concerned that certain situations may be rendered incompatible by design and by default. This movement has evolved into the formation of a safer but more prudent methodology labeled *progressive enhancement,* which avoids any technique that's obtrusive or demanding, requiring fallbacks not fail safes, to ensure that solutions aren't exclusively for a certain browser or user, but instead provide an added layer of integrity to your work, to assist those in need.

Progressive enhancement

Progressive enhancement is the flip side of the coin to graceful degradation. The graceful degradation method (discussed in the section, "Level 1: Graceful Design") works with a top-down approach, providing the most satisfying experience it can, while using patches and fail-safe solutions to offer an acceptable alternative experience. The progressive enhancement approach reverses this effect by using a bottom-up methodology (shown in Figure 2-4), demanding that less-critical features of a page be included only in a way that doesn't require crude fixes or hacks.

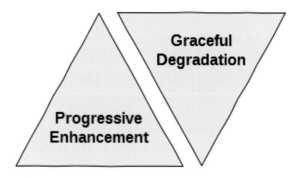

FIGURE 2-4: The top-down and bottom-up approaches rely upon how we apply the layers of the Web.

Almost everyone who designs sites is familiar with the concept of building a site's structure around the on-page content and then layering stylistic code on the structure, and finally adding behavior, or *scripting,* events on what's been built so far. The effect of separating structure, style, and behavior not only breaks these easily identifiable layers of the Web apart to make maintenance easier, it also forces us to design for situations in which layers such as CSS or JavaScript can be turned off. And yes, that does happen occasionally, too.

Regarding the design methodology, progressive enhancement is much more prudent than its graceful alternative because there must always be something to fall back on, even if it's the raw content. If the browser can handle JavaScript, then great, that behavior can be invoked, and the functionality will work; if it's not enabled, the page must still function. Ultimately, progressive design has the benefit of relying on numerous safety nets at every level so if one thing breaks — say, if CSS is disabled — something else, such as HTML, can take over.

Note

In graceful degradation, you keep the structure, style, and behavior separate, as each offers a range of advantages; however, unlike progressive enhancement, you won't be taking the time to finish and stress test each individual layer before moving onto the next. This is because you'll be fixing remaining quirks individually as a post-production process.

Progressive enhancement doesn't have the "aim high" philosophy of degradation, in which designers push for the best of both worlds, but the truth is that the Web has become far too diverse for anyone to have any real expectations of their users. As part of this way of thinking, attitudes toward progressive interfaces really tempt designers to remain with what's safe, mostly because they fear that any barrier to entry at a fundamental level is a high price for products that have no reasonable fallback (unlike the degradation crowd that patches fixes together).

To that end, the following components can be turned off easily:

> Images (embedded using HTML or CSS)

> Cookies, data caching, and local storage

> CSS and JavaScript (including jQuery)

> Flash, Java, Silverlight, and other plug-ins

To provide enhancements, you begin by ensuring that your content is marked up in a solid manner (semantics matter). Once that looks and works fine, you can provide CSS (perhaps some CSS3 if it has an older, stable CSS fallback for less-capable browsers). Then you can throw in some scripts to provide that extra push of interactivity without messing up what's already there. From that you could even layer Flash or other features with less support or recognition. As Figure 2-5 shows, it's all about layering one feature on top of its backup.

Rather than building for the best case, progressive enhancement provides a philosophy that reaches beyond simple browsers. Rather than assume features exist or that your visitors can take advantage of what you require, you start thinking ahead and testing as you go in preference to the graceful approach of "build now, ask questions later." Because it's a less-risky approach, many designers have gone with this as the de facto method of creating barrier-free layouts, while adapting its philosophy for other quirky situations.

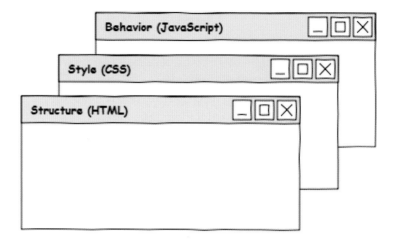

FIGURE 2-5: Processing a progressive site will involve the layering of features upon your existing content.

Justification for applying progressive design

The first tool in the progressive enhancement toolkit is feature detection. Suppose that you want to take advantage of the latest, greatest techniques, but you don't want to cause a compatibility issue by implementing something that may not be supported by older or less-capable browsers. What do you do? Avoid it? Not if you want to remain on the cutting edge! The easy answer to this question is to test to see if the functionality you require is supported. This may sound complicated, but it's used whenever you browse the Internet!

Note

Waiting for specifications to complete or browser support to be 100% isn't an option (if you want to have a durable layout). CSS media queries have shown that it's become a necessity to push languages beyond the "current," recommended specifications in order to be flexible. And with CSS3 evolving as it is (as independent modules), any hope of a general release that works for everyone equally seems increasingly like a pipe dream.

When dealing with code and browsers, by default, verify support before trying to use it. If you've used CSS3, you know that browsers that don't support it simply ignore it, which is great for code that can degrade well. The same goes for unobtrusive JavaScript in which the site's behavior is ignored and your fallbacks come into effect. By testing for support within your browser, you can not only customize a layout for the environment a user may be browsing in, but also provide some alternatives for when a component becomes unavailable for use!

Another example of using progressive enhancement to your advantage is through the use of unique experimental features called *vendor prefixes* (see Figure 2-6). We have already noted how adept CSS3 is at being ignored if it's not supported, which is good if a layout doesn't depend on it. Vendor prefixes within browsers go one step further to reiterate how you can add useful flourishes and features without worrying that your design will collapse. If a feature provides a benefit to the user's experience, it's worth attempting its utilization.

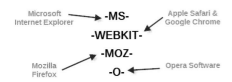

FIGURE 2-6: Each rendering engine has a unique vendor prefix, allowing for selective browser utilization.

While code is the backbone that allows you to take all these points into consideration, you must not forget that many aspects of progressive enhancement relate to concepts beyond what you'd put in a code editor. Sure, it's important to get those layers of structure, style, and behavior in check, but you can also deal some progressive enhancement justice toward less capable browsers, the aesthetic experience users enjoy, and the functionality you provide. You can even promote this progressive style toward your automated robotic friends.

Note

Search engines are big fans of context and easy-to-read information (as are the wealth of social networks that exist). You can increase the semantic relevance of your content by offering things like microformats, metadata, and text-based alternatives, too. In the context of "Web layers," these tools add an additional layer over your structure (HTML).

Regarding content, if you go down the reductionist route and weed out the material that is unnecessary (the Web is full of wordy fluff), you would offer those with slower Internet connections a better experience (Twitter, for example, limits the number of tweets per page until you ask for more). With functionality, you could have a script-free search form on the page, adding auto complete and other bonus features if scripting is enabled. And if you want to use tools like Flash, you could layer the implementation upon an existing, usable interface.

Putting this into perspective, I've come to like graceful and progressive design for very different reasons. Graceful design is a real force for good in maintaining a site, and the progressive route is an ideal way to begin building a flexible design. Arguably, people could state that because you want to keep things as simple as possible, it might be worth following the enhancing route in preference to degrading once it's complete (for consistency's sake), but as we shall soon find out, things have evolved in both camps to become more durable.

Considerations of compatibility: Progressive design

Compatibility in regard to progressive enhancement is relatively straightforward, which actually helps give it the edge over graceful degradation in regard to providing a useful and seamless experience for users. Up until the latest incarnations of both techniques (we take a close look at these later on in this chapter), sites suffered epic scale redesigns to take advantage of the increased flexibility and potential savings in both bandwidth and maintenance costs. Progressive enhancement isn't bulletproof or free of complications, however.

The first compatibility consideration you need to account for in your design work is that browsers and devices can behave very differently when asked to render something on the page. A browser's default fallback mechanism for a lack of viewport space may include the use of scrolling (in any direction), zooming, or some other unique feature. These inconsistencies in the way browsers handle variables and variations of those issues force you to think outside the box and provide a more considerate alternative for users.

Note   One downside of these necessary fallbacks is that they absorb added bandwidth and resources. Why? Even if that fallback code isn't used, it still takes up space. Also, if something falls back, the original effect (such as Flash) will be loaded. You really can't win as providing a fallback ultimately means that only one of the two options is used, and what remains is hidden.

Although users of a site are willing to scroll (the fold being a print design myth), requiring unnecessary scrolling can decrease the usability of the site. As another example, while a Flash video could prove itself a useful alternative to boring text (for users with a short attention span), you must be careful to provide something underneath that plug-in layer for users of iOS who cannot access the Flash plug-in at all. Enhancement is as much about offering substitute layered fallbacks as it is about letting variables drop to defaults.

Another compatibility factor to consider with progressive enhancement is that, as noted earlier, because of the way your work needs to be layered (to ensure dependency doesn't occur), such an implementation can become hard to achieve in existing sites that are extensive, multipage, or otherwise complex. A site with as much going on as Amazon or eBay could easily be excused for putting off the progressive move because of the fact that they'd likely have to invest in totally remodeling their code from the ground up, which would take a lot of time.

Here are some options for larger layouts:

> Roll out a revamped progressive layout over numerous iterations.

> Redesign an entire website from scratch to match user needs.

> Supplement useful tools that won't impact the existing design.

If you're building a site from scratch or trying to improve an existing one, the progressive route is a firm favorite to take. However, it's a given that deciding what's required and the work involved in ensuring that everything stacks up without breaking when something is turned off will take a great deal of planning. Rome wasn't built in a day, and unless you have a prebuilt CMS or template at hand, your site probably won't be either. Layering all of that useful material that could improve an interface requires plenty of consideration.

The final thing you need to know about the progressive model is that designers can get a bit heavy handed with the layering, so be sure to plan your site's production as if you were an architect. As many designers get used to the available tools and begin taking advantage of them, some get a bit overzealous and add "enhancements" that don't really do anything useful. Visual flourishes and animated effects can be a good thing if done in moderation, but just because a browser lets you do something cool, doesn't mean you always should.

Level 3: Adaptive Design

For all of its critics, graceful degradation has never been afraid to push boundaries in order to offer users the best-possible, technology-rich experience. From within the foundations of its parent, and the need for increasingly flexible layouts, appeared the ideology of adaptive design (like a phoenix rising from the ashes). Built upon the increasing usability demands of users, *adaptive design* forges an ideology that experiences shouldn't be identical, so designers should remain true to the graceful philosophy by just being both a bit more tactful and creatively flexible.

Adaptive paths to degradation

Before the explosion of the "mobile Web," which led numerous handheld devices among other devices to demand access to the Web and our sites, both graceful degradation and progressive enhancement could carry out their roles rather peacefully. The demands of ensuring everything worked on different devices wasn't taxing. So much for the good old days! As of right now, users demand something more flexible, something that can handle more variables than the older models can. And as of very recently, we can achieve that aim!

We're going to examine responsive design, the darling of the web design world, in a little bit, but before we get into that subject, we should, in proud tradition, showcase the modern-day evolution of the oldest of them all, graceful degradation. The idea for this evolution came out of the cries of one man who said something that really struck a chord with a few designers. That man, who is no stranger to controversy, was Andy Clarke, a well-known speaker in the web development community. He made a valid point: Why should we wait for stuff to become ubiquitous instead of using it now?

Arguably, the graceful degradation crowd has been demanding the use of everything new as it occurs, but its one critical failing point was that back in the day, the ultimate goal was to ensure that everything looked and worked the same for visitors, no matter their situation. Today, designers know that this expectation isn't realistic. So one thing that identifies this modern iteration over its predecessor is that we should actually cultivate different (even drastically different) experiences (see Figure 2-7) if the ideal solution can't be made viable.

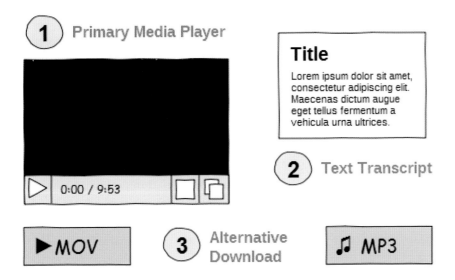

FIGURE 2-7: You can provide alternatives based upon the browser, the OS, or the device's capabilities.

Times have changed, the Web has evolved, and with this, we must now begin to reevaluate how the online world has produced revolutionary expectations of our work. By taking advantage of this philosophy, we still follow the ethos of planning for the best while expecting the worst; however, the way we deal with the worst can drastically differ. Adaptive layouts aren't about feeling a need to omit HTML5 or CSS3 because it may not be available; it encourages using them, but being more creative with necessary alternatives.

Consider how you code for Internet Explorer 6. Designers often try for a few conditional comments and hacks to resolve inconsistencies (that's the graceful bit); become selective in what they offer but ensure that it works if functionality is turned off (that's the enhancement bit); or refuse to support it entirely (that's the crazy bit). Adaptive design throws its hands in the air and shouts, "They deserve a great experience, too, but if they can't handle the heat, give them a different design, one that matches their browser's capabilities."

Tip

When building an adaptive site, the idea isn't that you would tell IE6 users to go away and upgrade their browsers. Instead, you would offer them a dedicated IE6 layout using conditional comments to provide something equally lovely, but less modern. Supporting old technology until it has too few users for the support to be worthwhile is the only way to go, as a ubiquitous interface cannot ever really go about denying access to anyone.

It's an intriguing idea that designers might prefer to avoid degrading or enhancing in place of a more drastic shift toward replacing the bits that won't work, and in today's ever-diverse and crowded marketplace of variables, admitting the failings of earlier approaches and providing a series of "fall forward" alternatives could really do the trick. For all the benefits that pushing boundaries can offer, however, many designers fail to go outside of their own comfort zone on the idea that they may upset the Internet gods (or more explicitly, IE).

This mechanism (which Andy Clarke refers to as *hardboiled*) forces us to rethink how we design, rework the way we test, and, if I'm being honest, it's a great evolutionary step to admit that we don't have much control, so we may as well throw caution to the wind and have a little fun while we're designing. When working with this method, you should treat compatibility as an opportunity to find useful solutions for the new and exciting gaps in the modern Web's texture, doing so with consideration of the consequences.

Reference   For details on the hardboiled philosophy, which I refer to as *adaptive design* because of its remodeling of a site based on the capabilities perspective, it's worth checking out the materials relating to Andy Clarke's interesting ideology: `http://hardboiledwebdesign.com/talk/`.

Considerations and justifications: Adaptive design

The adaptive technique builds on the ideology of graceful degradation by stating that a design shouldn't just be accessible and aesthetically pleasing, and it mustn't limit or restrict your realization of the finished design (or what you expect it to be). When it comes to fixing problems, you literally work backward, patching as you find limitations in the way a user's environment can be experienced. You begin by gracefully degrading as much of the site's interface and functionality as possible, and for more major issues, add a unique alternative.

You can't hope for a future-proof site without having flexibility in your approach, and you certainly won't be ready for the future if you remain trapped in the old mentalities held toward code. There are some things you can do by enriching your interfaces with visual treats (a few of you may have toyed with CSS3's box-shadow or border radius before), but that just isn't enough. Rather than limiting your potential for code usage, you should instead admit that *drastically different* doesn't mean *unacceptable,* and follow that.

Tip

The CSS3 target selector can help you achieve content on demand, but web browsers without its support would fail to show anything other than the default. Rather than just not using it because of compatibility, you could offer old browsers an alternative stylesheet.

Regarding compatibility, you want to equip a site with the best-possible features and offer whatever else that you could possibly imagine using, but then proceed to filter downward, intelligently picking alternative routes to deal with problems as they occur. Perhaps you'll find that some conditional comments will do the trick, perhaps you'll create an unobtrusive script to replicate functionality, or maybe you'll need to go overboard and offer a degraded stylesheet for the experience. What matters is that the user can enjoy it (see Figure 2-8).

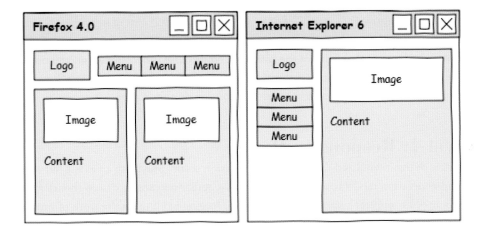

FIGURE 2-8: Visitors will make the most of whatever they're given, so don't be afraid to design adaptively.

Some web designers argue that the top-down approach isn't the most fluid method of working (perhaps because they're not used to it). You may have additional work ahead of you, but it's certainly a worthwhile technique to consider. An example of the top-down approach in action is how we approach font stacks in web design. We don't immediately restrict ourselves to what we know will work for everyone. We start with the best-case scenario and fall back with more recognizable iterations until the user hits something he will have installed.

Reference

Typography on the Web has been a problematic affair for years. Not only are there multiple ways of embedding a font into a page (such as directly from a file you own or by using a service like Typekit), considerations must be made regarding the fallbacks you want to use. The following site lists a few of the potential typefaces you can include: `http://www.speaking-in-styles.com/web-typography/Web-Safe-Fonts/`.

The truth is that the average web user won't really mind if things differ, depending on the interface they use. In many cases, they may be used to browsing with mobile-oriented layouts, which differ from the desktop ones (because of browsers trying to cope with a rather oversized layout by zooming). CSS3 will never be announced as complete, allowing everyone to upgrade in unison, and many of the traditional routes to compatibility cannot cope with diversity, so attack becomes the best form of defense.

The final thing to consider is to what extent you should employ such techniques. The idea behind being adaptive (or hardboiled) is to avoid the "graceful" part of degradation. While this might seem like a risk too far for some people, if you're determined to have a flexible layout that adapts to the needs of the content, compromise is necessary, and you need to make some hard decisions along the way. Building an adaptive design falls on your ability to iterate the degrading ideology in reverse; if you can do this, consider it carefully.

Level 4: Responsive Design

Adaptive design revitalized the graceful degradation scene, providing a flexible but stable second-generation model to work with. The now-popular responsive design theory makes the same philosophical leap, except in this case, forging itself upon the work of progressive enhancement. Knowing that various situations require a customized experience is only one part of this whirlwind romance with designers. The ethos of responsive design reaches into (and breaks) the old mentalities toward design (known as the one size fits all model).

Responsive design: A love story

Based on the discipline of responsive architecture, Ethan Marcotte (who, like Andy Clarke, is a well-known web designer) highlighted that because times were changing more rapidly than ever before, our old ideas of targeting environments or platforms with purpose-built experiences often weren't in a user's best interests. We have previously highlighted the ill-advised justification that some use for a separate "mobile" layout because of the lack of a good definition for what mobile constitutes and the diversity of devices. So what's new?

This methodology brings together three useful techniques into one useful implementation, which progressively increases the flexibility of our sites for the better. Traditional sites that used to be labeled *compatible* don't appear to be so these days because what looked great on the desktop doesn't fit well in smaller- or larger-screened environments. This technique interjects upon the work of progressive enhancement by offering the tools to better account for diverse user environment variables, and offering layouts added elasticity (see Figure 2-9).

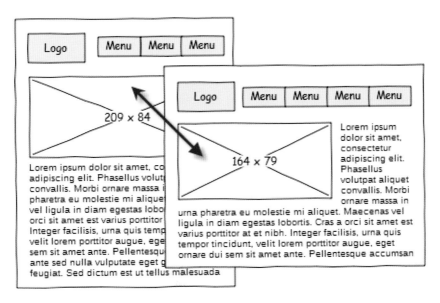

FIGURE 2-9: Being flexible in the responsive sense involves fluid layouts, with clever showmanship.

By using a combination of media queries (conditional comments for the viewport, rather than the browser), flexible images that scale to meet the demands of the available screen space so not to waste bandwidth, and a flexible grid (the tricky act of balancing everything into a non-fixed width layout that will further scale), you can produce designs that flex for the needs of what's using them more accurately. Basically, you're breaking down a design into "margins of scale," thereby offering multiple, flexible methods to achieve the effect.

When you think about it, the old "flexible" liquid layouts worked fine in the restrictive, old world of the desktop that only differed slightly in terms of resolution. Now that designers must accommodate a whole range of devices that can jump from 6 to 106 inches, the task of arranging content in that space becomes quite a task, and the issue is only going to get worse as the technology divide increases. Getting this accurate to scale would be impossible if you had only one layout to work with; media queries help in this challenge.

Tip

Here's an easy way to think of media queries. Consider the following clothes analogy. If you go to a store and find a shirt in one size, it would fit only a few people. Offering a range of sizes (while not tailor made) increases the audience for them. That's how it works! You're just providing visitors with a size that matches their own requirements.

Responsive design differs from progressive enhancement because designers don't use it just to go beyond the limitations of one situation; they try to take a bunch of interconnected situations (relating to screen size) and resolve numerous scenarios with some good, solid practices. Being progressive just means that you're willing to look at things from a holistic perspective, building upon early foundations as well as current trends. Responsive design is about pushing past some common barriers, and toning your site's muscles for flexibility.

These are the muscles' responsive design tones:

> The physical space users have, relative to the design

> Flexibility in regard to portrait or landscape orientation

> Fundamental layout options based on viewport sizes

Making smaller layouts more touch friendly is possible. Making larger layouts a bit easier to use with strange input devices (like remote controls) is possible. Redesigning an entire site to increase the usability of a complex interface on smaller screens (perhaps by using progressive disclosure) is totally doable! Each customization you provide, if done for the right reasons, can benefit the user, especially on restrictive devices. It helps you offer agile, sensible layouts that don't provide any more or less (time wasting) content than necessary.

Considerations and justifications: Responsive design

Responsive design isn't a silver bullet, and the facts are that there may be occasions where a different solution or separate layout may be appropriate. The cool thing about techniques such as this is that they force you to reconsider what you believe is important and they also help redefine what users need and how a site becomes more compatible for more obscure configurations. As a result, we should end up focusing on the variables and capabilities of a user's environment and cease thinking in terms of mobile, desktop, or other stereotypes.

One consideration with responsive design is that the widths applied to media queries or the image scales provided need to represent your visitors and their needs. Being prepared and knowing your audience's requirements are of critical importance. In the application of these techniques, or any other, it remains critically important that you source some reliable statistics and act on them based on the needs of your content and visitors, in preference to just following along with the crowd and building a layout that may not appease user needs.

Note

While media queries can be a useful tool in making your designs more responsive, they cannot be used without some insights into how our visitors will be using your pages. You will need to account for common resolutions, viewport sizes, and situations in which the visible space will be affected. You can't just rely upon a single consideration at work.

There is also a compatibility issue that needs to be addressed. Media queries are part of the CSS3 specification and as ironic as this appears, there of course will be a number of browsers (old and new) that only have partial or non-existent support for the lovely and useful technique. More worrying is that many devices and browsers still have quite spotty support for the @media rule in general (like handheld). This leaves you in a paradoxical situation in which your responsive designs must respond to not being able to be responsive!

If this issue confuses you, you're not alone. Working around such a quirk can be frustrating. But it's worth pointing out the adaptive philosophy in this instance as it really does justify the need to be flexible. It's not really a case of you either using media queries or nothing at all; the fact that you can use them and they both enhance and degrade well in equal measure is a justification to include the support they offer (amongst other tools similar to them) to benefit whatever a user has that can use them. Perhaps this is also a case for JavaScript.

Here are ways to layer flexibility using several mentioned techniques:

> Begin with a fluid or liquid layout that scales beautifully.

> Add media queries to scale the liquid into sensible portions.

> Increase the flexibility further with script-based solutions.

Either way, responsive design prefers a quite casual approach to the forging of designs. If we build layers from the lowest denominator within our field of vision (like tiny screens, low bandwidth, and measurable variables like the ones this book is based on), increasing to the more capable environments with the flourishes or nifty enhancements users may want, we're on the road to success. Some deem this specific methodology as *mobile first,* but in truth, no one really can say that mobile will remain the lowest rung on the stability ladder.

As a final note, one of the key components of responsive design is to be realistic in what you can achieve, focusing on the best performing and most agile solution you can use without your visitors suffering. It's about making the most of the space and the time you have, not making broad, sweeping assumptions about your users to dodge any common perceptions such as "only handheld devices need speedy sites" (consider that desktop users might have data caps or dialup access). Variables, after all, affect a diverse audience for different reasons.

Level 5: Reactive Design

Graceful degradation and adaptive design are a perfect representation of the modern way designers tackle the new range of technologies without limiting themselves to the safety net of the lowest common compatibility denominator. But this isn't the end of the story. While the preceding levels simply focus on the "design layer" in order to account for variables that affect an experience, by using clever code and behavioral engineering, we can build even more flexible, durable layouts, and it's with this that we'll introduce reactive design.

Reactive sites: Beyond behavior

By using scripting in your interfaces, whether on the client side or the server side, you can make interfaces and sites ever more responsive and adaptive. When you have the basics of compatibility down, you can look beyond the limited and restrictive power behind CSS media queries (which only tackle predetermined visual situations that occur within the browser) and provide something more assertive but proactive in your goal to help users receive the best experience possible. I call this methodology *reactive design.*

One of the major criticisms of responsive design and its counterparts is that for a layout to truly live up to the identity of being responsive, we must actually offer feedback or some form of response once an environment has been altered (or individual changes in the way in which they'd prefer to experience a site). Traditional compatibility techniques tend not to respond in the sense of offering feedback, but merely flex to an environment as needs occur. While being non-static is an incredible feat for a design, I feel we can do more.

These points can make a site work better within its environment:

> The ability to personalize a layout based on your identity and needs

> Customization tools that put users in control of content they receive

> Scripting aids that autonomously try to help users make choices

Rather than being responsive, a reactive site actually analyzes its situation and makes key changes as that variable is altered. If you consider something simple like bandwidth, while a responsive design would prefer the mobile-first "nothing more than is necessary" route, a reactive design would see what the environment would be able to handle, and provides more or less content as is appropriate. This isn't to say fluff would be inserted, but you could, for example, push more blog entries to users, or HD video to faster, more capable connections.

Previous compatibility considerations force us to look at statistics and feedback, so that we can code ready-built prefixed solutions for our users, but ideally we shouldn't need to do all of the hard work ourselves. A truly responsive site will account for necessary variable considerations and make an automated measured response by altering layouts accordingly (perhaps like in Figure 2-10). This may seem a little farfetched, but it's precisely what can be achieved using scripting if designers manage to create a framework to account for it.

With regard to durable scripting, you can see at this point that a designer would need to use a mixture of the client and server side because JavaScript can do things that can't be done at the server (but it can be crippled, limited, or disabled), and the server side can do things that the client-side cannot. The situation isn't perfect, and the technique to produce such a mechanized route to compatibility would be hard, but from the perspective of the bigger picture, this is an ideal place for a framework or project to begin, means-testing the user's environment and personalizing on the move.

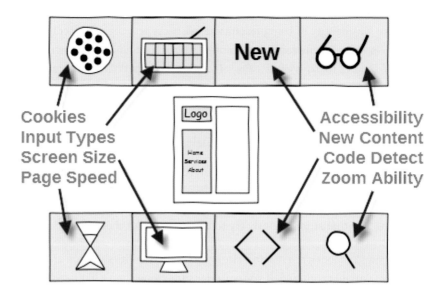

FIGURE 2-10: Dreams of a reactive framework. Who knows what we'll be able to calculate in the future?

In essence, reactive websites can be produced, and all you need to do is put some thought into how you can let a browser or script avoid the need for specifying defaults. If you were to perform chemical experiments, reactions would occur as the variables came into contact with each other. The Web may not be a test tube, but with the rapid rate of its evolution, a more scientific approach could be helpful when accounting for the variables mentioned in this book. One size will never really fit all, and not everyone will fit into ideal categories.

Philosophies of a reactive Web

Providing preset solutions isn't necessarily a bad idea, as we need to take baby steps to avoid going crazy with the markup and superglue. But the consequences for doing just enough to get the job done are that 95 percent of your audience will be happy. While the other 5 percent will demand more, it's also true that at a certain point, the cost of building a dedicated solution may outweigh the benefits. Ultimately, as reactive as we can make our sites, it's up to you to determine at what point you feel that a solution just isn't economical.

Note   One thing worth remembering is you can't satisfy everyone. Users will enter your site with preconceptions about what they believe makes a good design, and every user will have his own needs and limitations. The best you can hope for is a happy majority.

I discussed the benefits of client-side detection in making sites more reactive by letting the browser decide what is good for unique environments. Now, it's worth giving some credit to the work done in server-side development and how this could not only affect the visual web layer but the behavioral one, too. By letting users create an account with a site, and offering the option to manipulate objects and their positions upon the page as they see fit, you'll enrich the user experience, catering toward individual needs (see Figure 2-11).

User Profile		
	Name:	John Doe
	Age:	37 ▼
Profile Picture	**Country:**	USA ▼
Choose	**Job:**	Lawyer

FIGURE 2-11: At the server side, we can remember user preferences for an interface, no matter where they are.

Not only can you provide tools to improve the readability of your site's content, you can actually improve the overall interface by becoming more personable. Reactive layouts that allow for enriched customization can remember how a user browses, offer useful links that relate to her browsing habits, and eliminate unnecessary data, based upon her preference (say, if she didn't want to see images). While providing automation for compatibility can be a challenge, putting the power within the user's own hands can ease any learning curves.

Examples of reactive design in the wild would include any site that has a primary focus on customization or personalization, based either all or in part on user activity or her own explicit preferences. Experiences become more satisfying when they're easy to use, and if you can empower the visitor by giving her the choice in what appears, how the page will render, or even what features she has; you can take the presumptions and throw them out the window, leaving only individuals and their desire for a useful, handcrafted interface.

Note You could provide a control panel that allows users to decide what appears on-screen (in modes like small, medium, or large). Furthermore, you can allow your users to build profiles of the devices they use, catering a UI around it (like a programmable universal remote control). Also, consider how both preferences and content may be ported between devices.

Personalizing user interfaces is a common practice when dealing with content management systems. The practice is generally applied in behavioral engineering techniques online. For example, consider how Google caters advertising toward its visitors or how a blog can show related links to the material they've recently read. Being creative with these useful mechanisms can aid compatibility by profiling the visitor's concerns and site usage, offering meaningful details to help you cater content toward a user's specific requirements.

Ultimately, the Web is going to continue to evolve, and we must maintain our dedication toward giving the user the best experience possible. Using this technique doesn't mean that we should get privacy intrusive, force user accounts to be created, or start logging a user's every move. It's about rethinking the way we look at design beyond how we currently do, and then being able to look to the future and decide how we can provide an automated, manual, or preconfigured solution to the situation. That's what our job revolves around.

Ubiquity to the power of five

If your site has taken into account the ideologies of the first two levels, why not consider using adaptive and responsive design to provide some additional layers of functionality and flexibility so that it can cope with previous, modern, and future standards? The key to reimagining these techniques isn't so much in that we're going to just replace them or throw degrading and enhancing code out the door. Instead, it gives us a chance to push our code to new heights, embracing whatever the Web has to offer in a safe, useful manner!

To ensure compatibility, you will probably find yourself using a combination of different techniques to ensure your site can withstand all the stress testing that a user can place on it. Each technique has its own advantages and disadvantages, especially when certain types of variables are involved, and each has its own route to success, so don't feel that you have to limit yourself in your endeavors to maintain a future-proof site. After all, unless you're a psychic, it's highly unlikely that you'll predict all that will appear over the coming years.

Pick your weapon wisely, or create a hybrid:

> Graceful degradation

> Progressive enhancement

> Adaptive design

> Responsive design

> Reactive design

All of these techniques are best practices and it's worth reiterating that the future of design as we know it isn't something that's awaiting our permission from a far and distant land—it's here, right now! Handheld devices are on the rise, desktops are growing in diversity, web-enabled television sets are gaining adoption, and we might potentially find ourselves living in an Internet-powered house. Therefore, being both flexible and compatible *is* web design, and anything that contradicts diversity is a relic of a world long gone.

Designing for the Desktop

Accessing content and services from a variety of devices

ONE DEFINING ASPECT of an online experience is that you can access content and services from a wide variety of devices. Whether you use a cellphone, tablet, laptop, or desktop computer, your actions are restricted both by the limitations and features of your device (such as the display's quality and touch capability) and by the software running on it. In this chapter, you see how traditional desktop devices can affect your site's users by the mixture of hardware and software that makes a distinction between product models.

Knowing the Challenge: Compatibility

In the early days of online computing, desktop PCs were the only devices commonly used to access the Web. Even today, when thinking of average Internet users, many designers still think in terms of the trusty desktop computer. Of course, modern computers aren't limited to big, boxy machines. Laptop computers and their smaller cousins, netbooks and nettops, are in widespread use. These devices are gaining popularity because they make the Web more easily accessible to users while they're on the go. For your site to be successful, you must take all these devices and their differences into account.

In addition to looking at the types of machines available, web designers must consider the age of the machines. Although you'd like to think that each of your visitors browses your site using the latest equipment, lower specification, legacy machines are likely to still be commonplace (especially in large businesses where upgrade policies vary). As a result, you may have slower hard disks and processors, less RAM, and even an old version of an OS working against you. So, you must be open to addressing the needs of older technology.

Note   Often people have higher expectations of desktop machines than of other devices, but this isn't always accurate. Gaming laptops, for example, are often more powerful than an entry-level desktop computer, and unlike their desktop counterparts, laptops often come with webcams built in that can be used by creative web designers and developers!

Within the realm of desktop computers, compatibility is a real challenge. All the possible configurations can amount to a lot of unique machines. With all the possibilities and the different ways each component can affect individual users, you need a flexible approach. There is little restriction regarding what OS or software can be installed, and this uniqueness means that you cannot rely on the machine as a whole, but on the sum of its parts. If users can change their browsers, for example, the site may be visually affected.

In the past, testing for desktop computers focused less on the hardware and more on the software environment. But with the rise of cheap gadgets, some of which are explicitly for use on the Web, the form factor becomes worth considering. Pages with process-heavy CSS animations, hardware-accelerated scripts, and multimedia may find that they lag or drain the battery of lower-specification devices. As developers try to provide users with engaging, complex interactions, such optimizations have become increasingly important.

With a wider range of devices available to consumers comes the need to be more considerate of the devices' limitations and benefits. Each device will have advantages and disadvantages, and it's your job to analyze how your work may be affected. Whether you're dealing with the increasing numbers of legacy devices, or offering functionality to take advantage of the coolest, latest, high-specification machine, desktop computers and their more portable counterparts continue to be fundamental to how users interact on the Web.

Addressing desktop compatibility issues

When you consider the range of desktop devices on the market, it's not surprising that compatibility among device types is an issue web designers must deal with. As an example, suppose that one of your visitors is using an 11-inch netbook that is highly portable but not powerful. The visitor is inexperienced when it comes to Windows and hasn't installed any service packs in the Windows XP system. Even worse, he isn't even aware that alternative browsers exist (so he still has Internet Explorer 6 running as the default), and because the visitor lives in a rural area without low-cost broadband, he is restricted to dialup access.

When the visitor browses to your site, he recognizes the fixed width layout but isn't too happy to have to side-scroll because of a lower resolution. The visitor also isn't too happy with the heavy use of Flash automatically playing video on the home page to showcase your app. The video pushes heavily on his system's resources, causing the page to load slower than a delivery at the post office. Also, by not supporting the visitor's older browser, you inadvertently created a messed up visual interface, and although it may be the fault of the browser, the user just expects things to work and will blame you for the quirks.

Situations like this one aren't uncommon. Desktop devices are not necessarily free of the restrictions that handheld alternatives encounter. Many people still are restricted to dialup or low-grade Internet access, screen sizes can vary dramatically, and power behind the devices can vary, so diversity is as relevant for desktops as it is for mobile devices. The trouble is that when thinking of a desktop machine, many designers think of high resolutions, speedy machines, and the latest web technologies and browsers; in the case of a netbook and other devices, this isn't the case. Try to do all you can to work around these real-world issues.

Desktop

Many web-enabled form factors exist, but none have sustained like the desktop computer. From the early days of the Web, you've been able to use the traditional tower with a monitor, a keyboard, and a mouse attached to browse the Web (see Figure 3-1). Even today, these machines remain a popular choice for consumers. Desktop computers are highly customizable with a wide range of features. These machines remain popular among online gamers, businesses, and users who don't want the upgrade constraints of portable devices.

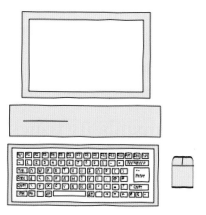

FIGURE 3-1: Desktops have existed for a long time, so you need to take older web-capable devices into account.

The following lists show this device's family tree and some issues its members encounter.

Relatives:

> Workstation

> Media center PC

> Gaming computer

> Kiosk systems

> All-in-one PCs

Considerations:

> Institutional longevity

> App configurability

> Hardware upgradability

Practical solutions

When designing for the desktop, the first issue that can affect your sites is institutional longevity. In many academic and government organizations, computers tend to have a longer "in-use" shelf life than you might expect, which can be particularly problematic if you use the latest technologies or have high-specification-based requirements. With older machines still in constant use and with demands for older, less-capable browsers (such as Internet Explorer 6 for corporate intranets), compatibility becomes essential.

Dealing with institutional longevity within your web designs doesn't have to mean being old-fashioned; it just requires you to be practical when building a site around the specific demands of a consumer's system. Though you might want to take advantage of the latest and greatest features of the Web, instead you should use either progressive enhancement or graceful degradation to provide a stable fallback for when the best can't be achieved. After all, it could be years before these organizations decide to upgrade!

One of the great things about desktop computers is that they often support a wide range of applications and browsers. In terms of the adoption of standards in browsers, desktops still lead the arms race. Although many handheld devices are getting better at keeping up-to-date with the Web's latest innovations, adopting web standards on these platforms often results from porting a desktop solution to the mobile environment. As a result, stability often comes at a cost to availability — and is affected by whether a user happens to have the right tools installed.

Note

One reason legacy devices and software exist in institutions is because the cost of upgrading can be enormous. If you have 100+ computers, you must deal with the cost of licenses, installation, maintenance, support, and more for each machine.

When novices buy a computer, they often use whatever is installed, out of the box. This practice is fine if your site supports all the major browsers and if users have products such as Microsoft Office installed (which opens up a range of websafe fonts); otherwise, this practice can create complications. So, you'll want to consider how ubiquitous a piece of software is before depending on its features for sites and services, including anything from typefaces, to frameworks (such as Adobe Air), to use of the Skype pseudo protocol.

With the latest hardware acceleration features included in modern browsers and with the amazing things that can be achieved (without Adobe Flash) using HTML5, jQuery, CSS3 animations, and more, many consumers worry about having a computer powerful enough to cope. Desktop computers are traditionally the most powerful device a user owns (they're also often easy to upgrade), so issues aren't as likely with desktop computers as they are with legacy or low-performance devices. Of course, even the performance of a really beefy machine can take a hit.

To help assure your site's stability, a good practice is to benchmark and stress test the heck out of your Hollywood-style effects. Although being able to produce an interactive comic book that uses more movement than a cartoon is great, effects that drain resources can stress even the most powerful machines. This is a very real issue for desktop devices and other computers, so avoid going over the top with anything that may cause bottlenecks (unless required for performance, such as in a game).

Best Practices

> Consider that your visitors may not have high-specification machines.

> Remember that users can disable or uninstall software and plug-ins.

> Avoid performance-heavy functionality, or at least limit its impact.

> Benchmark and stress test how long it takes for your site to process.

> Be flexible and compatible with various hardware and software types.

Laptop

The portable Internet dream has been around for quite a while, and the humble laptop (see Figure 3-2) has met the wishes of many surfers across the Web. Over the years, these small form-factored devices have increased in power, and for those who don't need the hardcore energy of a traditional desktop computer, these highly streamlined devices are a great alternative. In regard to stability on the Web, they do have limitations on the hardware they contain (especially in legacy devices), but they remain flexible in terms of software.

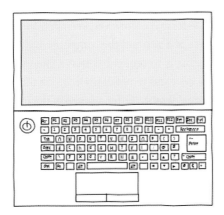

FIGURE 3-2: Laptops sacrifice upgradability for portability, which results in both benefits and pitfalls for designers.

The following lists show this device's family tree and some issues its members encounter.

Relatives:

> Gaming laptop

> Ultrabooks

> Desktop replacement

Considerations:

> Preinstalled systems

> Power supply limitations

> Hardware expectations

Practical solutions

Whenever you buy a new computer, software almost inevitably comes already loaded on the device. Sometimes, a piece of software is a useless component, such as a trial version of a graphic-intensive computer game, but in many cases, the software is beneficial to designers and websites. Many laptops come with plug-ins preinstalled (such as Flash), and often you get a range of websafe fonts in the machine, but preinstalled systems may also come with toolbars bundled with the default browser, reducing the amount of real estate for layouts!

Each manufacturer will install different products that, in general, will positively affect the ubiquity of formats (such as Adobe's PDF format). However, keep in mind that clutter can bog down a system, and the performance of a site and the computer may drop as a result. A best practice with preconfigured systems is to remember that some users may remove software, others may format their hard disk and reinstall their OS on purchase, and support for certain file formats may vary considerably. Offer a range of document formats.

Laptops, and especially gaming laptops, have one major consideration in web design. It's not their portability (though that is certainly worth considering); it's the amount of power they guzzle! When users are on the move with a gaming laptop, it makes sense that they'll want to be able to browse their favorite sites (hopefully, yours will be among them). As computers become more powerful, even if they're more efficient, users may suddenly find themselves running low on power, at which time, browsing becomes a time-sensitive issue.

Tip

Power supplies can affect computers in all sorts of ways. Screen brightness may be dimmed (so be sure your content has a good contrast), Wi-Fi may be turned off (so allow users to browse offline), and media could be reserved for later viewings. The implications are that you can't expect users to see things the same way you do.

Although you can't really do much to conserve visitors' use of power on your site (beyond limiting the use of plug-ins such as Flash and intensive browser effects), you can ensure that visitors take actions quickly and, if needed (when battery levels become critical), continue at a later date. Demanding that visitors complete a form in two minutes may seem like a great way to motivate them; however, what if they need to power down to prevent a crash? Obviously, in certain situations, you can't realistically expect them to continue on your site. Therefore, design your sites so that visitors can easily resume a session and, if they want, continue an action they weren't able to complete.

Finally, you need to examine hardware expectations. If you've ever owned a laptop, you know that these devices come with a great deal of technology carefully encased in the chassis. Pointer input devices (such as tracker pads and touch screens) have become a mainstay as an alternative to the mouse, speakers and microphones have gained added ubiquity, and users now expect to have the lowly webcam on many systems. Of course, these cool technologies have implications for designers, and you must factor them into your designs.

Because of the expectations associated with these devices, avoid assuming that users will have access to a mouse that can click with precision; remember that touch devices could be used in preference to more tactile tools like keyboards (laptops have begun experimenting with touchscreen sensitivity); and try taking advantage of tools that come with a machine by default. Why settle for textual comments when you can provide optional YouTube-hosted videos or an MP3 voice message via a laptop's built-in microphone or webcam?

Best Practices

> Check that third-party toolbars and sidebars don't obscure the viewport.

> Check that your documents work in a variety of viewer applications.

> Remember that your visitors may be working in a restricted environment.

> Power doesn't last forever; balance battery use against feature usefulness!

> Consider utilizing webcams, speakers, microphones, and other hardware.

Netbooks

Calls for cheaper computers that are also highly portable have pushed the netbook revolution into a successful market. These highly mobile, lower-cost machines (see Figure 3-3) are popular but can be tricky to accommodate. Many designers don't consider the issues that arise as a result of these machines' smaller screens and the fact they're less powerful than laptops. The differences among these devices are as substantial as those between a laptop and a tablet computer! They must, therefore, be treated with care as you work toward a stable site.

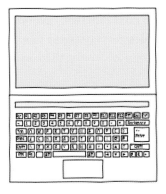

FIGURE 3-3: Netbooks may not be powerful, but they're very popular tools for browsing the Web.

The following lists show this device's family tree and some issues its members encounter.

Relatives:	**Considerations:**
> Chromebook	> Hardware fatigue
> Subnotebook	> Visitor choices
	> High portability

Practical solutions

Although netbooks are fantastic as low-cost web browsing devices, they're not the most powerful beasts in the digital jungle. They tend to have great battery life, but very little hardware power, so a real concern for designers is that lagging occurs if sites use processor-intensive animations or effects. Layouts and interfaces are becoming increasingly complicated, so think about how much pressure and stress you place on machines in terms of rendering and resources; otherwise, instability may occur.

Heavy Flash animations may result in unresponsiveness during rendering. Furthermore, if a site becomes unresponsive, there is an increased chance that the tab or browser will crash when interaction occurs. Obviously, crashing browsers and lagging, unresponsive sites are unacceptable, so if you can reduce or better distribute the load (using AJAX, for example), users will be happier. If a site crashes the browser consistently, users will likely avoid the site. Try not to just progressively disclose or hide content not in use; instead, scale it down (reducing the size to match the environment) and load it only when it's actually required.

Although hardware fatigue and crashing have a huge influence on the general stability and durability of a site, visitors' choices can be just as central to ensuring a future-proof layout. Today it's commonplace for sites to offer different environments for devices of varying capabilities and situations, yet site designers continue to make assumptions and decisions on behalf of users — for example, by not allowing them to determine how interfaces should be presented.

Note   There are movements toward offering netbooks a unique browsing experience not seen on PCs. The Google Chromebook, for example, is entirely web oriented because it runs Google Chrome (with nothing else). Although this places a strong emphasis on cloud-based services and limits system tweaks, users will be unable to change their web browsers.

If you provide alternative sites and decide to direct users toward a particular environment (such as a handheld-reduced layout or a desktop design), design your site so that visitors can jump between the two alternatives easily. Although there are debates about whether two versions of the same site are ever needed, it's accepted that there may be times when a capable handheld device gets a weaker experience or a less-capable computer is forced into using the heavy-going version. Choice is not only good in terms of usability but also because it empowers users.

Because netbooks are generally so small, they have the added advantage of being highly portable. This feature gives visitors the ability to access sites from many different environments, but the truth is that this ability can present its own fair share of issues. Beyond the obvious issues of security (see Chapter 10) and connectivity (see Chapter 9), an immediate concern is the environment in which users are working. They may be in a calm or busy location, a noisy or quiet place, or in a small, crowded, or large open space.

Designing sites that are easy to browse is critical to the longevity of your users' visits (users will quickly press the Back button if they fail to find what they seek). Large-click regions (links with plenty of clicking space) help users in cramped conditions or when a page is scaled out. Be sure that links offer the capability to confirm actions (such as the Delete option to correct mistakes if, for example, a user's arm is bumped resulting in an unwanted action). Avoid automatically playing audio (especially for users at work), and design your site so that every page has focal points to pull users away from distractions elsewhere on a screen.

Best Practices

> Ensure that your site and functionality won't crash a user's computer.

> Consider providing the ability to skip or turn off intensive flourishes.

> Always offer choices in how the content and service can be consumed.

> For perspective, browse the site in a variety of real-world situations.

> Avoid unexpected behavior that may embarrass visitors on the move.

Nettops

These devices, unlike netbooks, don't get the attention they deserve. Nettops are low-cost desktop PCs that have the same web-focused aim as netbooks (see Figure 3-4). They offer users an easy way to browse the Web, with few of the bonus features of a full power machine. Some people prefer a larger screen and added power over less portability, which nettops, unlike netbooks, provide. Nettops haven't caught the public's imagination like netbooks have, but they're web-friendly devices worth considering for the sake of compatibility.

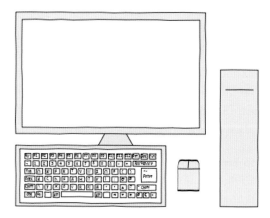

FIGURE 3-4: Nettops are like desktop computers, but they have much less power and are more web-oriented.

The following lists show this device's family tree and some issues its members encounter.

Relatives:

> Cloud PC

> Webtop

Considerations:

> Flexible form factor

> Cloud potential

> Single-use services

Practical solutions

Nettops are an oddity in that the form factor and experience differ greatly among models. Sometimes these devices are used as low-cost "nodes" to allow multiple users to share system resources (workstations); other times they work as plug-and-play media center units that can be hooked up to monitors as an alternative to a television. Nettops are even durable enough to be used as cloud devices (using Google Chrome OS or another OS to keep things web specific). As you can imagine, targeting this range of devices is tricky.

Consider an Internet café in a developing nation utilizing this technology to allow a group of people to share a low-cost web connection (via a central server). If such a site contains numerous resources and files making HTTP requests, users will be forced to wait as the priority system on the server delivers content at an inconsistent rate. As the designer, you can help avoid this situation by consolidating external files. By combining your CSS and JavaScript files, building image sprites, and caching objects, you can reduce waiting times.

Cloud computing is on the rise, and storing everything in a secure, continually accessible, and globally available location is an appealing thought. Service designers are starting to focus on this idea, taking everything online and using the hard disk purely for temporary storage. Businesses such as Google, Dropbox, and Apple are helping to push this concept to the maximum. So, as the idea of sustained user sessions evaporates and if you utilize cookies or personalized features such as user profiles, alternatives must be provided.

Note Nettops represent a new era of devices that are so bound by the constraints of the equipment that users could frequently find themselves unable to browse a site if it doesn't have a fallback to rely upon (such as the capability to save to Google Docs). Change isn't an option when these devices cannot have their hardware or software changed easily!

When you think of a user, you tend to picture a single person with his or her own computer and unrestricted access to the OS. However, the issue is that cloud computing forces local sessions to be treated like browsing at a public library (where you're bound by the vendor and their shared usage considerations). Data on a disk may be treated like the movie *50 First Dates,* in which memory is erased upon rebooting, caching is unpredictable, and cookies become unreliable. For a fluid user experience, you always need to think about what may happen if local data storage is lost.

Finally, you need to consider the case of single-use services. Never mind the minefield of shared devices and the problems they can cause in regard to tracking users, session data, and browsing habits. Have you considered how the site might be experienced by visitors who are simply testing a device (or using the Web) on an unfamiliar system? Imagine, if you will, a user in a PC retail store trying out a device or unit that could be his next PC. Or imagine that he borrows a friend's machine to visit your site. How do you handle this?

Part of having a stable site is making sure an experience is consistent on many platforms. Although you don't want to make everything look identical, you need an interface with a recognizable flow. If, for example, your users have multiple devices (like a phone and a laptop), the ability to use both devices makes or breaks the situation. When in the market for a new computer, they might factor how well your site works into their decision. If they use a friend's machine or a PC at work, they'll need their profile to migrate seamlessly to the new machine.

Best Practices

> Avoid using profiles and user scenarios; stereotypes are dangerous.

> Learn how different devices browse the Web; your education matters.

> Reduce HTTP requests to help visitors whose data priority is queued.

> Use cloud storage or backups for apps and services to avoid data loss.

> Treat computers like public devices and account for differences in use.

Helping Out the Handheld

Designing for handheld and ultra-portable mobile devices

DESKTOP DEVICES HAVE a long and established history as the pioneers of online experience, and the (to play off the song) times they are *a-changing*. The ability to take your web experience on the move is a compelling idea, and it's one that has gained mass appeal worldwide. This chapter analyzes the effects of small, handheld devices, showcasing why they matter. The chapter also covers the different experiences that each device type and model offers, and you discover how to be sure that your sites will work among them.

Benefiting from Portability

As far as web access goes, portability is the best game in town (if you need information and cannot afford to wait). You can't travel on the train, or go anywhere for that matter, without seeing people using cellphones, tablets, eReaders, or even web-powered watches to grab data on the move. Making your website usable on these popular platforms is essential to the success of your site, because as the world becomes increasingly connected, users are becoming more dependent on the benefits of technology.

Designing websites that are compatible with such a wide range of mobile devices poses a unique set of challenges. Many mobile devices differ significantly from one another in terms of hardware and software capabilities, which can make creating an interface that is stable on all devices difficult. Users who aren't web-savvy may not be willing to upgrade to smartphones, either through a lack of knowledge about the benefits they could bring or because the more capable and powerful smartphones cost more than traditional cellphones.

Note

Obsolete technologies tend to linger more on handheld devices (such as cellphones) than on desktops. WAP/WML, for example, still exists. It's hard to imagine that just five years ago, the capabilities of these handheld devices were primitive! Because this industry is evolving fast, the ubiquity of such devices is vital.

When choosing a layout for your website, keep in mind that mobile devices come in all shapes and sizes. Some phones may have larger screens than others, some have keyboards that are easier to use than others, and certain phones have better browsers than others. The distinctiveness of these products justifies the need to treat handheld devices as a new and exciting medium to work with. Responsive design will help to a certain extent (as will adaptive design, another useful design tool), but you must be willing to compromise to find a solution that meets your site's needs.

You also must consider the issues that touch screen devices present. They lack, for example, a traditional number-based keypad (which is commonplace on older featurephones) and mouse-click precision. Working on a small screen can be worrisome for designers wanting to ensure that user interactions are as stable as possible. Furthermore, many mobile devices have their own range of browsers, often with unique rendering engines, which means the testing methods and variables you use must differ from those used in desktop development.

A number of recommended best practices exist for dealing with the variables in handheld devices. These solutions usually stem from common hardware and software problems, such as the quirks for touch screens, highlighted in the upcoming sidebar, "The Apple fanboy." By dealing with these common issues (such as offering a purpose-built site or layout common for all screens under a certain size), designers can improve an experience and help resolve many well-documented complications. Make this one of your goals!

The Apple

A visitor navigates to your site, and like many people, this visitor happens to be an Apple fanboy. Apple products are pretty popular these days, so you need to consider them as a factor (whether you like the platform or not). In this case, the visitor has an iPhone and an iPad, using each device for different situations while visiting your site— the former while on the move (such as commuting to and from work), and the latter while at his office or at home, thereby overcoming the space restrictions that can occur in a crowded train car.

The problems your visitor encounters when visiting your site may differ widely, even regarding something as standardized as an iOS device. The visitor could, for example, have an older model that doesn't support Retina display (where HD video content will waste bandwidth) or could be using another browser apart from Safari, perhaps one like Opera Mini. Of course, all the devices are likely to have, or not have, certain things that can affect the experience, such as the lack of Adobe Flash support in the system.

Once the visitor gets to your site, perhaps he is doing fine and his mobile experience is equal to that on a desktop because of care and attention on your part. On the other hand, he may struggle to cope with the tiny click regions on the links or with the drop-down menu you provided because hovering events via a touch interface aren't too effective. Even worse, maybe those lovely, space-saving content overflows aren't working that well because of the need to use two fingers rather than one to scroll in such situations. Thinking about how these devices operate, and taking the time to code a workaround, can often eliminate these types of issues.

Tablet

Creating a stable interface isn't as easy as offering a desktop or cellphone solution. With their touch-screen interfaces and portability, tablet computers such as that shown in Figure 4-1 have many of the technical considerations of a phone. Tablets have a large screen, more power, and often more capabilities than a cellphone, however. Some tablets actually run a desktop operating system, and others run a mobile one. In this way, tablets bridge the divide between a laptop and cellphone (at least in terms of usage scenarios).

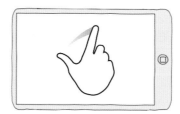

FIGURE 4-1: Tablets offer a lightweight way to browse sites on the move.

The following lists show this device's family tree and some issues its members encounter.

Relatives:	**Considerations:**
> Ultra-mobile PC	> Device sensitivity
> Tablet hybrid	> User environment
	> Device legacy

Practical solutions

Many tablet computers come preloaded with a desktop OS, and although tablet-friendly variants are beginning to make their mark, mobile operating systems are often used as a desktop alternative. Beyond the complexities that this can cause in relation to an interface's user-friendliness, hardware capabilities can be limited and underpowered. Combating such differences in scalability may require you to avoid behaviors that demand the user to manage windows (such as pop-up boxes and dialog boxes), and offer fallbacks to multi-touch gestures.

Anyone with fat fingers will tell you that trying to tap one of two tiny links next to each other is annoying, and nice chunky, easy-to-locate links turn this struggle into a pleasing experience. By clearly organizing your navigation menus and laying out your page to avoid squeezing too many interactive elements together, you can avoid such difficulties on touch devices. That's not to say everything on the page should be sumo-sized, but appropriately scaling an interface will make a big difference.

Depending on the environment, devices will often come with a method for allowing users to reference their sites beyond the browser. On iOS, adding custom iconic shortcuts to the home screen is possible; for desktop operating systems, the Bookmark and Favorites menus allow users to revisit their favorite sites quickly. Although it may seem like a small feature, the ability to add shortcut links (with custom-designed favicons) gives web designers an opportunity to bridge the gap between native and web-based applications.

Reference Creating a favicon or Apple touch icon is relatively straightforward, and Wikipedia has a fantastic guide detailing the conventions and formats you must provide for cross-device support (beyond ICO and 16x16 pixel formats): http://en.wikipedia.org/wiki/Favicon.

If you're providing a web app, it makes sense to include a favicon, an Apple touch icon, and a meaningful title (to act as the filename) to be sure that the process of adding shortcuts works well for software. However, don't forget about the little things that can increase a site's ease of use. Consider the on-screen keyboard in iOS, which lets you pick from a range of domains like dot com when you enter a URL. If you can get a domain name that tablets and other devices will default to (and users will easily remember), do it.

Tablets may be wonderful devices, but they can't be upgraded quickly and cheaply. As a result, many users hang onto their devices for a long time. Although this does give web designers an idea about how much power they might have to work with, it's also true that legacy devices become a real side effect of these situations. If the device, hardware, or software can't be easily (or cheaply) upgraded, users will tend to delay purchasing a complete replacement.

Take the time to understand the base configurations of different types of devices, not just the current ones, but also ones in the past. Understanding these defaults allows you to use data you find in analytics packages. If you have visitors using an iPad, you'll be able to determine what they can work with, and if they're using a device that has ten-year-old components and an outdated copy of Windows Mobile, you know it's time to despair! Knowledge is the key to successful website design, and without it, you're running blind.

Best practices

> Be sure interactive on-page elements don't require pinpoint accuracy.

> Tablet computer users hate tiny objects; scale your site accordingly.

> Remember to add favicons; doing so brings the device and site closer.

> Provide interface shortcuts within your site to aid efficient browsing.

> Learn about individual devices and their capabilities to guide your work.

Smartphone

Part cellphone, computer, game console, and just about everything else, these small yet durable devices have gained widespread popularity for their capability to undertake multiple tasks on the move. Because of their size and compact nature, smartphones (see Figure 4-2) are a genuine challenge for designers. Because they often sport high-quality browsers using the latest web standards, smartphones aren't as limited as many expect. Also, enhancing an experience by offering custom-built apps can supplement a site's usefulness.

FIGURE 4-2: Smartphones are capable devices, but scrolling a small screen can become tiring.

The following lists show this device's family tree and some issues its members encounter.

Relatives:

> Android (Google)

> BlackBerry (RIM)

> iOS (Apple)

> Symbian (Nokia)

> Palm OS (Palm)

> Windows (MS)

Considerations:

> Model abundance

> Popularity bias

> Function simplicity

Practical solutions

When dealing with smartphones, an immediate issue to contend with is the sheer number of these devices. Literally hundreds of different models are out there, roaming people's pockets, and as a designer, you need to contend with the diversity they bring. Some smartphones have their own dedicated custom-built browsers (and rendering engines), which can be a problem in terms supporting standards. Others put staggering ranges of component quality into the mix. Coping with the diversity in this market is a real issue.

Because of the range of smartphones, testing is also a challenge. Getting your hands on the physical devices is always the best practice because you'll get an idea of what the average individual is actually (or likely) seeing, but buying loads of devices could quickly become very expensive. As a result, many web designers rely on emulators to provide a simulated example of how sites will appear under the devices' constrained conditions. The great news is that emulators are usually free, and you'll need to search for each one online.

When it comes to choosing devices for testing, you will find a wide selection of smartphones. The popularity of these phones is without question, and the number of mobile users is set to overtake desktop numbers in the future. Knowing that these devices are increasingly important, you want to cover all popular bases. Although it would be nice to treat all devices equally, not all of them are born equal in terms of popularity or demand (and, of course, users' preferences change over time).

Reference

If you're looking for some free emulators, go directly to http://sixrevisions.com/web-development/mobile-web-design-best-practices/ and check the end of the article. If you're seriously looking for some cheap testing devices, perhaps look on eBay!

You can't please everyone. So, always test your site on the most-used devices first (this form of targeting will have the greatest effect on users). Often, the most talked-about devices aren't the most-used ones. Although iOS and Android often get the most media attention, unless your niche relates to Apple, Microsoft, or Google, a platform like Nokia is equally likely to have high usage stats. Research your options, set the most-used devices as a best-case scenario, and allow the site to flex beyond those proportions for other devices.

Because smartphones are compact devices without much space or many resources to go around, device makers employ all sorts of techniques to make life easier for users. Interfaces in browsers tend to be much more refined, and functionality is often simpler than in their desktop counterparts. This situation can cause problems when designers rely on browser-based functionality in order to use an interface, and it can also be a problem if the user's device (on any type of platform) has little to no functionality (such as the Lynx web browser).

Users often use the default browsers in smartphones to avoid incurring additional cost or complexity in an app store. As with the desktop, many users may not understand the advantage of getting a different browser and will continue to use what they've been given. Want users to make use of in-page searching? Looking to push a browser extension? Aiming to use some quirky JavaScript alerts? Beware. The resulting behavior may be highly unpredictable, so reduce your demands on their devices.

Best practices

> If you want to test on a range of phones for free, try some in-store models.

> Be sure that you don't forget older, deprecated versions of smartphones.

> Every device manufacturer has an emulator; don't forget to test on them.

> Find out about popular devices from independent sources like NetApplications.

> Avoid relying on browser functionality because it may not be available to users.

Featurephone

While the latest, greatest smartphones represent the best of breed in the handheld market, the classic featurephone (Figure 4-3) in its many task-oriented forms remains a popular option worldwide. Known for their low cost and availability, these devices come with access to the Web (a low-quality WAP browser, perhaps with HTML if you're lucky) and usually sport number keypads, low color or monochrome screens, and little in the way of general computing features. Essentially, they're a throwback to the old days of the Internet.

FIGURE 4-3: Featurephones may be basic, but they outnumber smartphones significantly.

The following lists show this device's family tree and some issues its members encounter.

Relatives:	**Considerations:**
> Cameraphone	> Information entry
> Musicphone	> Secondary features
	> Hardware quality

Practical solutions

One problem with older featurephones is that they often come with a very limited input method. Only having 12 to 15 tactile buttons can make life difficult if you're trying to enter data (and aren't a texting speed demon). Also, these devices are usually limited to supporting only basic HTML (on a good device) or WML (the norm), which makes organizing forms rather difficult. These devices are mostly oriented toward viewing textual content, so tackling the demands of interaction is critical.

Sites requiring input from users will have issues attracting users of these devices. Typing on a numeric keypad with support for alphabetic input takes time and energy; it's also an unnatural way to type if you're used to working on a QWERTY keyboard. Always allow your visitors to avoid filling in forms whenever possible, only requiring that they enter information when necessary; even then consider offering choices in drop-down menus. Progressive disclosure is the order of the day, and reducing the number of entry fields will save time.

The *feature* aspect of the featurephone has represented the diversity that can be achieved on these limited, single-focus devices. In particular, two types of featurephones, the cameraphone and the musicphone, have the potential to affect how your site will be accessed and used. For these low-quality devices, manufacturers must offer a unique selling point.

Tip   Don't spend too much time worrying about the different types of featurephones that exist. Instead, spend your time worrying about the quality of the underlying browser and whether users can successfully navigate your site with ease (when it's stripped).

Cameraphones in some devices may be able to take a snapshot or picture and upload that content to a site (which might be nice if you allow avatars in user profiles). Musicphones may let users hear podcasts or download MP3 files. Also, some featurephones may have superior-quality screens or perhaps a more technically capable browser. These differences can make or break a site, and there's little you can do about it. Still, they're worth knowing about — for example, you could offer MP3 formats for users who can't use a Flash player.

Face the facts: Featurephones are cheap, and with cheapness comes a lack of quality and generally low system specifications. One thing that particularly frustrates me is that despite their low quality (hardware and software), featurephones represent a huge portion of the Internet-browsing mobile-market share. Recent statistics show that up to 70 percent of all phone sales are for featurephones, not smartphones, and this reinforces the theory that the most popular devices often aren't the ones that are used the most.

With so many featurephones in use, you need to focus on the structure of your site. If the device supports only HTML or WML, you won't have the style you'd like to have available to help you define the site's quality. Working with these bare-boned devices requires a look back to the days of old. Forget all the flourishes and concentrate on a good navigation menu and some high-quality content. That's all these users can hope for, and honestly, when you boil the design process down, it's actually what the Web is all about.

Best practices

> Forms are the enemy of featurephones; make them optional if possible.

> Focus on ensuring content visibility to give cellphones a chance to work.

> Allow the use of a featurephone's camera, microphone, or speaker on a site.

> Structure your navigation menus carefully, with emphasis on simplicity.

> Write high-quality, succinct content; focus on reducing the fluff.

eReader

With the popularity of digital publishing, devices such as the Amazon Kindle have become popular reading devices. Built to improve the readability of print-based media on digital screens (using eInk), eReaders (Figure 4-4) deserve consideration in design. While these devices aren't powerful, the majority contain (at least for the time being) a black and white display and little support for animation or Flash. One feature that eReaders do have is that the devices are often the size of a book, and have rather unique screen sizes.

FIGURE 4-4: While eReaders may not be powerful, they often have good rendering engines.

The following lists show this device's family tree and some issues its members encounter.

Relatives:

> Cybook (Bookeen)

> Kindle (Amazon)

> Nook (Barnes & Noble)

> Pocketbook (Pocketbook)

> Reader (Sony)

Considerations:

> Visual content

> Vendor lock-ins

> Readability levels

Practical solutions

eReaders are built to view content (in the form of digital books). As such, when it comes to something like web functionality, they can become overwhelmed with the dynamic and less than static nature of the average site. Although many early eReaders might have a few problems viewing images in general, modern devices really do struggle to deal with intensive animated effects or videos. Times are changing, and this limitation may soon be overcome, but for legacy support, you want to at least consider offering a static fallback.

Dealing with online movement shouldn't give you too much trouble. Libraries like jQuery are built to gracefully degrade when accordion effects or visual flourishes aren't available, and if your scripts are not intrusive, the alternative shouldn't be a problem. Also, if CSS animations aren't supported, they will be ignored. Additionally, for the sake of accessibility, offer Flash fallbacks so that if a plug-in is unavailable, content will load. Dropping or reducing the use of animated GIFs may also be a good option.

eReaders are pretty strict, and for good reason. Although, as a secondary feature, they are Internet-enabled devices, primarily they are meant for reading content. Because of this, vendors tend to restrict their devices to supporting only the rudimentary tools that come shipped on the device to read online content. With firmware being upgraded only occasionally and with the dependency on device makers, you have to rely on choices that are offered or preset by default (which is different than the situation with desktops).

Note   JavaScript, in particular, has a few issues to contend with when it comes to the Amazon Kindle. Although scripting support comes natively with the device and can be used, it's unfortunately disabled by default. So you might literally have to ask users to turn it on!

Dealing with this feature, which is described by Amazon as an "experimental application," can be challenging because the end user will have a limited browser to work with. Yes, users can zoom in on the page. Sure, they can have the text read out to them (having the screen reader might be useful). However, there's no opportunity for users to get a better browser, use a different rendering engine, or use cool plug-in technologies. As in many cases, it's the content that matters most, and designers need to focus on that aspect.

It's definitely worth reiterating and placing emphasis on the eReader's readability levels. Looking on the bright side of life is a great idea when you're working with devices (after all, if you looked at all the negatives, you'd be too depressed to get anything done), and with eReaders, once you get the content on the screen, the reading experience is usually a very high-quality one. Therefore, focus on what these devices are good at, offering a great, elegant way to read content, free of interference and distractions.

First, pick decent, readable typefaces that scale in size to match users' needs. Users of smaller devices will always appreciate something that is highly readable without zooming. Users of eReaders in particular will love seeing some well-defined text and characters (so choose fonts well). White space (giving breathing room) and single-column layouts are also good choices because many books follow these conventions (small screen users will also benefit). If users expect book formatting, why not offer it?

Best practices

> Keep animation to a minimum for devices with a slow refresh frame rate.

> Avoid telling users to change browsers because they probably won't have that option.

> Don't expect functionality to always be enabled, even if it's included.

> Offer a print-friendly UI for devices that use them.

> Try to define appropriate font sizes for an optimal reading experience.

PDA

Before the days of smartphones and after the days of pocket calculators, the PDA (personal digital assistant) took the idea of computing into a tiny form factor offering a scaled-down experience with comparable features (think the Apple Newton). Although these devices aren't as popular as they used to be, their web enablement entitles them to support on your sites. Many PDAs (Figure 4-5) offer scaled-down keyboards and stylus pointers and sport smartphone-sized displays (but with fewer or no colors), and outdated and weak browsers.

FIGURE 4-5: PDAs were the precursor to smartphones, and many are still in use requiring legacy support.

The following lists show this device's family tree and some issues its members encounter.

Relatives:

> BlackBerry

> HTC

> Palm Pilot (Palm)

> WinMo (Microsoft)

> Other (Ogo & Sony Mylo)

Considerations:

> Layout degradability

> "Pen point" accuracy

> Postmortem viability

Practical solutions

Without pulling any punches, browsing the Web on a PDA is pretty awful. These devices, which are the precursors to smartphones, have a number of issues in usability, rendering, and a whole lot in between! The problems become critical enough that in designing for a PDA device, you need to try to patch together a stable interface by ensuring everything degrades with a fallback and a purpose. Consider something like Windows Mobile, which takes advantage (or should that be *disadvantage*) of dead versions of Internet Explorer.

Degrading your layout is as much a matter of making use of your space as it is utilizing the patching technologies available to code to regain some control over layouts. A few outdated PDAs have monochrome displays, plenty don't have a high pixel depth (making images look substandard), and with browsers comprised mostly of early adopter support for CSS 2.1, the result of your style and behavior could be crippling. If a site breaks upon testing, conditional comments, code compilation, hacks, and filters may be useful.

Browsing the Web on a PDA comes with an advantage and an input device that gets around the small screen issue: the digital pen (or stylus). By offering these tools with the device, users can tap the screen with accuracy (that is, if they don't just use their fingers, instead). Slightly counterproductive is that in preference to offering zoom functions, many PDAs predating the smartphone era overwrite CSS styling to scale content correctly or use scrollbars (in both directions) to simulate a full screen, keyhole preview in the window.

Tip   Looking for some PDA browsers? Plenty of archive sites and download portals retain their collections so that fans can still use the now mostly obsolete devices on the Web. While the PDA may be an old platform, it is worth finding some emulators for testing.

When dealing with PDAs, you must treat the device with care. Click-region sizes are probably not going to be a major issue because of the stylus, though small text could prove a bit tricky for those who want to actually read what's on the screen. In addition, PDA devices of old seem to have a few issues with images. I've encountered cases when images more than 150 pixels wide may not be rendered (correctly or at all). So, scale down your images for the device's capability, and in the process, save some bandwidth, too.

It may sound harsh, but with the advent of smartphones and the increasingly popular featurephone, the good old PDA has fallen into a bit of disrepair. Even though the devices may have entered retirement, retro fanboys and enterprising users of the devices continue to develop for these platforms, giving even the oldest of devices a better experience and a refreshing attempt at compatibility. Although users are required to download the apps and make the change, doing so helps to resurrect the dead devices.

Apps cannot solve hardware problems like a poor screen, a weak input medium, or a worn-out battery, but what they can do is provide users with a browser that (at least) supports the latest web standards and makes better use of the viewport. When designing for PDAs and older handheld devices, encouraging users to upgrade their software can help (if it's done responsibly as a request, not a demand). If users decide not to upgrade, check that links on the page function correctly, and try to ensure that designs offer a handheld stylesheet, too.

Best practices

> Be sure your images are legible on resolution-poor displays.

> Squeeze your content into one column, avoiding scrollbars.

> Try the site on a PDA without the stylus to really push its usability.

> Install a variety of browsers for each PDA platform for testing.

> Offer users a mobile handheld stylesheet for compatible devices.

Wristwatch

Although other handheld devices have already gained support, it's worth looking to the future and to what tiny devices like digital watches (Figure 4-6) may have in store. It may be surprising that something so small can be used as a web device, but with gadgets like the iPod Nano going mainstream, and companies already beginning to put WAP and web-capable watches into production, supporting micro-devices is surely going to be worth considering in the coming years. How does your site look on a 3-inch display?

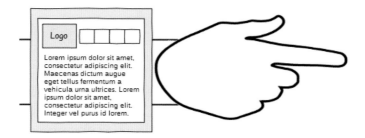

FIGURE 4-6: A web-enabled computer on your wrist? It's entirely possible and likely to happen!

The following lists show this device's family tree and some issues its members encounter.

Relatives:	Considerations:
> Fossil Wrist	> Device usability
> sWaP watch	> Update frequency
> ZYPAD	> Feed syndication

Practical solutions

Although the number of web-enabled wristwatches is fairly limited at the moment, the basic principle of creating technology that is smaller and lighter is making them a viable option for the near future. When designing for such devices, the main issue is that as devices become more compact, you have to work harder to prioritize content within the available physical space. Maintaining a usable interface on a 3-inch screen is tricky, and scrolling becomes a necessity. But as with life, all things are possible!

Without focusing too much on the screen, offering a usable interface for watches requires considerable visual changes to your layouts. One popular idea based on the iPod Nano is to turn your navigation menu into a series of icons that progressively disclose the content once a selection has been made. Achieving this could involve either using an entire page for menu options (for WAP-only devices) or using media queries and some other clever scripting toolkit to account for the exceptionally cramped environment and requirements.

Because, in the past, many of the digital watches were proof of concept designs rather than serious mainstream computing devices, updates for the platforms have been few and far between. Earlier models focused on single firmware versions with no upgrades, and this really pushes web compatibility to the limit. However, as with many of the old, retro devices, the rush of users with a renewed interest in this type of device has inspired individuals to hack or modify the devices into doing what they want. Fun for all indeed!

Reference

A number of apps offer VNC-style remote control of a normal computer (making it an input device). A couple of my favorites are Splashtop Remote (www.splashtop.com/remote/) and Mobile Mouse Pro (http://mobilemouse.com/).

Realistically, making a site compatible with this platform isn't something that many people should worry about (for now), but with the future of devices in question and with nanotech getting better, accounting for micro-devices and their future in browsing experiences makes sense. Another practical consideration is that watches could become remote controls for TVs, PCs, and more (affecting browsers as an input device). If this does happen, your content must be able to scroll easily, and the browser's UI (notably the Back button) should continue to function with stuff like AJAX.

When you have a page filled with content and a device with reduced capabilities, size does seem to matter. It would be unfair to place the entire blame on these devices' native capabilities because over the years sites have increased in size, density, and features. Previously, lots of energy was put into trimming pages into small, efficient machines, but in this modern era of broadband and high-speed connections, this art form has been all but lost.

Easy ways to deal with this issue are to work through the content, eliminating marketing text, unnecessary data, and fluff. Content management is something that more designers need to take advantage of, and tightening the copy helps in a number of ways. Beyond this (and the reductionist approach), many sites offer syndication feeds such as RSS and Atom to offer content to those who want quick, efficient updates. Finally, if your site isn't ideally suited for newslike updates, you could just break down pages into smaller ones!

Best practices

> Try experimental interfaces for more uncommon situations.

> Don't just focus on native capabilities; devices can be remote controllers.

> Ensure that default browser functionality isn't crippled by your code.

> Break down lengthy pages of content to reduce the pressure caused by scrolling.

> Offer your content in a variety of syndication formats.

Evolving for Entertainment

Designing for the latest generation of
web-enabled devices

ENTERTAINMENT DEVICES ARE shaking up the Web. Although we currently live in the age of a handheld revolution, it's correct to say that entertainment devices such as the humble television set are ready to join their digital cousins in becoming the latest web-enabled tools. In this chapter, you find out about the entertainment devices that have already shaken up the Web, and you also take a look at the practices that could help you retain a compatible layout.

Bringing the Web into the Living Room

In recent years, attitudes about the use of the Web have changed. Designers have been worrying about the impact of handheld devices on site experiences for a while, but the more subtle forces of beginner-friendly and web-friendly entertainment gadgets have been gaining momentum. The benefits of bringing the Web and its hours of entertainment into the living room are easy to see, and the simple, easy-to-use interfaces that such devices are equipped with make them worth considering.

When thinking of Internet television, you may consider the early experiments like MSN WebTV or a game console's multiplayer mode. Your sites and services can and will be accessed on these devices (game consoles and set top boxes act like intermediary bodies, giving an online experience to those who don't want to replace their existing hardware). However, because of their cost, the adoption of all-inclusive Internet TVs has been slow, though like HD and 3D, web access has become an expected feature of such devices.

Tip

Many barriers to entry exist in web interaction, and entertainment devices in particular will struggle with complex layouts. Bulking your interface with larger click regions and reducing the visible content per page will help the device and any TV it's connected to.

Regarding compatibility, the problems with multimedia devices don't often stem from the hardware they provide because they're mostly standardized. Legacy issues with older devices that fail to get any firmware upgrades are problematic and will remain a major factor, but unlike cellphones, the upgrade ratio for game consoles and set top boxes is a gamble these days. When contemplating old devices (retro gaming could keep old stuff in the mix for decades), the situation with browser quality and input devices becomes messy.

Television devices with web access, though not entirely ubiquitous or standardized at the moment, will very likely become a mainstay in future Internet use. These types of devices are highly appealing to those wanting to rent or gain access to onDemand media without needing to use or buy a computer (increasing the usefulness of their TV). However, the fact that this technology exists and will become a standard as part of the traditional upgrade technique means that it's a case of "sooner or later," not a vaporware pipedream!

As the Web becomes embedded in gadgets used for entertainment and the technology matures, your visitors will find themselves experiencing your work in evermore-diverse situations. If you make your work as flexible and platform-friendly as possible, your sites are more likely to attract the increasing audience for this medium. New breeds of Internet-capable devices also show that, even though many people assume that responsive design is aimed at handheld devices, these new devices can also be useful in catering to grander, more niche situations.

Accessing the Web with a PS3

Imagine that one of your visitors goes out to buy a game console such as the popular Sony PlayStation 3, and in addition to using it for movies (via the built-in Blu-ray player) and its native gaming functionality, the visitor decides at that point in time that she wants to see what's new on your site. Perhaps you've published a new video or screencast; perhaps you've included an exciting story; you might even have a live event going on! Any reason will work — for the last few years, most game consoles have provided built-in browsers.

Upon opening the PlayStation 3's native browser and typing your site's address (if she doesn't have a keyboard attached and frequently uses the built-in browser), the visitor's first issue may be that your site was designed with desktop devices in mind. Because few sites are designed with television screens in mind (not PC monitors and perhaps a cellphone or tablet), it's likely that the fixed-width layout you've built won't look first-rate. In addition, many game consoles currently do not have great browsers, so the latest web standards may be a problem for them.

Visitors on an entertainment device are likely to have significant issues inputting data if they're relying on a TV's remote control. Additionally, game controllers such as a Microsoft Kinect or a joystick can be particularly quirky to interact with. As users sign up for your service, they may find themselves struggling to fill in lengthy registration forms. In addition, your site doesn't scale well on their "40+ inch" TV set, which stretches things out as a result of its low resolution. These factors may all seem rather farfetched, but they present a situation that's on the horizon.

Television

Being able to browse the Web on a television (shown in Figure 5-1) isn't a new invention. Back in the 1990s, MSN offered a product called WebTV, allowing a browser-based experience to be served through a dedicated TV set (using a tweaked copy of Internet Explorer). Although the product is no longer available, its users still exist and require support. Modern TVs, unlike WebTV, sport widgets, standards-compliant browsers, and tools to make browsing easier. These modern TV offerings boost the general usefulness of the feature into something users want.

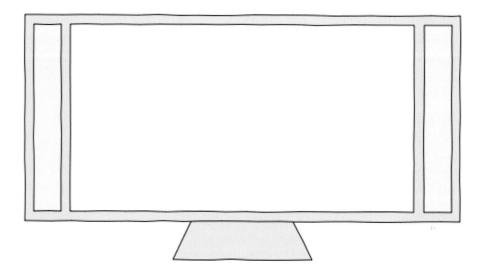

FIGURE 5-1: Televisions are an ideal way for novices to get a taste of the Web, without the expense of a computer.

The following lists show members of the television's family tree and some issues its members encounter:

Relatives:

> Smart TV

> Hybrid TV

> WebTV (MSN)

Considerations:

> Distance viewing

> Non-standard features

> Task efficiency

Practical solutions

Diversity in size is one of the defining characteristics of televisions. You can buy TVs that are anything from 10 to 100 inches (and potentially bigger, if you really have money to burn). However, even if your sites are scaled up to enormous representations of their desktop counterparts, you need to consider how viewing distance could affect the content's visibility. Televisions, in general, have lower resolutions than computer displays, so you can't rest on your laurels when it comes to ensuring good visibility of your site.

When most people use a computer, they tend to sit only a couple of feet away from the screen and are able to make out the crisp, high-resolution on-screen details. However, this is not the case with TVs, and now especially with large TV screens, people are sitting farther away from the device, allowing their field of vision to account for the larger screen size (greater distances may also relieve eye strain). To see how visible the content and imagery of your site is, try sitting in various positions and distances from the screen and then increase the size of your text if needed.

Another consideration with television displays is that a number of non-standard features can affect your sites. It's not uncommon in the electronics world for a company to put its own spin on a technology. Just think about how cellphone makers have turned the concept of a featurephone into an excuse to customize everything. However, the innovations that are produced can result in inconsistencies with browser rendering (MSN WebTV) or with a demand to use proprietary non-browser-based applications or widgets.

Reference Microsoft has discontinued the WebTV download, but you can still test on the WebTV platform using the Windows- and Mac-compatible emulator, available at http://web.archive.org/web/20070622144935/http://developer.msntv.com/Tools/WebTVVwr.asp.

If you look at the earliest example, WebTV, a number of proprietary elements were added into the browser to help designers make their pages better suited to television displays. In modern televisions, technologies like RSS or Atom feeds can be handled via a widget platform. Handling inconsistencies may seem tricky, but if you follow modern standards and ensure that your code is well formed, there shouldn't be too much of an issue. Although user-agents should render things correctly, you'll likely need to code around their oddities!

People visit websites to achieve goals, and this doesn't change when a television is involved. One of the critical issues with browsing the Web on a TV is that navigating around a page is more involved. Consider how hard it is to negotiate a layout using nothing but a remote control. Without a mouse or keyboard (which most sites assume will be used), the ability to scroll, zoom, or click links will require a great deal of precision. You want to make these tasks as easy as possible.

Dealing with the restrictions of televisual hardware requires you to reconsider how you design sites. Many designers concentrate so much on the visuals that they forget about efficiency. Being able to achieve a job in the shortest possible time and with the least amount of effort is a good thing, and psychology shows that visitors appreciate those attributes. Ensuring that navigation menus are informative, well described, and easy to access (without a mouse or pointer available) makes for a better, more useful, and accessible viewing experience.

Best practices

> Ensure that designs scale up effectively (try zooming pages, for example).

> Put yourself in a similar situation as users; check readability from a distance.

> Avoid proprietary features if you can; they only add additional complexity.

> As always, test on as many devices as possible (and the WebTV emulator).

> Try reducing the number of clicks or keys required to reach a destination.

Game Console

Game consoles such as the Nintendo Wii (see Figure 5-2) have gotten into the web ecosystem by embedding a browser (to varying degrees of success) within their devices. Consoles not only increase the ubiquity of browsing via a TV, but it brings a new set of interaction and usage concerns for designers. Unlike televisions, game consoles tend to upgrade their firmware frequently, leading to better browsers. Also, because of tools like the Nintendo Wii Wiimote, navigating the page can be a real experience.

The following lists show members of the game console family tree and some issues they encounter:

Relatives:

> Dreamcast (Sega)

> PlayStation (Sony)

> Wii (Nintendo)

Considerations:

> Unusual interactions

> Interface guidance

> Game mechanics

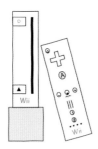

FIGURE 5-2: Unlike the Xbox, the Nintendo Wii comes with a browser.

Practical solutions

Game consoles are entertaining devices, and because they come with built-in browsers and are traditionally hooked up to a television, they offer an easy portal to the Web. Ensuring that your site is compatible with gaming computers requires being more aware of input mediums because users are used to having joysticks, gamepads, and gesture controllers attached to their devices. Moreover, consoles and televisions don't handle scrolling with dexterity.

When dealing with these devices, you first need to note the differences among platforms (consoles use desktop or mobile browsers). The browsers that are built into TVs don't particularly like the jagged movement of scrolling, so reducing the need to do so via progressive disclosure can be useful. Because hardware keyboards aren't common in game consoles, reducing the need for text input makes sense. Ways to achieve this include aids like autocomplete and autosuggestion features, breadcrumb menus, and drop-down menus.

One prize feature offered by many game consoles is the use of logical interfaces. Although many TV interfaces probably won't translate over to the desktop web because of their high dependency on video and audio, designers can learn a few lessons about the ever-evolving expectations of visitors. Depending on the platform they utilize, users will expect different experiences and features (suited to that device). Mobile users often prefer streamlined interfaces; gamers like visuals. So, be sure to keep these differences in mind.

Reference Best practices can be gleaned by looking at the components, uses, and features of a device. Go to `http://www.sean.co.uk/a/webdesign/webdesign_for_nintendo_ds_opera_browser.shtm` to find out how you can adapt a site for the Nintendo DS handheld console.

Consider something as basic, but essential, as a contact form. We've gotten so used to letting our hunger for information overload and overwhelm users that the basic usability of a site suffers as a result. When offering contact forms to devices with smaller screens or scrolling issues, consider dividing the forms into logical sections with boxes and progressive steps so that users can fill in the forms at their own pace. You can make such drastic UI changes with televisions by detecting the unique user-agent strings for browsers.

Modern gaming isn't the occupation of geeks with no friends; instead, it has become an event that brings together entire families or groups of people, socially connected around the world. With the Web being an equally expressive and communicative medium, taking advantage of the TV platform to encourage interaction within a site makes perfect sense. By utilizing game mechanics, you can add another dimension to your layouts and also help a website retain a diverse audience, which is necessary for a site to survive.

Examples of game mechanics that encourage interaction and sustain interest levels include offering user profiles, statistics, and point systems. These common game console features may seem trivial to the owner of a site, but their addictive nature means you may achieve a sustained presence on your sites. You'll also want to consider gaining feedback by using simple tools such as polls, which, unlike surveys for getting user feedback, don't require a lot of time or energy to answer. Gamers tend to become easily frustrated or impatient, so they'll want to perceive whatever they undertake as offering them an inherent benefit.

Best practices

> Progressively disclose your content to avoid information overload.

> Visitors expect interactivity, but ensure that it functions smoothly.

> Employ game mechanics to tempt console users to open a browser.

> Everything must have a purpose. If it doesn't, then don't include it!

Handheld Console

Although game consoles are bringing their unique charm to the browsing masses, more mobile products are getting into the arena, too. Whether you're browsing via a handheld gaming device that's provided by a console maker (like the Nintendo DS, see Figure 5-3) or a dedicated gaming device with web connectivity by a cellphone manufacturer (like the Nokia N-Gage), access to the Web is easy. Many have customized browsers to deal with small screens and a range of unique inputs, and like featurephones they are tough to design for.

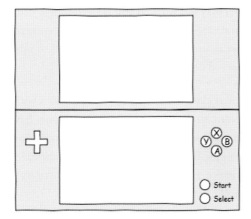

FIGURE 5-3: Handheld game consoles can be just as web-friendly as their TV-connected counterparts.

The following lists show members of the handheld console family tree and some issues they can encounter:

Relatives:	**Considerations:**
› 3/DS (i) & Wii-U (Nintendo)	› Multitasking
› N-Gage (Nokia)	› Friendly URLs
› PSP (Sony)	› Region responses

Practical solutions

Although desktop consoles can take advantage of a wonderfully large screen, the smaller brothers of these giants of entertainment tend to be more restrictive, both in the viewport they provide sites and in the durability of the experience. Consider something that you take for granted, such as multitasking, or the ability to have a number of tabs hanging around the top of a browser window. Being able to render windows side by side is something you may expect (such as opening a new window), but it's not always available to your users.

Handheld gaming consoles tend to follow the notion of keeping everything in one field of vision to reduce confusion. For designers, this means your requests for pop-ups or a new window or tab (scripted or otherwise) may not work. If you're designing a site that'll work for everyone, avoid trying to do anything that draws attention to two separate pages. Always allow users to choose whether to use pop-ups and new windows or tabs, especially because their use can affect low-powered devices.

I've already mentioned the issues that data input can have on devices with limited or more unusual input tools. Now, I want to discuss the effect these tools have on URLs. Software-based on-screen keyboards are usable; however, they generally don't have the accuracy or tactile quality of a traditional keyboard. Although this feature differs greatly based on the make and model of a device, it's better to be safe than sorry by using short, easy-to-read URLs, and avoiding complex strings of characters.

Tip

Extra windows and tabs make using a handheld device a little confusing, but other on-page media may be detrimental to a user's experience. Frames and iFrames, for example, are known for poor accessibility and, if possible, should also be avoided.

One of the more obvious ways to ensure that your site is data-entry friendly is to give it an easy-to-type, friendly URL (using mod_rewrite) that doesn't have misspelled words and that an autocorrect feature (as commonly found in handheld devices) might overrule. Another issue to contend with is the need for international domain names because input could be limited to the language of the country in which the device was purchased. Finally, it makes sense to avoid excessive character strings because inputting text can become hard work.

Handheld gaming consoles can be useful little browsing devices, offering good resolutions, plenty of colors, and a standards-compliant browser (or at least one that's close). Taking on the challenge of building a site that's compatible for these devices requires determining what your visitors need to know, when they need to know it, and how to ensure that when they click a link or do something on the site, that site does what it's told to do. There is nothing worse than an unresponsive layout, and you can remedy this issue in several ways.

Because handheld game consoles have relatively small screens, users must be able to undertake actions on the device *and* know where those actions will lead. If the site offers a lightbox effect, make the image appear at the center of a user's field of vision. If users incorrectly type a phone number (say, by slipping an alphabetical character in there), they will appreciate receiving an alert about the issue next to or near the input box. Users don't appreciate unwelcomed surprises, and all actions should be accompanied by a reaction.

Best practices

> Sites need to be self-contained; avoid spreading them into multiple tabs.

> Frames within a page are an unnecessary evil; avoid them at all costs.

> Keep URLs short, sensible, and in English, if possible or applicable.

> Pages should be well-structured, so use friendly URLs to help visitors.

> Keep warnings, dialog boxes, or alerts within the user's field of vision.

Media Player

The idea that your MP3 player can provide Internet access makes perfect sense. If you're a fan of Apple, you know all too well that certain iPods (Figure 5-4) provide such a feature. In addition, Microsoft's Zune and a range of other manufacturers offer a browser with their devices. Like cellphones, media players tend to be compact with tiny screens and a browser that does the job well. Plenty of these media-playing devices also use a mix of touch screens with on-screen keyboards to limit the size of the physical hardware.

FIGURE 5-4: Web-enabled MP3 players are like cellphones, but without the phoning capability.

The following lists show the members of the media player family tree and some issues they encounter:

Relatives:

> Archos

> Cowon

> iPod touch (Apple)

> Zune (Microsoft)

Considerations:

> Media richness

> Proprietary media

> Usage demands

Practical solutions

Many sites, even to this day, have failed to comprehend the help that media can give a design. Providing video and audio that automatically begins playing without the user's permission certainly isn't a good plan; nevertheless, utilizing the power of dedicated media-playing devices with web capability is central to surviving in the home entertainment market. If you have a product you want to sell, have you considered guided tour videos? How about podcasts on news sites? An MP3 player can take advantage of many options.

The use of media on a device can be affected by the support and playability of supported media formats, and certainly you need to account for browser plug-ins (such as the availability of Flash). However, if you want to offer media to consumers, you must first consider the quality of the devices. Although an MP3 player will likely have a great set of speakers and a good sound card, other devices may not have the same screen quality (for video) or audio capabilities. In such cases, offer alternative, optimized content.

When dealing with MP3 players, you have two types to consider. First are the ones that are dedicated to playing music with only a browser as a bonus feature. On the other side of the equation are the tablet hybrids, such as the iPod touch, which are media players that can perform other functions on the side (and can be treated like small computers). These variations are central to understanding how media-focused these products are and more important, how well they can handle the needs of someone browsing your site with them.

Tip

When offering multimedia on a site, consider how compatible the content is in terms of web accessibility. Providing audio descriptions, captions, subtitles, sign language, or translations can go a long way toward giving disabled users a chance with a device.

If you provide media on your site, be sure that your loyal viewers can access this useful content. Two issues that dedicated media players experience are that they tend to support streaming directly from the source, rather than downloading, and they can have a low-quality browser with good levels of support for formats. Hybrid devices, with their multi-function capabilities, often have a good browser with solid media support, offering various video sizes and quality or compression levels to ensure that your users get the best fit for their model.

Media players are like mobile phones in that people carry them everywhere. Particularly interesting for web designers is that, with this kind of travel, using audio or video content can be advantageous in certain situations. Podcasts can be listened to in an office or during a gym session (when you need to multitask), screencasts can be watched on a bus or when you are sitting down, and both need to be as user-friendly as possible to encourage users to return. When it comes to online media players, resumability and tactility rear their ugly heads.

Dealing with *resumability* (the ability to resume a media session) is critical because you don't want readers to be cut off during a session with no means of checking their progress. If the user's MP3 player (or mobile device) runs out of power, if a browser or OS crashes, or if the user loses connection with the Internet, having their playing book-marked is helpful. Beyond offering this help, remember to ensure that a media player (if you have any control over this) isn't too fiddly to work with because the visitor may be playing media on the move.

Best practices

> Consider offering podcasts or screencasts to expand content relevancy.

> Offer a range of compression and video sizes to match device capabilities.

> Provide a range of popular formats to compensate for a variety of devices.

> Always allow media to be resumed because connectivity isn't guaranteed.

> Users play media in all sorts of places; players need extra flexibility!

Set Top Box

A number of providers have begun building dedicated boxes, called *set top boxes* (Figure 5-5), which offer the power of WebTV without needing to replace your equipment. These devices are gaining popularity, not only because of brands like Google embedding Chrome OS to offer a seamless experience, but also because many onDemand providers now allow their media to be broadcast and integrated, giving bonus material and exclusive content via the cloud. This capability offers non-gamers the opportunity to browse the Internet on their sofas.

The following lists show members of the set top box family tree and some issues they encounter:

Relatives:

> Apple TV

> Boxee

> Google TV

> TiVo

> YouView

Considerations:

> Jailbroken devices

> Single-task focus

> Lacking in expansion

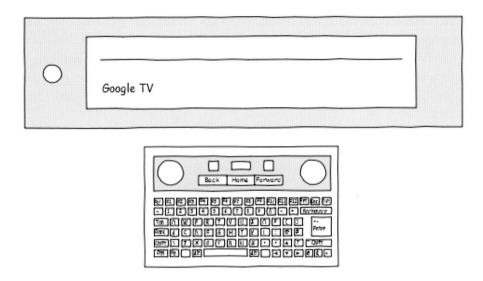

FIGURE 5-5: Set top boxes provide web-browsing functionality to televisions that don't have the native capability to do so.

Practical solutions

With the Internet television revolution on the horizon, a good number of device makers are working on building set top boxes that can offer web-browsing functionality to TVs that don't already have web capabilities built in. Many of these devices offer a wide range of functionality, but there are always going to be a number of enthusiasts who want to push the technology beyond what it was built to cope with. Jailbroken iPhones show that web experiences can be dramatically altered with a hack, so let's focus on the TV equivalent.

The great thing about compatibility for jailbroken devices is that in many cases, better or more universal solutions present themselves. If a good browser can't make it into an app store, the jailbroken version may offer that extended (potentially better) functionality to devices in a less-restricted environment. However, jailbreaking can go in another direction and leave devices open to malware, so you need to be sensible in how you support or use such options. In terms of solutions, only support jailbroken technology if there's a demand for it.

Set top boxes in general aren't known for their multitasking capabilities. Although people do complain about how limiting a certain MP3 player's methodology is, the truth is that set top box devices are so bound by their infrastructure that multitasking is often out of the question, which isn't a bad thing because it can help to focus users on achieving one goal at a time. However, visitors may find that Web browsing is challenging if they're forced to go from one site to the next, with little more than bookmarks or their History tab for aid.

Note

Design is as much about anticipating and providing solutions for when something goes wrong as it is about trying to keep things looking right. One variable may topple a site by a quirk of nature, but a single, well-crafted feature can save a site many times over!

Because these devices are always focused on the here and now rather than the journey leading up to that point, you need to ensure that your visitors don't become trapped in a dead-end scenario. Examine your site's visual hierarchy and provide relevant crosslinks and a visible global navigation menu to content that will interest that particular niche (perhaps this is where video content could be showcased); always be clear about the route through your site (to avoid wrong turns); and provide some good documentation to help lost souls.

Set top boxes aren't known for their *expandability*. Although some offer a USB or HDMI port to allow media to be transferred to another device, or in the latter case, a good connection to a high-definition TV (these boxes are the middlemen for browsers as are game consoles), you're unlikely to be able to attach a printer or mouse to the box (though certain devices might offer a keyboard). The legacy consequences for such imposed limitations may be huge.

If a set top box has firmware that isn't upgraded frequently, browser support may not move with the times. If the hardware locks itself into vendor-approved devices, how you interact with the medium will be inhibited. With these boxes of destiny or doom, you must follow the vendor's specifications and guidelines if you want to explicitly cater experiences to their users. As with the W3C specifications, you must RTFM (read the fluffy manual), make appropriate changes, and test on the affected devices. There are no shortcuts here!

Best practices

> Support jailbroken devices in your workflow, if your users have them.

> Regularly check your site to ensure that harmful exploits don't exist.

> Reading a manual may be tedious, but doing so can be very helpful.

> Don't punish users for making a mistake; instead, help them recover.

> Documentation is worth its weight in gold. Don't forget to write it!

Automobiles and Appliances

Considering compatibility with household appliances and automobiles

HOUSEHOLD APPLIANCES HAVE gained connectivity on the Web, so it's not surprising that compatibility considerations go far beyond just desktop, handheld, and entertainment mediums. Of course, sci-fi films have always promoted the idea of living in some kind of digital home, with robots and weird, yet wonderful, gadgets — and now the future is here! In this chapter, you examine the ways in which household appliances, transportation, and even buildings themselves are gaining connectivity to the Web, and how you can design for these new environments.

Preparing for Your Dream Reality

A few years back, people were making jokes about how Apple's next product would be an iToilet (perhaps based on those Japanese toilets that have more technology than a NASA space mission). However, here we are today with big-brand companies such as Samsung and LG embedding web enablement in household appliances like microwaves and refrigerators, and Microsoft has created cool Internet-enabled furniture (Surface). In addition, you can now browse the Web in your car or in an airplane. It's all becoming like a reenactment of wacky races!

Although these devices may seem like gimmicks, they have potential and our vision of the Web is changing even more than we may realize. A true digital home may be a long way off, but that's not to say that a web-connected house won't happen. Rather than browsing a traditional interface, these tools parse content and display that data in a unique way, much like "feed readers." Simply put, it's still the Web, but not as we currently know it.

Note Manufacturers use heavily customized systems, so limitations will be imposed on users based on the device maker's API. Objects like a web-enabled refrigerator will be targeted toward performing specific tasks, so unless you're signed up to the system manufacturer's API, your site probably won't be directly affected by such devices.

Some of this fabled technology already exists in a commonplace environment. Consider transportation and the range of Internet-ready gadgets found in planes, trains, and automobiles. Many of us drive around with a SatNav, some cars even have some form of entertainment system (such as televisions or DVD players), and lots of us take our MP3 players on the move, which in the case of the iPod touch means remote web access. Even car dashboards are becoming more digitally aware, which, of course, could interfere with concentration!

To further complicate matters, many of these devices rely on touch screens because they're easier to clean and take up less space. In addition, web connectivity is likely to become an immediate issue as carrier coverage isn't guaranteed, and to help avoid traffic accidents, the car may limit or disable your access to gadgets while in motion. Using hands-free navigation (perhaps using screen reader software that will audibly read content from the screen) and voice activation may help in this case, but it demands that your sites be very accessible via the Web.

Regardless of the odd devices that piggyback existing products or those that do the interacting on our behalf, there is an important lesson. Times change, devices change, and visitors will continue to dictate which products you need to support. Ensuring that your site works is fairly straightforward, but having a stable site that unconventional devices can use is a challenge. With such interactions taking place, what you see isn't always what users get — it's a marvelous environment that an increasing number of devices are using.

Creating a futuristic travel site

Imagine that a client has asked you to produce a travel site that offers guided tours to popular destinations. Taking advantage of geolocation (GPS) capabilities and built-in assistive technologies will be a useful addition to your site. Perhaps you want to allow users to learn about a place they're visiting by offering easy-to-read articles of local attractions and directional maps. Also, you want to offer them the ability to connect to the sites of those places and book any necessary tickets online. All within a car!

As cars connected with some form of web technology become roadworthy (some already exist), you may want to make your site increasingly accessible for the hands-free aids that many cars offer through voice navigation (this technology is similar to that of screen reader tools). Assuming users have access to the required technology, they can hear articles read aloud and continue driving safely. The use of friendly URLs will also help them choose pages based on filenames or keywords.

By using voice assistance to read content, give directions, and potentially book or reserve tickets, the only other things users will need to know are where the car is located and what local attractions are available. Scripts could use geolocation and location awareness (as in many smartphones) to confirm users' locations (using a secure connection), and then proceed to guide users through the various options that are available from their cars. All of these capabilities are currently available to consumers.

Embedded Gadgets

The use of integrated technology within buildings or structures is likely to increase. Many UK hospitals, for example, provide patients with a pay-to-use device containing a basic phone, television, and web access, and although not perfect, they're at least better than nothing in situations where phones must be turned off and cleanliness is king. In the future, you may see more in-house technology, such as interactive walls, but for now, just keep your eyes open for innovative ways to access the Internet in various situations and environments, as shown in Figure 6-1.

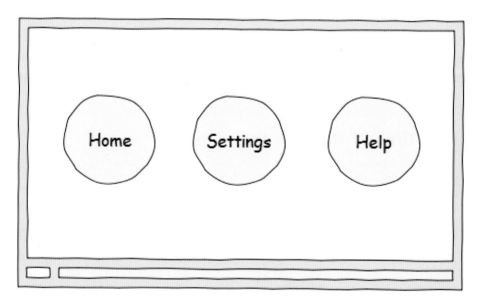

FIGURE 6-1: Embedded displays, such as those at conferences, offer clutter-free, icon-based navigation.

The following lists show members of this device's family tree and some issues they can encounter.

Relatives:

> Home automation

> Interactive displays

> Patient TV system

Considerations:

> Shortcut routines

> Shell redundancy

> Baseline support

Practical solutions

One of the biggest lessons you can glean from the adaptation of buildings into digitally connected habitats is that achieving simple goals is important to users. Consider functional tools like a light switch. Its purpose is straightforward, but while we appreciate the ability to achieve the goal with one action, we often forget how fortunate we are to have such a feature. When you apply this concept on the Web, always try to reduce the complexity of a site as you try to achieve maximum user satisfaction levels.

To deal with the increasing need for fast, relevant results, provide a range of shortcuts to common locations in your site (such as features, sale items, or links to popular sections). Never force users to learn about or use features that are of no interest to them, and offer only relevant links to pages. Calls to action and keyboard shortcuts can reduce the stress of a site by lowering the number of steps users must take to find what they're looking for (saving bandwidth), and doing so helps avoid the stagnation and erosion of your information architecture.

If there's one thing that the movement toward the digital home has taught us, it's that manufacturers enjoy using proprietary solutions. Perhaps it's because of the Web's need to reinvent itself, but every home automation device and household display unit seems to run within its own unique environment. Although having other programs piggyback on your browsers isn't a new thing (just think of all the browsers using Internet Explorer's renderer), it can be a troublesome gremlin to deal with in terms of ensuring compatibility for a device type.

Tip

Never underestimate the lingering power of old products. Internet Explorer 6 managed to sustain its lifespan beyond what anyone could have predicted. If you stop supporting something (reducing stability for a good reason), be sure to notify users about the situation.

Solutions for dealing with these proprietary shell apps that can connect to a site require less in the way of targeted code and more in the way of testing on archived equipment and software. Because these devices (like many others) depend on firmware upgrades, you cannot be sure that users will have a modern system (Patient TV, for example, might use an old version of Windows CE). Also, because of their limited ubiquity, it makes sense to test on these devices only if you know that people in your niche use them.

Embedded systems are a concern for legacy support because they're often tied into your devices. With many gadgets, we're lucky that manufacturers treat customers to frequent (or infrequent, as the case may be) updates. The lifecycle of many consumer products tends to be a year or more, and software in general has a good reputation for release cycles (even if you need to pay an upgrade fee to get it). However, this isn't often the case in these embedded system devices. For example, it might seem unbelievable, but Windows 3.1 may still be in use on some of them.

When it comes to the technology behind a digital home, think very carefully about the length of time you'll continue to support certain devices. If you produce web apps, you could find yourself tied to using an aging system for an extended period of time (this is especially true of the fragmentation affecting certain niche devices). As you plan the site, determine sustainable thresholds for long-term support and publish the details for your users to see. Education and awareness are as important as implementation.

Best practices

> Reduce the number of steps to success by providing in-page shortcuts.

> Only test on niche usage scenarios if you're affected.

> Check to be sure that the use of custom interfaces won't affect your layout.

> Provide a support policy for your site, describing your lifecycle process.

> Extend your support for older browsers, operating systems, and devices.

Connected Objects

Household appliances are going digital, and I'm not just talking about a refrigerator that tweets (Figure 6-2)! Because a mix of technologies can be used, household objects such as certain microwaves are becoming web enabled. With the potential for API-based interactivity on social networks, designers could soon be dealing with users through the limitations of third-party services. Some devices, such as digital photo frames, have gained huge levels of popularity; others, such as kitchen appliances, are still in their infancy (but they do exist).

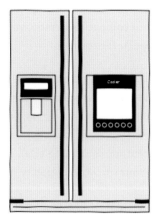

FIGURE 6-2: Refrigerators with Internet access are no longer science fiction — they're science fact now!

The following lists show members of this device's family tree and some issues they can encounter.

Relatives:

> Digital photo frames

> Internet radios

> Microsoft Surface

> Smart appliances

Considerations:

> MIME-type support

> Niche-explicit needs

> One-function fads

Practical solutions

The first issue to examine is the increasing diversity in support for niche device formats, which is an ancient foe of the Web that has turned many a site into an undecipherable collection of random files. Think of the standards that exist for images that work within every browser (such as JPEG), the standard downloadable document format (PDF), or the types of web languages that are recognizable everywhere (like HTML, CSS, or JS). Some devices may use a non-standard format, which could create incompatibility.

With some devices, such as digital photo frames, you can expect (or hope) that product makers will support a wide range of formats. Although it may seem premature to get out the champagne and begin throwing RAW or PSD files onto your site, you should consider that, in an attempt to be competitive, certain manufacturers may "choose" not to support their competitors' files. To ensure the greatest compatibility ratio, your best bet is to keep things simple and use the standardized, popular file formats.

Designing a site for a particular type of device is totally different than designing a site to be compatible with as many devices as possible. If you're in a lucky position and only have to work an interface around a particular device, app, or niche system, you know what you're dealing with! Because there will be times when you need to design a site for specific situations (whether it's an intranet, in-app content, or something else), I want to offer a few essential tricks that can help you maximize your site's compatibility for the environment.

Best practices for dealing with such a situation include building a complete list of business and device requirements, ensuring that the site matches in-house stylistic or behavioral requirements, and trying to sustain the visual flow of connected variables (such as an app, which will often reflect the device's look and feel). If your site can match an app's interface, the UI should feel like a natural extension of the product. Intranets can be particularly difficult for compatibility because of slow upgrade policies (it's one reason why Internet Explorer 6 has held on for so long), so be sure to cover every base.

Tip

Connected objects are often very basic, which affects how users interact with sites. Some devices may have no screen; others may have few options. For your interfaces, it makes sense to follow the KISS principle: Keep it simple, stupid!

Let's face it, for every device that can accomplish loads of wonderful things (leaving you with an endless checklist of potential factors to consider and deal with), a dedicated group of devices with a single purpose or function will remain. Having a microwave check the Internet for cooking instructions is one example (and, yes, such an appliance does exist); another example of a device built to do one thing particularly well is a pager. If your site offers something that may affect such a device, consider offering it support.

If the device requires the use of an API or a specific piece of software (the tweeting refrigerator, for example, is built around that functionality), make sure the service performs as expected in that environment (for example, use Twitter to allow its audience to find you). The last thing users want is for a service to change and, as a result, find that their tool no longer works. Build layouts to match the capabilities of the browser or variables in effect. Asking users without access to a mouse to make precision clicks just isn't practical.

Best practices

> Devices may not support odd proprietary formats, so stick to common ones.

> Ensure that the formats you provide work outside the niche device's application.

> Optimize solutions around an individual device's functionality and capability.

> Account for limitations or expectations that exist within a niche environment.

> List ten critical factors to deal with, and implement them on a priority basis.

Transportation

In recent years, vehicles have become increasingly like computers. Being able to connect an iPhone to your in-car entertainment system isn't the only way to access the Web in your vehicle. People and manufacturers have been modding cars to include PCs, voice-activated systems (Figure 6-3), and dashboards—and even windshields—are being digitized. Although they're still in the early stages, consider supporting these technologies because browsing on the move is gaining momentum. Trains and planes are receiving limited web enablement, too, in the form of embedded tools.

FIGURE 6-3: GPS navigation systems are just one type of transportation device with web capabilities.

The following lists show members of this device's family tree and some issues they can encounter.

Relatives:

> SatNav devices

> In-car dashboards

> Web-enabled vehicle

Considerations:

> Micro-activities

> Aural communication

> Localization tools

Practical solutions

Keep in mind that when devices with visual displays (rather than just sound) are used, being on the move means that the ability to look and interact with a screen may be limited by various situations. Users may visit your site while stopped in heavy traffic, but when the traffic starts moving again, they'll need to look away and get back to driving. Similarly, in the case of trains and aircraft, you may be trapped into using their facilities for the duration of the trip. Of course, ordinary web users may need to take breaks, too!

In Chapter 5, I talk about the importance of resumability and provide some easy, sensible principles that you can use — for example, allowing users to pick up where they left off and ensuring that your content has logical breaks and is formatted so that it can be read in easy-to-consume sections. Offering presentations and slide shows that progress only when a user clicks is great because they allow users to take simple steps and micromanage their time while driving safely. These are just a few ways to ensure that content is resumable and consumable.

When designing sites for transportation, your first consideration relates to the expectations for input. When you drive a car, your eyes should be firmly on the road. Although cars are starting to offer displays that let users access useful information (via projections on the dashboard), don't depend on this option because it may be distracting. Some device makers had the great idea of porting screen reader software into these in-car systems, thereby allowing a car to do all the reading for you (aloud), while you continue on your journey.

Reference

Test content in a screen reader for clarity (the web browser Opera has a built-in read-aloud feature that can emulate such functionality), check that the content is ordered correctly (text browsers such as Lynx may help), and help train pronunciation by using the speech CSS3 spec at http://www.w3.org/TR/css3-speech/.

When focusing on aural considerations in web design, visuals won't be part of the equation. Because the focus is firmly on the content, be sure that what you do write is concise, conversational, and easy to understand. Using unusual wording can be a problem if the car's voice-training doesn't recognize or know how to pronounce what you've written. A practical solution for this issue is to use CSS speech stylesheets (and DFN and ABBR tags in HTML to better explain underlying meanings).

A major benefit of web browsing on the move is that a large number of sites offer travel information and contact details. The SatNav inside a car allows you to find what you want, when and where you want it. If you own or build sites for a business that relies on brick-and-mortar locations (be it a store, a museum, a school, a landmark, an office, or something else), you can use localization in your work to provide more country-specific features. By including location details like phone numbers or an address, GPS tools can help localize the results.

To ensure stability when working with localization tools, design your site so that visitors can override their location (in case the detection is incorrect, or if they want to plan a trip outside the country they reside in). If you're working on something like a travel site, engage users by allowing them to input target destinations and distances they're willing to travel, and refine the site's content to match their needs. Avoid bombarding them with irrelevant data, and offer a wide range of ways for them to input data on their destination.

Best practices

> Make your site screen-reader friendly, to allow in-car dictation.

> Ensure that your site is structured in logical sections for readability.

> Visually break down content using slide shows and presentations.

> Avoid time-sensitive code (marquees and auto-refreshing pages).

> Allow users to change their locale or have it dynamically updated.

Physical Goods

When you have something that could be web enabled but isn't, what can you do? Create a custom solution! People have been building web-friendly hybrid devices for some time now. From RFID-tagged smart objects (as shown in Figure 6-4) to cat feeders (I'm not kidding here, either), pretty much anything is possible. The end user will be niche, the functionality will be limited, and you can't guarantee that anything will be as you expect. Strange as some of these innovations may seem, if they become popular, we may all end up designing for them!

The following lists show members of this device's family tree and some issues they can encounter.

Relatives:

> Evrythng.net

> Touchatag

> Violet

Considerations:

> Device context

> Outsourced parsing

> Custom solutions

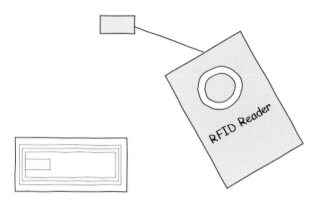

FIGURE 6-4: RFID is a technology that allows you to tag objects with useful digital information.

Practical solutions

Each item you see and own has expectations associated with it. You expect your tables to withstand the force of whatever objects you place on them, you expect chairs to be comfortable to sit on. When it comes to the Web, you expect it to work using whatever you use. On the Web as in real life, context plays a huge role; therefore, when it comes to going forward and turning a non-web-enabled object into one that'll connect and undertake a task, you need to consider the extenuating circumstances and adjust your work accordingly.

Imagine that you own an eBay-like site, or want to resell goods, which is fairly common these days. You could use RFID to track an object's ownership and history, verify its authenticity, and more! When scanned the chip could help users understand where their products originated (great for transparency and warranties), and this verification process could be processed anywhere. It's the same kind of technology sites use with barcodes, and it could be tied in with other useful technologies like near-field communication.

In addition to track-and-scan or track-and-pay options, which retailers can use to help users get to know their products better, outsourced parsing is another example of how supporting such objects can enhance a site's flexibility. We all know what bar codes have done for the retail sector. Well, as a designer, you have another form of bar code that can help non-web objects get a digital presence: the QR code. Very common in Japan and Asia (and catching on elsewhere), this code helps you offer real-world web interactivity.

Reference To find out more about the digital applications of RFID, go to the University of Washington website: `http://www.cs.washington.edu/homes/magda/papers/welbourne-ieeeic09.pdf`. Also, IEEE has an excellent paper on what's been dubbed "The Internet of Things."

Attaching one of these codes to physical goods means that you embed it with digital data! You can design the code to produce an image, text, or something else, but most useful for web-savvy readers, you can have them encode a URL or e-mail address that opens when scanned. If users sell physical goods or packages, or if they have a business that sends out letters rather than e-mails, by using a clever mixture of something like PayPal scripts and QR codes, you can accept quick payments. Or more traditionally, promote your stuff in print.

Luckily, beyond the track-and-scan potential just mentioned, variables that affect physical objects are few and far between (regarding web enablement). People will always build new devices and customize objects for web-specific purposes, but all you need to know at this point is that everything the bandwidth touches will generally be made up of hardware components in a hybridized fashion. Ultimately, dealing with custom builds isn't that complex if you're open to the limitations and factors that each component brings.

Best practices for dealing with devices vary, depending on the purpose of the object and the capabilities it offers. Although future chapters in this book push deeper into the issues that underpin all devices, a holistic approach doesn't hurt! If a new web-enabled gadget enters the market, don't just walk into the corner of an electronics store and begin crying; don't ignore it either. Show your enthusiasm and curiosity by learning about the object and what it offers users. To quote the movie, *Galaxy Quest,* "Never give up; never surrender!"

Best practices

> Research whether RFID can increase users' levels of trust for your brand.

> You can use QR anywhere; if visitors have smartphones, use them!

> Keep looking for new web-enabled devices that your visitors are using.

> Universal site stability requires adaptation, and it's a long-term goal.

> As future devices are released and gain popularity, ensure compatibility with them.

Designing for
Input Tools

Examining human-computer interactions

DEVICES REFLECT HOLISTIC views of interactivity and show a unique combination of variables affecting your layouts; however, not every device behaves the same. One of the primary variables that dictates how we interact with the Web is the hardware lying under the hood, and with customization being commonplace, data input methods can vary. In this chapter, you explore the hardware that translates human actions and responses onto interfaces, allowing users to explore the Web. Essentially, you examine human-computer interactions.

Just Point and Flick!

Designing sites with input tools in mind is rarely something designers think about. They regularly measure usage in terms of users and devices, rather than the components that comprise them. However, when your visitor's ability to interact with your offerings is affected, the cause is almost always related to an issue that many devices containing similar components will experience. Screen size is a typical output variable, affecting PCs to PDAs. Yet other input factors such as browsing a site on a keyboard are frequently overlooked.

There are many types of input tools, and each can provide a substantial amount of control over interaction within your pages. Some input tools can increase the precision on a page to a fixed point of reference (such as a mouse, rather than a tracker pad); others can be rather clunky and procedural, requiring users to hack their way through sections (for example, with a keyboard or number pad). Perhaps users may be lucky enough to have a choice of varying input methods, but as with many variables, you cannot simply count on that being the case.

Tip

Keyboard navigation can become complicated online, especially if your site uses AJAX or functionality that resets or refreshes pages, which can easily cause loss of focus on elements. Too much content or a lack of organization on a page can also affect keyboard navigation. Be sure to test the site using a keyboard to ensure that input tools have a chance.

Although you don't need to buy and test on every existing input tool, you can follow a number of best practices to maximize the compatibility of your sites. In addition, it's worth looking at how some of the more unusual input tools can affect and benefit certain types of sites (benefits will vary depending on the tool used). Options include voice browsing, video input via webcams, gesture input on a gaming controller, and even quirkier niche tools that can be connected using a USB port. If they can be connected, they can be used online.

It's actually very hard to measure which input tools consumers will use. Although sales data exists about the devices that use such tools, and data exists about the volume of sales for specific hardware (for example, digital drawing tablets), neither scripting nor analytics can interpret what kind of input medium is used, how sensitive it is, how restrictive it might be, and what you can do about it (it's beyond JavaScript's capabilities). Also, when dealing with the compatibility of input tools, don't assume that every user will have components identical to yours.

Always ensure that your site is compatible with all common methods of input that visitors may have access to (tools preloaded into devices, and sold separately). Also, consider the benefits that tools like webcams and microphones can offer sites. Interactivity is the focus of most online experiences; without the ability to communicate with pages, accessing new content will be impossible. These tools simply act as a "middleman" between humans and the Web, so you need to consider such issues seriously to retain stability within your sites.

Alternative navigation

For perspective, say that you have a visitor browse to your site on his laptop. He is in a good position to successfully navigate your site. He can use the keyboard built into the base of the device, and he also has a built-in webcam, microphone, and touchpad, all of which can be used at any interval to undertake actions on the device. Although some laptops may have more features (and some fewer), this visitor has a good range of methods at hand for visiting your site.

Designers tend to expect users to have the ability to move a cursor around a screen by using point-and-click technologies. But what if your visitor is unable to use his touchpad for some reason, but still wants to be able to visit your site conveniently? In this case, his next best option is the keyboard, but without keyboard shortcuts and the visibility needed to identify selected links, browsing the site is difficult and stressful for your visitor. He then tries the last option, voice input, but soon realizes that training the speech recognition would take time, so he gives up visiting your site until his laptop is fixed.

Providing support for device-native hardware is important, even if it's not the most popular or obvious route to browsing a website because sometimes a particular input tool may fail, become unusable, or simply not exist on a particular device. By making a few changes to the code you build or the design you engineer, you're more likely to guarantee that no one entering your site will have a low-quality experience. By offering fallbacks (for example, skip links and ensuring that images contain alternative text for voice navigation), you enhance the usability of your site.

Pointer

Among the various types of input tools people use when browsing a website, few tools are as suited for interaction as the *pointer*. Many different types of pointing devices are on the market (the most well-known being the mouse; see Figure 7-1), and they allow users to move around a screen with precision. Pointing and clicking wherever you like is highly valued (as is the ability to drag and drop), and these devices have sustained their popularity and ubiquity for many years. So, ensuring compatibility with these tools is worthwhile.

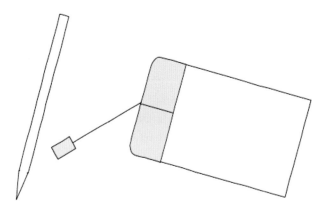

FIGURE 7-1: Pointing devices like the mouse and pen stylus allow users to click with accuracy.

The following lists show members of this hardware's family tree and some issues they can encounter.

Relatives:

> Mouse

> Trackball

> Joystick

> Stylus

Considerations:

> Drag-and-drop interfaces

> Click support

> Cursor style

Practical solutions

Interactivity is becoming an increasingly critical part of designing, so web designers are spending a great deal of time considering how their sites' interaction can better serve its users. Many applications are moving from the realm of desktops to the Web's cloudy back-bone, and one feature showing potential is the drag-and-drop interface. This interface can help visitors use the relevant parts of a site. Think for a minute how handy being able to visually organize content would be, and how it would revolutionize how sites are read.

Through scripting, drag-and-drop mechanisms are already being implemented. However, because these tools rely on JavaScript, the code doesn't work if scripting is unavailable or disabled. If your visitors are likely to have access to scripting, using such techniques could help you offer a choice to users by allowing them to use their pointer input tools to group content that matches their interests. Users could then prioritize relevant parts of a site, reducing how far down a page they have to travel if on a restricted screen (and be less distracted as a result).

Empowering users to decide how they consume your content will surely be an important step in ensuring the longevity of your interfaces because friendly interactions often invite frequent use. However, click requirements are just one issue that pointer tools experience, not only in drag-and-drop actions but also in other areas of user interactions. Users will always have specific expectations of an interface based on the capabilities of the input tools they use; designers must now try to encourage users to use their available tools effectively.

Tip

Although you can intercept actions such as right-clicking or text selection to enhance or disable a browser or script-implemented feature, remember that users expect actions to work a certain way. Ignoring their expectations and blocking their natural responses could have consequences. As such, avoid messing with a pointer's capability to do its job.

Does your interface anticipate that users will right-click? Does your site and its scripts support feature buttons or other unique properties such as those found on gaming mice (middle clicks, wheel scrolling, gaming buttons, and more)? Another critical issue concerns what happens when users can't hover (if, for example, they have a PDA and stylus or certain smartphones). Remember, pointer tools aren't born equal, and because users with different input mediums will experience sites differently, your site needs to adapt to their particular gadgets.

One common feature of pointers that everyone recognizes is the cursor. Although this often underappreciated part of an OS may seem trivial, that assumption couldn't be more wrong! Users must know where they're clicking and what they're hovering over; otherwise, they're flying blind. The cursor represents more than a distinction within text, white space, and links; it represents a digital positioning system that designers can take advantage of.

CSS allows you to customize cursors, and although swapping the expected cursor with something a bit more fun may seem harmless, doing so can confuse users and reduce their productivity. For example, if you change the cursor to an animated snowflake, it might look appealing, but you'll lose the precision of the usual pointer. Also, if you use the hand cursor on anything other than a link, users may think that object is clickable. Only change the user's cursor if you have a valid reason!

Best practices

> Use scripting to enhance existing behavior, but make sure the code degrades.

> Never, ever cripple functionality to attempt to stop piracy; it doesn't work.

> The only action you can realistically expect of users is a single, left-click.

> Use custom cursors on non-hyperlinked objects that respond to users' actions.

> Avoid needless, stylistic cursor changes, especially if they reduce visibility.

Touchpad

With the rapid adoption of tablet computers and smartphones, the race to move away from the traditional mouse and keyboard is on. These tools' capability to offer both input and output interactivity means that devices using them require less physical space, but achieve a more fluid experience. These tools, although notably lacking the high precision a mouse offers (fingers rather than a cursor), are ubiquitous enough to warrant your attention, and multi-touch features, such as pinching (shown in Figure 7-2), allow natural interactions between hands and displays.

The following lists show members of this hardware's family tree and some issues they can encounter.

Relatives: **Considerations:**

> Touch screen   > Sensitivity level

> Multi-touch   > Multi-touch issues

                                                                > Click precision

FIGURE 7-2: Multi-touch devices like the latest iPhones allow actions such as pinching.

Practical solutions

When adapting your sites for touch-friendly devices such as the tablet, you must consider a number of things to ensure the usability of your interfaces. The first issue relates directly to the sensitivity level of the surface being used. Sometimes, for example, visitors will have a touch screen; other times, they may have a tracker pad, as commonly found on laptops or netbooks. Touchpads tend to provide more precision than a touch screen; they often also have multi-touch support, and you can also see the screen as you use the tool.

Sensitivity levels of these tools can differ depending on a number of variables. First, the device could just be a poor-quality tool that isn't very sensitive to an easy touch, and perhaps it also doesn't support multi-touch. On the other hand, something on the tool's surface (such as dust) could make it a bit jerky. The best course of action is to offer a buffer or margin for error, such as increasing on-page white space so that clicking and actions like drag-and-drop won't demand too much precision.

Also, touch screens are becoming more adept at interpreting users' actions. In the old days, you could instigate only a few core actions like click and double-click and the basic movement of the cursor along the screen. Now, with the aid of technologies like multi-touch, you can make the computer do all sorts of things based on actions like strokes, flicks, and pinches. As touch screens gain precision and added gesture support, their capabilities will increase, leading to better support for such features in sites.

Tip

If you use a script library like jQuery, you'll be happy to know a few scripts have been created to allow gesture and touch interactions (beyond what a browser natively uses). A great example of this is Apple's iOS multi-touch event-handling API, which can be targeted with JavaScript. Just remember that not all devices will support scripting!

First, you need to know that many touch screens cannot initiate a hover action. Because a touch usually equates to a click, drop-down menus requiring a hover event will likely require an alternative route of access (perhaps click, rather than hover). Also, some devices have a unique method of dealing with overflowing content, if scrolling is required. By default, it may require two finger motions rather than one, and because iOS doesn't show scroll bars until you're scrolling, users need to be notified about which direction scrolling can occur.

Beyond coping with the complexities of scrolling when you can't see the scroll bar or its position on the screen, there are the potential issues surrounding the ability to click on the screen when using a touch device. For many users, the idea of prodding a device to click is a bit unnerving. Why? Because many people have fat fingers! It stands to reason that if we need to make a gesture or click a link on the screen, we want to do so with precision; however, unlike a mouse, fingers tend to have a wider surface area.

To ensure that your site works for touch interfaces, provide all clickable objects and links with enough space so that users can avoid making accidental errors. Providing anchor links with padding via the CSS property with the same name is one easy way to achieve this; another is to provide adequate white space between links. To understand the issues involved, imagine that you own a smartphone and suddenly find that a site's links are hard to click because the layout is being panned and zoomed out or links are too close together.

Best practices

> Touch experiences may not be smooth; don't expect lengthy interactions.

> Use scripting to enable gesture support (iOS offers some custom events, too).

> Avoid overflow scrolling and hover events, or at least provide fallbacks.

> Enlarge click regions and input boxes for people with large fingers!

> Avoid disabling the native zoom feature that iOS offers for input fields.

Keyboard

One of the oldest pieces of hardware, the keyboard (see Figure 7-3), has been gracing PCs for many a year. Designers could be fooled into underestimating this tool's capability to browse the Web because the mouse and touchpad offer much cleaner, optimized methods of interaction. However, for those lacking a better option, the ability to tab or cycle through your UI is a critical feature. Beyond the traditional keyboard, some users may also use shortcut keys, custom buttons (such as function keys), and even a numeric keypad!

FIGURE 7-3: Keyboards come in all shapes and sizes, but users are most familiar with the QWERTY format.

The following lists show members of this hardware's family tree and some issues they can encounter.

Relatives:	Considerations:
> Input buttons	> Access shortcuts
> Numeric keypad	> Visible tabbing
> Function keys	> Auto completion

Practical solutions

Browsing with just a keyboard is something that most people avoid if at all possible, and a good reason is because many sites aren't equipped to handle the effect it has on users' experiences. Taking the time to bounce around objects that can hold an active state on the screen (by way of the Tab key) is a tricky process for average users, though there will always be situations in which keyboard navigation is the only option. Therefore, reducing this burden on users is central to compatibility.

When it comes to lowering the hassle of keyboard navigation, the most obvious solution is the humble shortcut. We've all used shortcuts at some point (such as Ctrl+V to paste content from a clipboard), and with some scripting, it's entirely possible to assign them. The thing holding designers back is that some shortcuts (with browser defaults) are inconsistently implemented, causing cross-compatibility issues. Use scripted solutions (rather than access keys) because they can be unified to match conventions.

If you browse via the keyboard regularly, you'll recognize the key that is used most often when navigating a page: the Tab. When you press Tab, you jump to the currently most active element (with the highest `tabindex` value) on the page, and the page will scroll, placing the object within your field of vision. Unfortunately, because of the complexities of many dynamic layouts, things may not always work as expected. Because the keyboard is unlikely to disappear anytime soon, it makes sense to allow such navigation on your site.

Reference Although ensuring the visibility of an active link is tricky, partly because you may need to alter your site's visuals to make the invisible outline surrounding a link visible, doing so is well worth the effort. A site explaining the issues surrounding the CSS "outline: none" property/value combination is located here: `http://outlinenone.com/`.

To overcome the issues of keyboard navigation, try to reduce the number of active links within a page; this reduces the number of Tab keystrokes needed to select a link for navigation. Also make sure every link on your site uses the CSS outline property so that keyboard users can identify which link is currently in focus, avoiding any hidden content in preference of AJAX or some scripted focus switching event that'll cause key presses to be ignored or hidden on the screen. It's all about trying to maintain visibility.

Finally, you have another handy little feature that many products enjoy: auto completion. This feature attempts to correct typos and all sorts of mistakes as they occur, helping users make faster, more accurate decisions. It can reduce the need for changing or adding input and, thus, enhance speed. Many sites and browsers implement such a feature, which can be both helpful and a hindrance, as it attempts to assist with search boxes, sign-up forms, and other input mediums.

The accuracy of auto complete varies among countries and devices because it's dependent on the dictionary used and on previous entries. To avoid having users wonder if they've made an error or letting the device try to (unhelpfully) correct something, use autosuggestion in search boxes. Unlike auto completion, autosuggestion tries to provide alternative search terms, not guesswork. Also, for the sake of consistency, unless you're aiming your site at a specific nation, default to U.S. English.

Best practices

> Avoid access keys and instead use common, script-powered shortcuts.

> Ignore your mouse and browse with a keyboard to test your site's usability.

> Provide actionable objects with a CSS outline to highlight what's selected.

> If you use progressive disclosure, ensure outlining avoids hidden content.

> Make sure typos, nicknames, and abbreviations are accounted for in code.

Remote Control

Since the dawn of gaming, the ability to slouch into a chair and press an odd range of keys on a remote control or gaming pad has been a pastime for many users. However, since the incorporation of browsers within these entertainment devices, compatibility with such input tools has become a serious affair. Including the absurdities of controlling a site via a universal remote control (which is more restrictive than a keyboard), we're on the verge of gesture browsing. So waving your Wiimote (shown in Figure 7-4) like a ninja is a serious business!

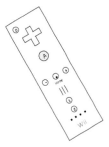

FIGURE 7-4: The Nintendo Wii's Wiimote turns physical gestures into web-browser controls.

The following lists show members of this hardware's family tree and some issues they can encounter.

Relatives:

> Remote control

> Gamepad

> Motion-capture

> Gesture sensors

Considerations:

> Multi-tap stress

> Motion fatigue

> Hybrid inputs

Practical solutions

Dealing with remote controls in your site's interactions comes with many cautionary tales, but none as widely recognized or frustrating as the stress of multi-tap inputs. If you think back to the issues affecting featurephones, inputting data with only a limited amount of buttons is challenging. The issues surrounding multi-tap also apply to other forms of input like television remote controls, where the expectation of data entry is rarely considered. To ensure that your site works on such devices, you must work around this common issue.

Because of the expectations surrounding remote controls, we assume that as each button is pressed, a particular reaction will occur (such as changing the station). Visitors expect the effect of these limited devices to go a long way, so it might be worth exploring the option of offering in-page *microsites,* in which each part of your site will have its own "station." Offering a highly visible navigation menu on TVs with numeric shortcut keys would allow users to quickly jump between sections, and CSS3 selectors could be used to achieve the effect.

In regard to relieving multi-tap stress by using techniques like keypad shortcuts and reducing the need for form entry, there is a downside: You automatically restrict the interactivity levels afforded to users. The benefit of being able to avoid such tools is a great idea, but with physical demands on users increasing, the chance of causing injury or fatigue over time rises, too. Granted this style of input wasn't intended as a mainstream alternative to a keyboard or mouse, but because it's used to interact with a site, you need to cater to this style of input.

Fitt's Law describes how motion and distance can affect users trying to browse a site, and how user interaction is affected by an object's size and position. Although the rule also applies to other pointing devices, Fitts's Law particularly applies to the compatibility of tools like gesture controllers. Because people stand farther away from a screen when taking advantage of these input mediums and because of the three-dimensional space in which they're used, selecting parts of a screen becomes more difficult. To deal with this issue, decrease the amount of movement required to browse around a page by reducing distractions and keep the navigation simple.

Reference   The psychology of human-computer interaction is interesting. To learn how motion and distance can affect users trying to browse a site, read this article about Fitts's Law (it applies to your designs): `http://particletree.com/features/visualizing-fittss-law/`.

The one remote control tool that has the biggest implications for your sites is ironically the one device that seems to swallow up most of the others: smartphones. In this age of an app for almost everything, clever people have built hardware and apps to provide a fully functioning remote control to anyone with access to the device. Often, it's not just a TV remote or a mouse; it's a touchpad and virtual keyboard, too. Put testing against tools that turn a device into a functioning input tool at the top of your priority list because they're very popular.

Dealing with these virtualized remote controllers forces you to consider a couple of things when users enter your site using a device. They could be using a virtual PC application such as Splashtop Remote, which allows a smartphone to be used as a portal for a desktop computer. This kind of functionality lets people use plug-ins like Flash on iOS devices . . . exciting news! Once the user initiates such an application, compatibility rules for devices will change because although the hardware remains identical, software will be desktop oriented.

Best practices

> Try to offer the maximum effect with minimal input demands from users.

> Allow users to select from a range of options in preference to entering text.

> When designing web interactivity, try to group related objects together.

> Allow for unstable physical motions — for example the Wiimote or Logitech MX Air.

> Determine whether a virtualized environment will affect your site's usability.

Microphone

Modern computing has become incredibly adept at dealing with unique input situations (such as the need for hands-free use), and with modern speech recognition software, the age of microphone-based browsing (see Figure 7-5) has become a reality. If you speak certain commands into a device, the software will translate the requests into actionable responses. What is particularly cool is that the technology has, in recent years, matured enough that you can even use voice browsing to accomplish more complex web-navigation tasks.

<small>FIGURE 7-5:</small> With microphones and voice recognition, you can use voice instructions to direct a device to carry out actions.

The following lists show members of this hardware's family tree and some issues they can encounter.

Relatives:

> Aural commands

> Voice recognition

Considerations:

> Accent interpretation

> Language support

> Background distortion

Practical solutions

On the surface, it may seem apparent that voice control has little functional purpose within your sites and that compatibility for something that requires a voice recognition application is of little use to your visitors, but you would be rather surprised as to the impact a little bit of audio input can have on a site. When you think about it, such features go beyond a sci-fi fantasy or the tools found in a car; they can also help users with specific accessibility needs by enabling them to navigate a site without requiring limb usage or tactile input.

Over the years, voice recognition software has matured to such a level that the accuracy is pretty decent, and by using these tools, users can bark browser commands and have them undertaken, or perhaps leave a voice comment on a site or even contact a site owner using Skype. The trouble is, when you go from regular voice input to voice-to-text input, things can get a bit muddled; for example, individuals with strong accents may be misinterpreted. Avoiding this problem involves using common keywords that can be easily pronounced.

Beyond the lost-in-translation issues that could leave us all with a mild case of insomnia, not everyone speaks English, so the rules that apply to content will also affect vocal input within sites. Perhaps that Flash voice input feature you bundled in a site can't understand Spanish; ensure that users know that. Maybe you want voice comments you can moderate. If so, the obvious solution is to stick with a standardized language. As for any CAPTCHA mechanisms, don't even hope that voice-dependent users can input that without difficulty.

Overcoming language issues when dealing with voice input depends upon your audience's needs and if support for the language is required. Luck is on the majority of our users' sides in this situation because most computers come with multilingual support. In addition, if users own a smartphone and want a quick way to leave voice comments (in text format) on your site, they can get an app like Dragon Dictation, which will do the hard work for them. So, even if you don't offer voice support natively, it can still affect site-based interactions.

Reference Dragon Dictation turns your speech into a fully formed paragraph of text. This has some really awesome potential for situations where typing is less than ideal, and touch isn't great for data input: `http://itunes.apple.com/us/app/dragon-dictation/id341446764?mt=8`.

One problem that can readily occur with voice input tools but doesn't affect other styles of online interaction is the issue of distortion. When you press a key, you perform a function. Distortion won't occur because there's a limited channel of input for it to deal with. With any kind of voice recording, however, background noise and other ambiguous information can interfere with the quality of the results. Because of the distortion, in some cases the content loses its usefulness and should not be depended on for critical site functionality.

Dealing with the discrepancy in the quality of sound often requires manual intervention from the site author, though in speech-to-text cases you won't have to worry because the processing is done from the users' machines, and they'll be given an opportunity to both proofread and verify the content before submitting it. Justifying the use of audio input with this issue present is a leap of faith. However, with microphones being built into so many devices these days, it's a shocker that few designers have pushed the medium any further.

Best practices

> Identify potential functionality for this underused, hands-free input tool.

> Remember that not everyone speaks English; always offer alternatives.

> Convert uploaded audio into a compressed format to save bandwidth.

> Test using voice-to-text software, and ensure that the output can be used.

> Allow the reporting of any low-quality audio comments, for moderation.

Imaging

Photography has become a hobby and obsession for many socially connected Web users. From sites like Facebook allowing digital albums to be stored in your account to sites like YouTube letting people become stars, the age of the imaging input device has really come into its own. Although many dismiss the potential of using image-capturing tools, which professionals and amateurs use regularly, some devices like cellphones or laptops with webcams provide imaging input tools, so their uses are worth investigating. Figure 7-6 shows a webcam.

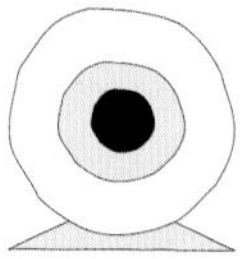

FIGURE 7-6: Users who own a webcam provide an entirely new level of potential interactivity.

The following lists show members of this hardware's family tree and some issues they can encounter.

Relatives:

> Camera

> Camcorder

> Webcam

Considerations:

> Plug-in dependency

> Metadata support

> Hardware quality

Practical solutions

One of the first issues to contend with regarding this type of input is that it's not exactly a standardized or simple process, which is why it probably hasn't had much attention lately. Although photographs have managed to gain a level of support with devices containing built-in upload mechanisms to certain sites, video input potentially requires using numerous video formats and a player that requires and depends on Flash or the less than ubiquitous, but gradually gaining adoption, HTML5. As for webcams, it's a plug-in or nothing situation.

Although this may seem like a lackluster opportunity, to be fully supportive of the way sites may evolve in the future you need to keep an eye on any technology that can help your users communicate with your site. For the lucky people with smartphones, a custom app can give them some real image, video, and webcam interaction, by either streaming the media you capture, or by using some post-processing effects. Overcoming third-party dependency issues will take time, thus this high-end feature should go on the waiting list.

Because images are exposed to the Web in a number of ways (such as through progressive disclosure slide shows), and with support for image formats fairly standardized and usable on many devices, you want to ensure that the greatest number of people can benefit from the photos and the data captured and uploaded using camera tools. Because images can be disabled and aren't appropriate for the visually impaired, you'll need a good fallback in place. Offering textual fallbacks also enriches images for other purposes (like SEO).

Tip

If you do offer a mechanism that encourages users to get involved with your site, and thereby add their own content, remember to ensure that the provided content has the necessary required fields to ensure a suitable fallback. Not everyone can see video or images or hear audio, and it's important that you be fair to their situation.

When you take a photo, the camera will usually build up a whole series of metadata in a format like EXIF, which can contain cool metadata like Geodata and more. Drawing this information from an image and putting it to use in image attributes or figure references will help make the image more semantic and potentially useful. Because text is the only online format that has no barrier to entry for visitors, it's important that all images and captured media from imaging devices offer a metadata-rich, descriptive explanation of the visuals.

Although these input tools come in all shapes and sizes, quality is a real problem with the imaging variable. Low-quality cameras and webcams often result in low-quality images, and low-quality images essentially degrade the quality of content. As a consequence, low-quality media input could be illegible. Keep in mind that the use of low-quality media will affect how the site ages. Certainly, it's worth compressing images as a post-production event to avoid bandwidth sapping, but quality is an important issue to consider.

Just like the issues that PDA and E Ink users suffer in regard to quality and color, you can't do much to improve a poor-quality input tool, though with high-quality cameras appearing as standard in modern devices (and on shelves at consumer-friendly prices), the situation is getting better. A best practice for dealing with this input tool is to simply make the most of what you're given; allow users to crop and/or scale down their files and try to improve the quality of the content. Once completed, check that the format works and publish the media.

Best practices

> Keep up-to-date with any media input-formatting best practices.

> Use server-side code to make the most of the user's input tools.

> Offer a range of imaging-input consumption features like subtitles.

> Consider exploiting any EXIF metadata and putting it to good use.

> Determine quality versus compression ratios based on user needs.

Scanner

Cameras have gone the distance in providing us with the tools to offer photos and media in our web experiences, but scanner devices (Figure 7-7) have made their own mark in our ever-growing pursuit to digitize the world's information. Hardware scanners, for example, can reproduce print formats into web-friendly images. As for software scanners, they take data that already exists in the digital (or real) world (like bar codes or QR codes) and turns that seemingly random image into a feature (with hidden context) that users can use.

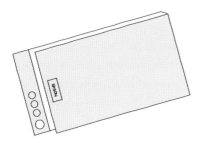

FIGURE 7-7: Document scanners can be useful for submitting digital forms that are filled in by hand.

The following lists show members of this hardware's family tree and some issues they can encounter.

Relatives:	Considerations:
> Biometrics	> Limited potential
> QR code scanner	> Physical verification
> OCR imaging	> Cloud conversion
> Bar code scanner	

Practical solutions

Scanners are an interesting case for the Web, because, while they're not exactly the most ubiquitous of objects and don't have a direct web connection, they offer a wide range of niche web purposes, depending on the scanner used with the device. Consider the classic example of biometric fingerprint scanners now widely used in business laptops. Because of their limited potential online, they might not be the most obvious source for providing bonus functionality, but if you consider tools like biometrics, scanners could help a lot.

If your site can support the outputted code that a biometric fingerprint scanner provides, you can use the scanner as a simple security feature, and if you can use QR codes (digital codes with web applications) or identify bar codes (if they're relevant to the products you offer), smartphone users can capture the data they need in order to find details about your products. With each unique scanning implementation, potential benefits for certain sites become apparent, and if the cost of implementation is isn't high, support can be justified.

Now that you're aware of the justification for offering tools with limited online potential, an opportunity will exist for you to implement support on your sites and services for such interesting features (depending on the likelihood of user adoption). Certain scanners may prove more useful in certain niches, such as biometric fingerprint scanners, which can be found within laptops offering a solution to more-secure passwords. But in every case, the idea that something physical can be digitized certainly still has value associated with it.

Tip   I've already highlighted the potential of QR codes in being able to launch a URL from a physical product, but the technology can also be used virtually by embedding the code within a web page. Consider it as another layer of interaction as you can provide links, e-mail addresses, phone numbers, and a wealth of useful "snap and save" information.

Getting users to verify their identities or provide secure-enough passwords on sites is always a challenge. Complex passwords tend to be forgotten, simple ones can be hacked, and often, people use the same password for every site, which isn't good. Using the software provided with a fingerprint reader and supporting the outputted code could reduce issues relating to security. Enabling this support can be as simple as not placing limits on the length of passwords, allowing non-alphanumeric characters, and enforcing case sensitivity.

Although many things are being transferred to the Web, and physical tools are becoming more web aware, plenty of analog pieces of data are still lying around, sometimes held in books, other times in rough printouts of pages that no longer exist in a digital format. A time may come when you want to recover such data or allow this free-range information to be used on your site in some way, shape, or form. Because scanners are incredibly useful for making hard copy files digital, it's no surprise that they have Internet potential.

The process of transferring analog to digital requires a few steps, but the output can be worth its weight in gold. If you use a business management app in the cloud, being able to store all your paper receipts, documents, letters, and invoices is critical. Depending on what you offer, this may or may not be useful to you, but as an input tool that can be used to take things online, it's worth a mention. Supporting this could include a PDF transfer of the uploaded file, or if you're adventurous, using OCR to turn images into bloggable text.

Best practices

> Not everyone has access to a scanner; don't demand one for data input.

> Smartphone cameras can work like scanners; offer support for these, too.

> Biometric codes are unique; allow them to be used for secure passwords.

> Supplement scanning functionality by allowing prescanned image uploads.

> When using OCR, allow users to verify its contents (to reduce error ratios).

Other Tools

Although scanners have rightfully earned their place in the digital ecosystem by offering a bridge between print and digital goods, there is something to say for the thousands of other gadgets that can be connected to a device to offer some innovative, new level of interaction via a USB, Thunderbolt or Firewire port, or even using Wi-Fi or Bluetooth connections. These gadgets range from practical (like credit card and RFID readers, see Figure 7-8) to outright silly (desk robots that read your RSS feeds aloud), but they're all web connected!

FIGURE 7-8: RFID allows you to associate physical objects with data that can be used by readers.

The following lists show members of this hardware's family tree and some issues they can encounter.

Relatives:

> Card reader

> Nabaztag/Karotz

> GPS positioning

> Brain-powered

> USB devices

Considerations:

> Feature demands

> Secondary usage

> Reduced ubiquity

Practical solutions

If you're planning on offering support and sitewide compatibility for any number of the thousands of niche tools, I salute you! Not only do the tools in this category often connect to sites or undertake activities through a controlling third party, just using them requires meeting demands and expectations that can be undeniably harsh. Although the general rule for dealing with any of these devices is to read the manual, do nothing unexpected, and hope for the best (praying to the Internet gods may help), there are some things you can do.

Something like the absolutely adorable Karotz talking robot will read a site's RSS feed but nothing else relating to individual sites, at least for now, but more capable robots like it may well appear in the future. It may seem like a pointless product, but if you offer a site aimed at kids or people with children, the animated talking toy might encourage learning (or be a great way to get update alerts). This is, of course, just one example of an alternative tool in action. The point is that even if a product supports only RSS feeds, be sure to offer them.

Another issue that can affect your site's stability relates to unusual tools with the potential to offer secondary enhancements, which may be deemed as bonus features in the hardware world. Many web-enabled USB devices don't just connect and do the job on their own; they often use existing devices, OSs, software, and more. The use of enhancements on sites is dependent on the environment on which they're used, so you'll want to determine the popularity of such tools before supporting them (ask your users and check site analytics).

Reference   Because of space, or because they just aren't in users' hands yet, only a few unique devices are touched on in this chapter. For a few friendly faces and some new ones, see this article: `http://sixrevisions.com/user-interface/the-future-of-user-interfaces/`.

Ensuring compatibility for these devices can be relatively easy if the environment is self-contained (as in the Karotz example), but in cases where the technology relies on drivers, software, or other mission-critical components, you may need to offer basic details on how to get the equipment up and running (or link to the manual) to help users take advantage of these enhancements. Perhaps the tool will need a runtime file or a Windows update; maybe the tool will need configuring. To use the tools, you may need to help users get started.

There's one final point to consider with these more exotic types of hardware; because of these tools' limited audience, ubiquity and the need for support and compatibility are less than you'd find with other input mediums. GPS these days could be deemed the exception to the rule because many smartphones (and some tablets) have location awareness built in, increasing the ubiquity of GPS input tools and making support justifiable. As for the rest (like mind-controlling tools), it's up to you to decide on appropriate levels of support.

Encouraging any new tool with a good idea is always worth the effort if you can spare the time and if it can benefit the users of your site and the tools they have access to, but most designers are busy people, focusing on the stuff they must cater to in the here and now. Giving support to underdog technologies helps enhance their ubiquity, forcing others to adapt or fail, and helping useful technologies online encourages further innovation. However, every audience will have different needs of an interface, so nothing should be taken for granted.

Best practices

> Check the gadget's demands and provide whatever it needs (within reason).

> Identify new technologies and ask your users if they'd find support useful.

> Offer basic (if not full) support to deal with issues common to getting started.

> Prioritize the hardware your users need support for, and work in that order.

> Support innovations if they can help visitors achieve specific goals easier.

Designing for Output Tools

Managing visual displays, printers, and other hardware

HARDWARE ISN'T ONLY about the interaction and input that users can provide to our sites. What visitors get out of it and how they interpret the feedback and responses of such tools matters, too. Hardware exists to help users consume digital data, and your job is to ensure that sites are compatible with these personable tools so a user's journey can be successful. In this chapter, you explore the displays, printers, and hardware that can impact what we see, uncovering best practices to account for their inconsistencies and differences.

Your Digital Eyes and Ears

Output tools within specific categories such as visual displays are generally fairly similar, but don't be fooled into thinking that they're all the same. There are many different sorts of displays, from mainstream monitors and self-contained displays (with computers built in), to projectors and tools utilizing more unusual technologies, such as E Ink. Also, don't forget touch displays, which have gained widespread popularity. In the future we may likely find mainstream wearable displays that allow displays via projection glasses and contact lenses!

Because output tools achieve their tasks in quite unique ways, compatibility with various types of tools can be particularly hard to account for (universally). For example, the output on a display that refreshes as you browse a site has little in common with a printer (even if the function is similar). Obviously, you want to ensure that your work accommodates a wide variety of output mediums, so don't forget factors such as the quality of the tool and the technological limitations of particular variables (as future tools will likely remain diverse).

Tip

Keep in mind that the screen on a device may not be accessible or useful to all your users (such as the visually impaired). Although expensive applications do exist for testing in these scenarios, you could install a screen reader and turn off the display to see if your content can be read aloud. Sites need to remain accessible in the future,

While visual output is a critical feature in terms of the Web's beauty and elegance, other output tools exist, and some are critical to certain audience niches. For example, speakers, though an optional piece of hardware, are key technologies that allow the blind to visit a site. Another is the printer, which still manages to linger on, offering hard copies of your work, despite pushes to the cloud. Being compatible with these tools makes perfect sense as they offer alternative, friendly methods of consuming content and enriching experiences.

If your site is media oriented, understand the value of providing visual and aural content that users can initiate. Engaging multiple human senses adds richness to an experience, and certainly you want your sites to use these forms of content. Sometimes, optimizing a site for different output tools is a challenge; for example, consider varying screen sizes. Other output tools such printers have a more direct, universal solution (print style sheets), though in every case, users must have access to at least one usable output (and input) tool.

From a compatibility perspective, often it's the variables within a computer that affect the visuals that users see on their screens, which makes it harder to design around output tools (while input tools often just rely upon an event being triggered, whether that be a click, tap, or key press). Often, it's not the hardware users own that breaks a site visually; instead, it's usually something interjecting at a lower level, such as a browser or the code being used. That said, differences do exist purely at the output level, and they're worth investigating.

Working with a variety of display sizes

Try to imagine for a moment that one of your loyal visitors who has previously experienced your site upon their 21-inch LCD monitor bought a smartphone and tablet combination to complement their workflow. Upon buying their choice of smartphone (in this case an Android device) and a tablet (an iPad), they decide to try out their coveted new gadgets by visiting your site only to find that your layout isn't flexible enough to be friendly on the tablet, and the separate mobile site you provide makes the visual experience unfamiliar.

Confused by the differences on the mobile site, they look for a link to visit the full version of the layout and find that one doesn't exist, meaning that their powerful device is trapped by the assumed limitations of the screen (because of its physical size and viewport). Additionally, the user isn't exactly happy about browsing your work on the tablet, as it's nether touch friendly nor able to cope with the unique screen size without initiating scroll bars in every direction. Alas, this isn't an out-of-the-ordinary situation; in fact, with many older sites, the issue is common.

Ensuring that your layouts work for a variety of display sizes, types, and models is critical in determining that your content is readable. If there isn't enough contrast, flexibility, or scale in your work, small screens or displays with little brightness may simply become unusable. In addition, with the range of displays being so diverse, it's quite likely that the visitor may have subtle yet different experiences simply by using a product with unique dimensions. This issue is similar to that of printers that can differ based on the type or output capabilities of the tool.

Display

Beyond a shadow of a doubt, your device's display is the most frequently used hardware output tool. In terms of engaging your senses, there's no comparison: Experiencing a site with your eyes will beat just experiencing it with your ears every time! This tool regularly trips up designers wanting the mythological pixel-perfect layout, because of the available range in quality, features, or size. It's important to ensure that every site caters to various displays gracefully to ensure layouts continue to work within various unique situations. Figure 8-1 shows the type of visual display typical to a television.

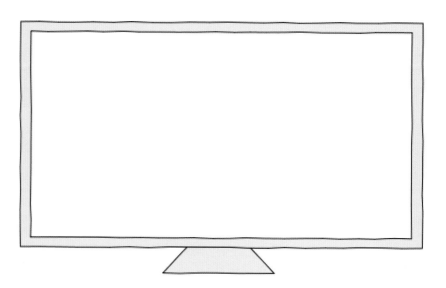

FIGURE 8-1: Displays visualize your content using technologies like CRT, LCD, Plasma, and OLED.

The following lists this hardware's family tree and some issues its members encounter:

Relatives:

> Monitor

> Touch screen

> In-dash

> Television

Considerations:

> Technology used

> Size and resolution

> Visual orientation

Practical solutions

Different screens have different effects on visual objects. Not all screens have equal pixel density, not all have the same luminosity, and not all are equally popular. If you want to cater to the widest-possible audience, you need to consider the effects of different screen technologies (such as how black the blacks really are) and the extent to which they can be calibrated within the gadgets that contain them. The importance of this is because contrast and color visualization play a huge role in how images are interpreted by the human eye.

Dealing with the wide range of formats is tricky because users may have an old-style CRT screen, TFT, LCD, or Plasma screen attached to their computer (as commonly seen in TV sets). You also have other display technologies of note such as LED, Retina Display (for Apple), and OLED. Dealing with different compatibility quirks will require you to read up about the mechanics of the technology (a good place to start is Wikipedia, as it has quite a bit of information on the subject, and some useful comparisons), and try them for yourself.

When ensuring stability with displays, the most obvious issues to consider are the physical dimensions of a product and the resolution being utilized. Obviously, a 5-inch display will show content differently than one that's more than 100 inches (in the diagonal); and an 800-x-600 resolution will offer less space than a 1024-x-768 resolution. Accommodate diverse audiences and their devices by embracing and accounting for these differences, as in the future CRT may totally disappear, and high definition OLED may be the standard.

Reference

CSS3 media queries can help you better define and use the available viewport space. It's also one of the primary tools used in responsive design. To learn how to target both resolution and orientation, offering a range of flexible layouts that work within a range of defined dimensions, read this W3C specification: www.w3.org/TR/css3-mediaqueries/.

Dealing with different product sizes can be mystifying because not all large screens will have a high resolution and not all small ones will have low resolutions. Some may support HD, and some may support only standard definition. You can't do much about the size of physical objects except consider how the content will scale and cater to different window sizes (no matter how they scale up or down). Rather than offer separate fixed-width sites, you should use liquid layouts (that utilize flexible units like percentage widths) and CSS3.

As I continue talking about displays, it's worth mentioning their capability to work in both landscape and portrait modes, as popularly utilized in smartphone devices that need deep, lengthy document displays and widescreen video and gaming visuals. On the Web, you must consider the differences between these two modes of orientation, if only to ensure that your sites are as responsive as you hope they are! CSS3 media queries, liquid layouts and content, and object and image responsiveness are central to achieving such flexibility.

If you tip your screen into landscape mode, you'll obviously have less space above the fold (visible on the vertical scroll line) but have a wider angle that can be ideal for sites needing multiple columns. By turning things to portrait, you provide more space to show a full, vertical document, but with less room for columns. Every site should work in both modes, which you can implement using the viewport `Meta` tag (to avoid scaling); so test, using fewer (or collapsible) columns, and reinforce this with well-defined CSS3 media queries.

Best practices

> Research different visual technologies; screen quality can differ greatly.

> Avoid using small text as it might downscale on various screen sizes.

> Never build for resolutions; instead, scale to relative, satisfactory levels.

> Learn CSS3 media queries; it's the visual bread and butter of web design.

> Devices can turn on their side, so test in both portrait and landscape modes.

Projector

Being able to look at a glass display with a range of colors and pretty visuals is great for many browsing experiences, but if you've ever been to a conference, you will know that sometimes a monitor isn't enough to meet an audience's needs. While projectors such as the one shown in Figure 8-2 have been around for a long time, they aren't as popular as other displays like computer monitors, though you shouldn't let that keep you from considering them because your design's effectiveness and the visibility of content can be affected by these external units.

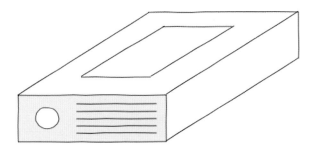

FIGURE 8-2: Projectors allow entire groups of people to see a Web site at the same time.

The following lists show this hardware's family tree and some issues its members encounter:

Relatives:

> Head-mounted display

> Virtual-reality headset

> Projection glasses

Considerations:

> Brightness problems

> Split concentration

> Upscaling distortion

Practical solutions

Projectors are unique output devices that transmit images onto another physical object, rather than keeping them within a device. Compatibility with such tools isn't as common as with desktop monitors, and to be honest, not many of them will be found in a user's home. That isn't to say, however, that projectors aren't heavily used, because they are in business and education, for example. Still, if you've seen a projector in action, you know screen brightness is a real issue, and this is one of a few projection factors that we must deal with.

A projector is normally used in a darkened room, such as an auditorium or a theater. Because of the beams of light transferring the on-screen visuals onto a wall or specially crafted canvas, heavy amounts of outside light or reflections can seriously distort what's being displayed. As a designer, you can't do much about such interference; however, you can be aware that sites will need a good amount of contrast to counteract potential low-visibility situations. A more common light situation can be seen with cellphones used in sunlight.

Projectors are like TVs in that they tend to have low resolutions (preferring to upscale content as required), and projectors that augment reality can provide endless entertainment. Avoiding upscale distortion in projectors can be achieved by increasing the physical size of objects on the page (so that clarity isn't lost in the scaling). Avoiding the other issue of wearable projectors (like glasses, which can give users the opportunity to browse sites as they walk) requires keeping the display aspect as a secondary feature to the real world.

Tip   Projection glasses already exist! One common brand among gadget sites is Vuzix's iWear range, which projects a virtual screen to a user's eyes. While this technology is more of an enthusiast product, it could soon catch on for browsing the Web while on the move (especially for users who like the idea of gaming or watching movies outdoors).

Because projections are normally shown to many people sitting together (monitors are more for one-on-one experiences), such as at a conference, the user's concentration levels may wane as a result of outside distractions such as other people or objects in the room. In the case of a regular PC display or touch screen, attention deficits are less frequent as the eyes focus on objects rather than a region. Because of the natural displacement between user choices and the environment they view the displays within, holding attention is tricky.

Keeping a user's attention is difficult when that person has no direct, interactive route to visualize content, sits some distance from the screen, and just follows along with the host who is presenting the visuals. Moreover, the projectionist can encounter problems because he ends up having to browse between the device and the projection to ensure what appears on one also appears on the other. For compatibility within your designs, try to keep the site's content visibly clear and concise, and a splash of multimedia can keep things lively.

Spiderman fans around the world will know by heart the phrase, "With great power comes great responsibility." It's one of those statements that applies to many facets of life. In the case of projectors, these powerful producers of visual output can showcase a site like yours to hundreds or thousands of people in one shot. Yet, with this awesome tool at a visitor's disposal, the likelihood of distortion, blurriness, and quirks increase, as does the likelihood of issues such as problems with viewing angles, distance, and partially blocked viewpoints.

Best practices

> Provide a high-contrast layout fit for poor lighting conditions.

> Increase visibility by allowing increasing typography sizes.

> Consider where attention will be focused within each split second.

> Aim for clarity and provide visual shortcuts to aid reading flow.

> Never distort a user's vision while moving (via projection glasses).

E Ink

In a quest for more natural-looking visuals that are frequently less affected by reflections from natural sunlight and consume less power, E Ink screens in the form of digital paper and glass displays have gained popularity (see Figure 8-3). Most commonly found today in book reading devices like the Kindle and the Nook, the technology has gained a level of Internet ubiquity with the attachment of browsers into the devices. However, E Ink can be hard to design for as it lacks things we take for granted (like color—that's coming soon).

FIGURE 8-3: E Ink displays aim to give a more natural reading experience (free of reflections).

The below lists this hardware's family tree and some issues they can encounter:

Relatives:

> Electronic paper

> Digitized glass

Considerations:

> Low refresh rates

> Monochromatic

> Readability impact

Practical solutions

Electronic ink is a funny sort of display medium when you think about it. Unlike many of the others, it has a paperlike look about it. However, when it comes to ensuring that your sites work with each output medium, E Ink is one of those unfortunate examples of where the technology hasn't caught up with the feature sets that many Internet users expect. In many E Ink devices, low refresh rates and ghosting (pixels getting stuck) is a considerable problem, which means moving objects aren't treated with much dignity or durability.

Best practices when dealing with the aforementioned issues on eReaders or related gadgets require that sites avoid page refreshes and Flash effects unless absolutely necessary. Some sites, out of fantasy that their actions are beneficial, automatically force pages to refresh at set intervals. Not only does this "feature" affect screen readers, but it causes E Ink to flicker the screen to reset the pixels. As for low refresh rates, avoid any animation on a page as older eReaders either won't support the technology, or it may hurt users' eyes.

As I mentioned previously, E Ink isn't just limited in its capability to render animated effects on a page; most E Ink-powered devices of this type are still incapable of viewing any color (the display uses a gray palette). In the future, color eReaders will exist, and the technology is really being pushed in that direction. For now, though, you can expect the lack of color support to affect how your pages visually appear (in most eReaders). To ensure sites work on monochrome displays, try using a color-blindness filter to see how it affects visibility.

Note Color E Ink products (like the Hanvon eReader) exist, but the refresh rate they employ is unfortunately still very low. So, although the upgrade to such a device could bring some lovely color to your layouts, animation still will not be a stable feature to display.

You can work around monochrome screens by testing how your site stacks up against the lack of color availability. Most decent graphics applications can take a screenshot of a page or an image and produce a grayscale or monochrome version (if the image is readable, it can stay as it is). If you do find the grayscale doesn't work that well, try to increase the contrast and use stronger background and foreground shades. The aim isn't to turn your whole site into a gothic wonderland; it's to help your visuals work in either situation.

The main selling point of E Ink is that, above anything else you'll find it's seriously easy on the eyes and built for looking at over long periods of time. Not only will the device work well in bright sunlight (absorbing and reflecting the light instead of glaring it back in the user's face), but also it has an encouraging battery lifespan because of the lack of backlit elements in the display. However, while it may have a superior reading experience (when the technology catches up), you still need to support it to maximize compatibility chances.

First, while E Ink may be a great reading experience, you need to ensure that the legibility of the text transfers from traditional screens well. By testing on a device that uses E Ink, you'll gain perspective on the clarity of the platform and an idea of how legible content will be. Ensuring that your text is appropriately sized and not too small will help with readability, too. Additionally, because E Ink devices have a lengthy battery life, don't time-out sessions for on-screen activity (as users might pause reading for hours on end).

Best practices

> Avoid forcing a page refresh as doing so causes E Ink displays to flicker.

> Block animated content and video multimedia from various E Ink devices.

> Although animated GIFs are supported, it's safer to avoid using them.

> Check your site under a monochrome filter to see how it's likely to look.

> Don't time-out sessions (the impact of sites on the battery is negligible).

Speakers

Let's face it, when it comes to outputting your data into something that users can consume as they like, we tend to default to supporting displays and little else. Yet, as you know, the ability to provide audio content within your pages is worthy of your attention. In terms of output tools, many of us have in-ear headphones, headsets, or speakers, such as the ones shown in Figure 8-4, either built into a device or attached separately via a sound card. With such a cool implement at many users' disposal, it makes sense to consider the availability and usefulness of sound.

The following lists show this hardware's family tree and some issues its members encounter:

Relatives:

> Headsets

> Media speakers

> PC speakers

> Earphones

Considerations:

> Automatic playing

> Integration methods

> Portability issues

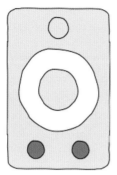 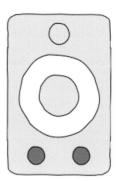

FIGURE 8-4: Speakers play sound, so why not use them to further help users consume content?

Practical solutions

When considering the implications of audio and ensuring a site's stability, the web design community regularly frowns on one commonly used technique: automatically playing music. Although doing so might seem like a logical step toward tapping into emotions, setting a beat to a page, or perhaps introducing users to something you've created or the content that a band recorded for purchasing. However, in the Web hall of shame, auto-playing media has a permanent spot as one of the most annoying things you can do to a visitor.

If you imagine a situation in which a user is multitasking, perhaps listening to tracks on an MP3 player or iTunes, the seriousness of the mistake is obvious. Having audio you didn't ask for blasting from your speakers, bleeding into something you're already playing (or annoying everyone in an office) doesn't do anyone any good. Audio or video use must be user-initiated or accepted by them. So, never make the mistake of forcing "noise" on users! This not only counts for the audio that you create, but video or Flash multimedia as well.

Speakers and headsets come in all shapes and sizes. Some are better suited to channeling the sounds to an entire room, whereas others focus on the personalization of the output (to one user's ears). Not all speakers are going to be of the same quality, and some will have better clarity and quality than others. Web designers aren't expected to be some kind of supernatural audiophiles who can make out every tone, but it's worth noting that some users will be more critical of the output quality than others, depending on their personal tastes.

Note

Environment plays a big role in how sites are consumed; it can actually increase the level of use, too. If users listen to a podcast of your site's news while driving or working out, they'll accomplish more things at one time than they would otherwise be able to; and like listening to music while moving, it's a popular method of consumption.

Hardware speakers, headphones, and the software these products offer allow the alteration of the volume of the output media (within a control panel). Because users may be listening in a busy environment, your content needs to be audible at lower levels. If you're offering a recording of a speech, avoid having too much background noise behind the track (such as a loud soundtrack) or keep it at a lower level than the speaking volume level. Also, avoid being monotonous and signify and structure the file accurately to aid the file navigation.

With the rise in online piracy and worries about the security of their media, many sites try to encase audio files within media players that prevent downloading or copying. Sure, it makes sense to want to protect what you own; however, when trying to protect any object published online (images and content included), know that once it goes online, you cannot control distribution. Tools like Audacity can record "what u hear" and form an MP3 file as a result. Moreover, to be compatible with every type of user, physical files are needed.

Because of how some audio output devices offer docks for popular MP3 players, you first must recognize that the way users access your audio may differ greatly. To cover the many integration methods, you must not only provide an inline MP3 playing application (using Flash or a relative system), you also must provide compatible fallback formats that match the needs of your audience (popular formats like MP3 are always a winner). It's also worth setting up an RSS feed for podcasts, as dedicated streaming apps may request such a feed.

Best practices

> Automatically playing audio is a sin worthy of abandonment; don't do it!

> Offer a range of varying quality levels to offer users quicker downloads.

> Volume or EQ levels may vary, so ensure sections are as clear as possible.

> Don't just offer a Flash player; offer physical files that can be downloaded.

> Podcasts need an episode feed and submission into directories like iTunes.

Printers

Finally on the list of output tools is a golden oldie: the printer. Sometimes found attached and integrated with scanners but mostly as a separate gadget, printers (shown in Figure 8-5) have been enabling you to make paper copies of digitally formatted sites since the inception of the Web. These products have high ubiquity levels and are almost the polar opposite of scanners in terms of functionality (as they turn digital files into print, rather than print into digital files). As you can provide dedicated support for them on your sites, why not do so?

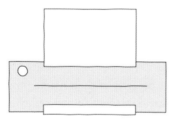

FIGURE 8-5: Printers format Web pages for paper (and thus require a unique styling approach).

The following lists show this hardware's family tree and some issues its members ncounter:

Relatives:	**Considerations:**
> Desktop printer	> Printworthy objects
> Label printer	> Eco-friendliness
> File printer	> Stylistic formatting

Practical solutions

Compatibility with printers no longer requires having a dedicated printer-friendly site as it did in the 1990s (because of innovations in how we can format layouts). Along with the evolution of CSS came the benefits of the print media type, letting you offer a customized experience on paper unique to what users could expect on their screens. Rather than leave browsers to either strip away all the style or squeeze everything onto a page, you can easily improve the core compatibility of your content in that environment, without a lot of work!

One critical factor in providing a stable and useful print experience is to determine what is relevant to the user and what translates well onto a printed page. Things like the navigation menu, search box, and functionality provided in sidebars aren't usable (or clickable) with paper and ink, and showing them doesn't make sense as they have no practical function on paper. Instead, hide them using the CSS *display* property. Links can be made useful if you use the CSS *content* property to showcase the URL for retyping from the paper document.

It's worth noting that in the current endeavor to be environmentally friendly, we all need to do our part to reduce the amount of ink and paper we waste. By helping users reduce their print output, you can actually save them money in ink and paper costs (which will give you bonus points in places where printing occurs regularly, such as within schools), and you'll reduce the ecological impact of your work as well, helping you to boost your business's green credentials. Removing fluff is, of course, a great start, but there's more you can do.

Reference

I suggest reading two fantastic guides for ensuring a great quality print stylesheet. The first guide can be found at `www.webcredible.co.uk/user-friendly-resources/css/print-stylesheet.shtml` and the second at `www.alistapart.com/articles/goingtoprint`. Many of these practices have been recommended by designers, and do improve Web experience.

Although CSS2 offers you the option to target printers with some predefined stylistic effects, CSS3 and the power of media queries can help you offer monochrome displays and printouts a customized style sheet of their own (to further optimize the experience). It makes sense to remove stylistic, unessential images and objects from a page, as well as things that aren't appropriate for printing. Animated images, banner adverts, and media files, for example, are common features that serve no purpose on paper-based formats.

You also need to think about the paper layout because few designers give the same level of care and attention to what their printed pages look like as they do to what appears on a digital display (most just assume it works and little else). Printing to paper may end up being gradually phased out as everything goes digital, but for the sake of maximizing and ensuring the flexibility of the format, try to be a bit creative with your layouts and continue to offer printer-friendly versions, as printing to PDF or other formats will remain popular.

Because printed documents are static, they're the only format on the Web where responsive design and the other flexible layout techniques hold little relevance. Take a page out of print publications in order to see what layout, color, and typography choices will work best in print formats. The great thing is that printers are adept at turning a printable layout into an exact (or nearly exact) copy of what's shown on a page; however, be warned that using fixed-width layouts may result in content being cut off and/or spanning additional pages.

Best practices

> If it has no purpose on a printed page, it should be marked for removal.

> Use the CSS *display: none* combo and print media queries to target fluff.

> Optimize your printed layouts to ensure they're as eco-friendly as possible.

> Flash-based sites require an HTML fallback to ensure print compatibility.

> Design stylesheets for what looks good on paper, rather than on-screen.

Environmental Influences

Ensuring stability with components, connectivity, and bandwidth

HARDWARE CAN BE a tricky business. When it comes to ensuring that sites remain compatible with a user's needs, you often must look far beyond the obvious demands of existing input and output tools. The internal components of a device that users rarely get to see (such as the hard disk) and the Internet connection that provides access to sites affects how stable your site will be. In this chapter, you examine these environmental concepts, their consequences, and what (if anything) you can do to avoid complications.

Internal and External Factors

Manufacturers release faster and more powerful hardware regularly. Upgrades frequently become available for hard disks, graphics cards, audio cards, processors, and RAM, and all have an impact on a device's performance. However, not all users will upgrade as soon as these components are released. Try to design with every user in mind, from the user with an older device to those using the latest equipment, and avoid overtaxing their hardware, as our sites will increasingly utilize hardware to boost performance in the future.

You need to consider the connection between the visitor's computer and a site. Obviously, without connectivity, a site isn't useful to the consumer, but as with many other variables, things just aren't that simple. Today, many web apps are designed to offer some degree of offline usage capabilities to ensure that work or access to critical services won't be lost if the user's connection fails at any time, and there are always server issues and issues related to bandwidth, speed, and roaming charges that can interrupt the user's online experience.

Tip

Determining how large or small to make your pages is difficult. However, excluding content (text and images critical and unique to a page), I recommend that the design (code and graphics) ideally be under 100K. Keeping pages to a predetermined limit helps to ensure that download times won't become excessive on slow connections.

Environmental issues are often outside both your control and the user's control. Although the problem can't be entirely averted, you can make a number of tweaks and optimizations to your sites to aid users and to help reduce the likelihood of such complaints occurring. In recent years, Internet speeds have increased for many, but the old enemy, dialup access (or speeds equally as slow), is still in circulation around the world. Also, handheld device users are increasingly finding that data charges can be costly, especially when roaming abroad.

Compatibility with slower computer systems is important because lagging can result from the intensive utilization of too many Flash or feature-rich components. In addition, be sure that sites aren't too bandwidth heavy and they don't misuse precious system resources in other ways. The days of limited connectivity may seem numbered as Internet access gains increasing levels of adoption, even in the remotest of areas; however, for some Web users, such issues could be a reality that's as harmful to their experience as it was in the 1990s.

Ultimately, the most stable sites on the Web are easy to maintain and require few system resources. Small sites tend to load quicker and put less strain on users' devices, and they're often more flexible in low-yield environments (for example, being friendly to cellphones as well as desktops). This is because, in part, to browsers having less code to render and fewer files to load. Don't downscale everything on a site unnecessarily, but use simplicity and avoid redundancy as they're gifts that we should treasure that benefit everyone involved.

Dealing with slow connections

Consider users who live in a rural part of the country, use a fairly old computer, and are still getting used to the Internet. One of these users finds your site by using a search engine and decides to give the site a read. As the site begins to load, the user suddenly finds herself in a spot of trouble. Her computer is really lagging under the stress of loading a Flash intro, and everything is excruciatingly slow. In this scenario, the user with the slow connection wants to invest in faster access and get broadband, but because of where she lives, no ISP will support her.

As the user manages to push past the Flash introduction and onto the site, things go from bad to worse. Large images seriously affect her dialup connection, the graphics-accelerated material provided to the browser starts cooking her humble processor to high temperatures, and the frameworks being batch-loaded into each document starts to absorb bandwidth like crazy (and in this case, little of it was actually being utilized to achieve effects). Moreover, not all of the styles and scripting were being cached in external files, resulting in large file sizes.

One solution is to use external stylesheets and scripts to offer a lo-fi edition of the site that eliminates surplus flourishes. This will improve the overall flow of an interface, even one being used on older devices requiring legacy support. So, even with the excitement offered by new standards and innovations, you should offer a reasonably optimized experience for all users. If you can reduce the size of a site and avoid bundling unnecessary resource-heavy features, do so. More often than not, users have a lower emotional threshold for loading times than errors, so efficiency is a worthwhile goal (it could have helped that visitor to browse more easily).

Components

Many hardware components, such as those shown in Figure 9-1, can affect your website's performance, and with the browser's rendering increasingly being tied to your machine's capabilities, the relevance of this trend is certain to increase. As a designer, it's critical that you know your hardware and that you ensure the stability of even the weakest link, from storage mediums to the processors that render objects. These components range from the tools that give us speed like CPUs, GPUs, or RAM, to the tools that store or affect our content's playback capability.

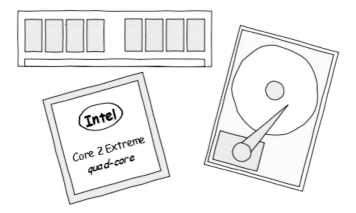

FIGURE 9-1: Memory, processors, and hard drives are internal components.

The following lists show this hardware's family tree and some issues its members encounter:

Relatives:

> Hard disk

> GPU

> Audio card

> CPU

> RAM

Considerations:

> Hardware acceleration

> Local object storage

> Resource overhead

Practical solutions

When determining whether a layout is sustainable and compatible with internal hardware components, you must consider the hardware's stress levels while the browser is viewing your site. If a user's device suffers performance issues while the site is open, she will not visit your site again. If performance excels, or is at least reliable, the site is likely to survive even the oldest of machines. Hardware acceleration in browsers is perhaps one of the best examples of the developing relationship between web designs and computer hardware.

Making sure that your site works with some device's hardware isn't just about using some neat piece of code or ensuring your site renders to a recognized speed benchmark. Often rendering happens automatically in modern browsers. Except, rather than rendering like in the old days, browsers now use the system's CPUs, GPUs, and RAM to process and churn through graphics, scripts, and other heavy-going files, at epic speeds. The only way to help users with weaker devices is to reduce the level of resource-intensive scripts in designs.

Reducing the demand on resources in your pages is relatively straightforward, as you just need to make your work as clean, lean, and mean as possible. However, everyday actions can affect the performance of your hardware. Consider, for example, the humble hard drive, which handles caching, offline storage, temporary files (like cookies), and does so by writing data to the disk when required. If the user has other programs that intensively read and write from the disk (like an antivirus product), performance issues may occur.

Reference Cookies and local storage have become a perilous subject with the controversial new EU laws becoming effective. You might want to consider taking the hit and transporting all of your stored user data into cloud-hosted (secure) solutions as a safer option. For details, check out the article, video, and eBook at http://www.silktide.com/cookielaw.

Everyone on the Web makes a big deal about HTTP requests and the latency they cause, but from a desktop angle, levels of cached or fresh content vary greatly. Although SSDs (solid state disks) are becoming more ubiquitous, plenty of older, traditional disks are out there, and having to keep writing data to the disk and grabbing it back adds to machine stress. When possible, reduce the number of files you use. Also, caching keeps files on the disk for longer, reducing the need for constant rewrites, which lowers the load on the machine.

The resources required for data are enormous. If you open your operating system's process-management application and examine how a browser absorbs memory when loading a page, you'll be shocked. The average site is increasing in size, and the use of extensions and other features (like plug-ins) increase the scale of the issue. This double-edged sword is equally problematic because downloading and uploading files between the client and server side takes additional time. Weighing your options allows you to plan for the future.

If your site is to withstand the demands of different device types, you should balance the needs of a site with the capabilities of the tool being used to access the Web. Don't burn resources on needless features and effects. More importantly, deciding where to store user settings can make a real difference. Data stored on the client side is great for data that will be requested constantly. Server-side storage costs more in terms of latency (awaiting files to download) but offers portability for multi-device users. So pick your methods wisely!

Best practices

> Reduce the level of intensive-rendering scripts for performance gains.

> Splash screens are an example of wasting resources. Don't use them.

> Try to reduce the frequency of disk-writes to assist slow hard drives.

> Keep repeat requests local as disk-writes are faster than bandwidth.

> Resources are precious; don't squander them on pointless or large files.

Connectivity

While you can applaud the Web's many useful innovations, the availability of sites remains an issue to this day. The problem could be on the client side, ranging from issues involving lack of Web connectivity (see Figure 9-2) to DNS issues; or it can be on the server side, ranging from a server's availability, domain pointers, and downtime, either accidentally or purposefully. Of course, no one will ever eliminate every issue surrounding connectivity, but it's worth determining how your site may be affected, and what you can do to ensure its availability.

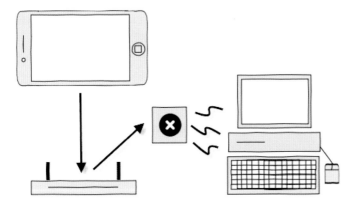

FIGURE 9-2: Problems can exist on the client side, caused by lack of Web connectivity or DNS issues.

The following lists show this hardware's family tree and some issues its members encounter:

Relatives:	**Considerations:**
> Web connectivity	> Archive mirrors
> Domain pointers	> Issue handling
> Site maintenance	> Offline browsing
> Server downtime	

Practical solutions

Naturally, when you talk about connectivity on the Web, availability of the site matters; otherwise, the site is basically offline. Downtime still troubles designers, but there are potential solutions at hand, so you're not entirely defenseless against the tides of hosting providers. For example, many hosts provide backup solutions that can help reduce the potential for downtime (such as distributed hosting, cloud architecture, backup devices, and other features that are designed to ensure that if one server fails, another kicks in).

When talking to a computer user who understands the dangers of hard disk failures, you'll keep hearing that they wish they'd backed up their data. Regularly synchronizing data to backup sites, mirrors, or archives offering identical sites may not seem that useful, but it's probably one of the single most important aspects of running an online service. Using backup hosts comes the added cost of maintaining this second tier of hosting; but, if your site requires 100% uptime (or something close), you might want to consider investing in it.

Ultimately, no matter how hard you try, problems will occur on sites. Compatibility and ensuring a future-proof layout doesn't mean a total lack of downtime, which unfortunately, is unavoidable (so you can't be blamed for what is often out of your control), though you'll want to reduce the likelihood of it occurring. The old adage, "An ounce of prevention is worth a pound of cure," makes perfect sense here, and having a protocol or plan about how you'll deal with unexpected failures or situations can help preserve a site's longevity.

Tip Many of the world's largest companies have seen the benefits that social networking can provide in terms of user satisfaction and maintaining an online presence when their sites have issues (thus upholding the stability of a site using flexible approaches). So get yourself a Twitter or Facebook account and keep users abreast of systemwide issues.

Monitoring your sites for bugs and issues relating to connectivity is important, whether the problem is that the entire site is unavailable or there's a bug in an PayPal IPN script. Rather than leave minor errors to fester, resolve them immediately. Also, regularly back up your data to reduce long-term harm to a site, especially one that has a rich, active community, such as a forum filled with members and feedback in public view! When things go wrong, informing users and providing good communication are just as important as resolving the issue itself.

Finally, you need to cover offline browsing. Offline browsing has been around for years, and the technology has moved on a bit because people are using scrapbook apps, snippet managers, capture tools, and offline readers to use sites without connectivity. Because users are beginning to save files to read later, be sure to allow and encourage that behavior. Yes, there are issues about piracy due to content being downloaded, but as many handheld devices encourage offline reading (for if connectivity isn't available), it should be allowed.

Offering a PDF version of an article, for example, is a great route to offline reading (and it has the benefit of letting visitors read your work anywhere). Rather than make users copy and paste entire blocks of text, you can use DRM or features that are non-intrusive and not distracting. When users can't get online for some reason but want to promote something they found on a site, they may open what they saved in their Web browser. In the future, offline availability will become less critical because of advances in Internet coverage.

Best practices

> A backup site is a great way to dodge downtime and increase bandwidth.

> Whenever downtime is noticed, immediately try to resolve the situation.

> Use social networks to alert users about situations and potential timeframes.

> Don't demand that a page connects to the Web unless really necessary.

> Users may want to browse content offline, so test if your site saves properly.

Bandwidth

Since the inception of broadband, users have enjoyed a rich online experience filled with media and imagery. While some visitors have speedy connections (Figure 9-3), many have issues with slow connections and a lack of bandwidth (especially in small countries and third-world nations). Don't neglect these less-fortunate users. Additionally, with the mobile handheld market pushing worldwide connectivity to its limits, you should consider the legacy of dialup, data limitations, and whether offline browsing can aid your audience.

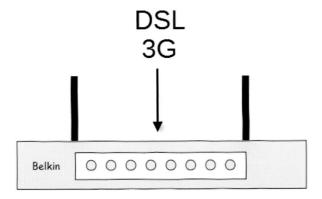

FIGURE 9-3: Users may have a fast DSL connection, or a dialup or limited 3G Internet connection.

The following lists show this hardware's family tree and some issues its members encounter:

Relatives:	**Considerations:**

Relatives:

> Reduced speeds

> Bandwidth caps

> Data throttling

> Roaming charges

Considerations:

> Semantic separation

> Compression options

> Caching utilization

Practical solutions

If you've been building sites for a while, you'll understand the need for easy-to-maintain, small file sizes. Even today, many sites have scripts and CSS scattered throughout their HTML files; even worse, designers are still pumping deprecated tags and dead attributes for stylistic properties into code (and web editors that don't know better). With the goal of availing your site work to the widest possible audience, be careful about including such features because they're not exactly bandwidth friendly (bloated code uses more data).

Some legacy devices and browsers may not recognize new code, but very few people use technology that can't do things semantically (which is as good a reason as any to ensure your code is well written). Maintain clean, efficient source code by eliminating duplicate junk, and separate structure, style, and behavior as much as possible. By doing so, you not only make updating the sites easier, but also you'll often reduce the amount of bandwidth used. As code becomes more complex, code separation will remain essential in the future.

Bandwidth is a well-documented issue on the Web. Because Internet speeds aren't always consistent for everyone and because of the data caps and roaming charges being applied by ISPs and carriers alike, be careful that you don't waste user resources needlessly. Kilobytes soon add up when multiple pages and objects are being loaded frequently. Beyond keeping code clean of deprecated, useless tags (in favor of well-supported options with temporary fallbacks), the best and most useful weapon at your disposal in this battle is compression.

Tip

Handheld devices tend to reserve less disk space for storing temporary files so you may find caching less efficient than on the desktop, which is a shame because that's where the benefits are needed the most. So try not to cache enormous MB+ sized files.

You can compress quite a few things on a site with mixed results. For example, you can shrink video or audio files by reducing the quality, or in the case of video the size of the media and by using a good compression format (such as MP3 over WAV). Images are much like media, except you have a few more compatible formats to work with. As for code, you can remove white space and use other tricks (such as enabling GZIP on the server) to reduce the size of files, though maintaining minified source code can be harder.

Caching is another option you can use to give users the most efficient experience possible. Earlier, I said that with excessive disk writes, hard disks can develop a bit of latency, but people choose to use the feature anyway because of its capability to shave megabytes, or even more (gigabytes), in terms of data and hosting costs as revisited files are less frequently downloaded! When using a smartphone roaming abroad, users could save a lot of money, but even if they do have an unlimited plan, it may still speed up subsequent page loads.

When a file is downloaded, it will automatically attempt be cached by the browser (if that is possible) and held until an updated file is detected online. This is almost like a hybrid form of online and offline browsing. The fewer times the file is updated, the fewer times it needs to be redownloaded for use, which is why designers frequently break their styles, scripts, and resources into external files. Caching lets users recycle code they've already downloaded and avoid duplicate downloads, so leverage this technique when possible.

Best practices

> Structure, style, and behavior do not belong together; separate them.

> Utilize server-side includes to separate and cache common content.

> Images and media take up the most space; compress them if possible.

> Enable GZIP compression if supported on the server side for savings.

> Prevent large files from caching as handhelds have a small datastore.

Influencing Operating Systems

GUIs, controls, typefaces, colors, and more

THE WEB ISN'T a physical entity that you can touch, and the layers involved in securing a stable layout go beyond the devices and hardware at your disposal. Deep inside every device, you'll find a range of software variables that allows you to turn interactions with devices into something meaningful and responsive. First we'll examine the operating system (OS) and like ice cream, everyone has their favorite OS (popular ones include Windows, Mac, and Linux). OS directly affects how sites render, look, and feel.

Inside the System Shell

The idea behind an OS is to manage a computer's hardware and software. Each OS has a unique user interface and also a unique way of handling browser windows and other Web-enabled applications. Visually, the most prominent differences relate to how much space the components absorb. Consider the Windows taskbar: Some users may have it enabled; others may have it disabled. The taskbar (or dock in OSX's case) comes in different sizes, can be modified, and absorbs a screen's real estate (helping users manage open windows).

In addition, when running different operating systems (or versions of an OS), the most popular browsers render websites differently. For example, font anti-aliasing, which is OS controlled, makes the text in browsers render differently. In other words, your site may appear differently on Safari for Mac and Safari for Windows, all because of how the OS decides to handle the text that appears on-screen. To give users a consistent experience, you must consider such differences upon each platform.

Note

Expected behavioral functions may not always work the way you want them to. An example is the way browsers open a new window. Some mobile operating systems will refuse to allow more than one instance of an app, and others may not even allow pop-up windows to initiate. So, it doesn't make sense to push such features upon users.

Moreover, desktop computers aren't the only game in town. Mobile operating systems function in drastically different ways, and often their platform is more limiting in terms of customizability than their desktop counterparts. The number of variants to account for also jumps significantly from the three we know about for traditional computers to a range that includes Android and iOS (which are, in part, based upon existing desktop systems). As the operating system controls both hardware and software, it should be taken quite seriously.

Getting users to change OSs is more difficult than getting them to move from a damaged browser. If, for example, they use a handheld device or a tablet such as the Chromebook, they're locked into using the OS included on the device, because of restrictions imposed by the manufacturer. When changing OSs, the learning curve for the average user is significant. Making the most of an environment is a challenge, but with new operating systems being developed constantly, if you can ensure compatibility over time, you'll have happy visitors.

Many other aspects of an OS can affect your site, and different systems and shells can affect a user's interaction with your offerings. However, for the sake of simplicity, this chapter focuses purely upon some of the more essential and game-changing factors, from how the OS handles applications like browsers; to the color, typeface, security, and file-handling capabilities they offer by default. Operating systems have considerable control over what users see, so test upon multiple platforms, resolving any quirks you encounter.

Rasterized antialiasing

The user's OS is instrumental in her journey through your site. Say that you just had your site overhauled, and it takes advantage of the latest, greatest toys in CSS3. You reference a beautiful, customized anti-aliased typeface to provide an emotional connection to the content (using CSS3, which is now widely supported, but still requires a legacy support fallback using font stacks) and some subtle low-contrasting shades in the background, and your user is browsing on a solid browser like Opera. All good news for you and the site's visitor, right?

Sadly for this user, things aren't going well. Although her browser does support the CSS3 font-face technique, which allows typefaces to be embedded within a page, her brand of OS (Windows XP) doesn't have ClearType enabled by default — something that her browser cannot work around. The lack of anti-aliasing on the font makes headings look so jagged and blurry that they're illegible. Also, her PC's color calibration settings are set up inaccurately (by OS default or user customization) and are uncalibrated; the subtle shading on the site is lost to the site's visitor!

Resolving such an issue is tricky because the process of enabling a tool like ClearType or calibrating a monitor requires users to go out of their way to do so. And with certain types of displays, there's no guarantee that things will actually look clearer because one bad move from the user could mess things up further! There's no real answer to this dilemma except to carefully consider the use of supporting typefaces. Beyond this, it makes sense to build a traditional font stack so that if the typeface you want isn't installed, alternatives will kick in.

GUIs

The graphical user interface (GUI) dictates how objects appear on desktops (and screens, by association). These powerful, visually engaging components control and restrict the space a site can use, including everything from windows, dialog boxes, and pop-ups to the many types of bars (status, menu, task, side, and so on). The GUI (Figure 10-1) controls what happens between a browser and the OS it's on. Although OSs come with a default setup, users can customize these shells to a great extent, which in turn can affect a layout.

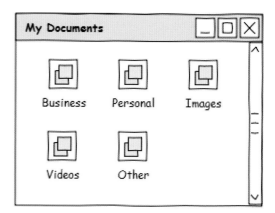

FIGURE 10-1: GUIs control and stylize the aesthetic of everything outside of a browser's window.

The following lists show members of this software's family tree and issues they can encounter:

Relatives:

> Desktop environment

> Window manager

> Interface shells

> Desktop metaphor

Considerations:

> Dialog notifications

> Quick window scaling

> Theming and skinning

Practical solutions

Regardless of whether we're on a mobile platform or a desktop computer, our online experience seems to revolve around dialog boxes and notifications. From a real-estate perspective, notifications are more effective on a mobile platform than on a desktop, but with their recognizable icons (which depend on the OS or browser) and notable penchant for disabling app interactivity unless the message has been answered or acknowledged, it's true that your users will take notice of these distinctive tools, regardless of the platform.

Sites have been using dialog boxes within layouts since the dawn of JavaScript. Because they are highly intrusive and overused, however, many users don't care for them and get annoyed at their use. Alerts and prompts have become so problematic that many browsers limit how many can be shown (in sequence). To ensure consistency in interfaces, avoid using them at all; instead, use a lightbox or related technique except on mobile platforms, because there, dialogs match behavior expectations and reduce the potential for user errors.

Every OS has title bars that provide a product (and/or document) title along with buttons that aid window management. The capability to minimize, maximize, and close windows will play a role in how a site appears to users. In addition to default functionality (like zooming on a Mac), certain products can extend the functionality of the title bar and offer features like pinning a window to be always on top. What's more, users can resize windows, which can affect viewport space (say they wanted two sites, running side by side on a monitor).

Tip

Some browsers and applications defy an operating system's GUI conventions and offer customized interfaces. With this becoming a regular practice, don't assume that a user will have the same viewport (rendering space) or dimension limits by default and avoid assuming the size, appearance, or behavior of objects like buttons, scrollbars, or menus.

In terms of compatibility, your site will not always be visible to users; for example, you cannot expect visitors to keep their windows maximized or in full-screen mode each time they browse to your site. So, rather than thinking in terms of resolution, instead look at the physical amount of space available for designs to appear within (this is commonly called the *viewport*). Many users with large screens will not have their browser maximized, and if the screen is small enough, horizontal scrolling may occur if responsive design isn't used.

Another interface complication is the capability to theme or skin the desktop. For many years, companies like Stardock have been producing simple, effective software to give the GUI an extreme makeover, which makes depending upon the look and feel of objects unreliable. Plenty of alternative products exist, and to some extent, the OS also allows customization. Consider how users can choose between the modern and classic Windows themes. Now, imagine how this behavior can affect your website's appearance as menus visually change.

Users can increase or decrease font sizes within the title bar through skinning software or the OS's display properties, which will reduce or increase the viewport space available in a maximized window. Also, users can alter default text sizes, native color schemes, and do other things that globally affect screen real estate. To resolve theme-related issues, try to avoid any precision JavaScript calculations that start from a base resolution, and account for default object sizes that may reduce the overall viewport space to avoid scrolling.

Best practices

> Avoid using alerts or prompts except when a small screen is utilized.

> Use a lightbox script to create a customized, less-obtrusive dialog box.

> Try your site in a variety of different window modes, such as full screen.

> Avoid depending upon an OS's look and feel in case themes are used.

> Avoid trying to calculate usable screen real estate by way of OS objects.

Controls

The capabilities of an OS extend beyond the desktop it maintains and regulates. Objects used in browsers, such as tooltips, scroll bars, and input controls (like text boxes, drop-downs and buttons), all garnish some default styling, and while they can be customized to varying degrees, they largely remain the focus of the OS's theme renderer (with exceptions where a browser takes over). As shown in Figure 10-2, a range of input elements can be affected by control rendering, and with HTML5 offering several new elements, interactivity is set to increase.

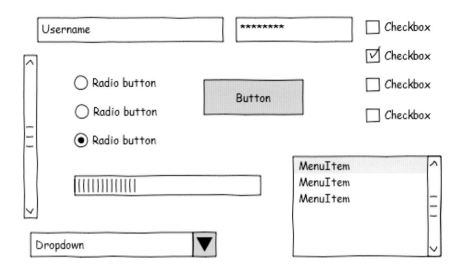

FIGURE 10-2: Input controls affect how users interact with sites; if they fail, users are silenced!

The following lists show members of this software's family tree and issues they can encounter:

Relatives:

> Graphical UI widgets

> Interface controllers

Considerations:

> Input and output

> Websafe widgets

> Screen behavior

Practical solutions

Elements allowing interactivity are critical to the success of the Web. Each input widget, whether it be a drop-down menu, text box, or any other embeddable element, has a specific goal to achieve, and each OS has its own way of implementing the widget to give it the look and feel users can recognize and use throughout their online experiences. Consider something like iOS. When you select a text box, the screen zooms to give the object focus and the on-screen keyboard pops up, ready for input (this behavior is unique to the OS).

When dealing with these interactive widgets, first you need to know that each browser will have its own policy about how much the object can be customized. With critical feature (for example, scroll bars), it's best to leave widgets to their own default styling mechanisms (as the user expect them to appear as), rather than replace them with special effects or more exotic replacements that users may fail to spot. To help reduce confusion, try disabling widgets that users may not need when performing a particular task (like filling out a form).

A range of input widgets has existed since the early days of HTML. For many years, this select group of objects has been the center point for interactivity and inputting data online. However, with the push to HTML5, a new bunch of input widgets has been created with the intention of improving interactivity online, like being able to enter and parse e-mail addresses, number values, URLs (in iOS it activates the URL-oriented virtual keyboard), ranges (represented as a slider), search, and date or color pickers. Very exciting stuff!

Reference If you want to have some fun with HTML5 forms and the new input widgets, read the following article. It covers only a few general principles, but it shows the potential for these new, exciting features: `http://24ways.org/2009/have-a-field-day-with-html5-forms`.

Unfortunately, as is the case with all new HTML5 features, browsers that existed before their creation will not be able to support these tools. Additionally, because some of these objects don't have an OS default control to fall back on, they can be very different in style and function, especially between browser manufacturers. If you do use these new widgets in sites, you'll need to provide a fallback, or in the case of elements that function similarly to others (such as e-mail to text), a script that can replicate the specific effect.

To reiterate, different environments may treat input widgets differently and thereby they will render uniquely upon the page in those situations. Although they are not ideal for those who take pleasure in styling every aspect of the page (because the level to which you can customize these interactive objects is somewhat restricted), the lack of custom styling options, which force users to see recognizable, non-stylized objects, does provide some comfort in terms of usability because objects will be immediately identifiable on-screen.

If you own an iPhone, for example, and have completed a form, you will have come across a drop-down menu and watched that beautiful roller wheel with the clicky noises appear.

If you, the designer, demand that users enter a specific value into a drop-down while the menu is active, they may find doing so tricky because they can't see the page, and would have to understand what needs entry by reading provided instructions before clicking the menu (such as knowing they need to enter a country of origin rather than the destination).

Best practices

> Avoid coloring or replacing the scroll bar; doing so may confuse visitors.

> Input widgets can be styled, but don't expect effects to work cross-browser.

> Utilize HTML5 inputs, but provide easy-to-use alternatives and fallbacks.

> Clearly state what users must do before asking them to interact with widgets.

> Input selection can trigger zooming, so keep form objects close together.

Associations

Most users maintain default settings on their computers. These settings affect the visual style of their OS, the file associations (which determine how their applications open or what file types will work), and other aspects of their computing experience. Understanding such behaviors helps you assess what users may encounter while browsing with default settings intact (Figure 10-3); for example, scripting could be turned off, support for XLS files may not be offered, or the browser's capability to input form data automatically may be disabled.

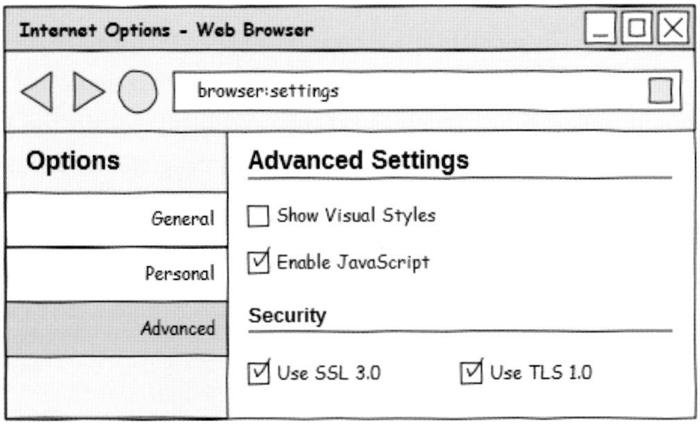

FIGURE 10-3: Browsers come with default settings, and this could determine feature availability.

The following lists show members of this software's family tree and issues they can encounter:

Relatives:	**Considerations:**
> Operating system defaults	> Native behavior
> Manufacturer configurations	> File associations
> Default format compatibility	> Browser defaults

Practical solutions

The native behavior of an OS, browser, or device is important to consider. Although more technology-minded individuals are able and willing to push equipment to its limits, the average user isn't likely to share this enthusiasm or competence. If something in an OS must be turned on or off before it can be used, then it becomes intrusive. Don't force users to undertake such activity any more than necessary and use default behavior as the norm when deciding whether to implement something that's dependent on custom user settings.

When designing, consider a system's default browser, the tools or plug-ins that may be available and installed (ready to use), and the default theme or shell used within an OS. It's not that users are lazy and unwilling to work outside the box and make changes if there is a real justification to do so; it just makes sense to reduce the learning curve and barriers to entry so that beginners can browse without complications. For example, look at what each browser has upon installation (in terms of default settings) to get you started.

One of the biggest issues regarding the availability of content in specific formats is what application (if any) will open files by default (associations). It is true that some file formats have the luxury of ubiquitous support (such as txt, gif, and html, within the Web browser), but other recognizable, popular formats have trouble getting the default support they need. This can be problematic if you depend on such formats because lack of support or wrong file handling can affect your sites, reducing the availability of potentially critical content.

Reference

Processing e-mails with a form and script combination is the best way to go, but you can also launch the default e-mail client from within a browser. The following reference describes the `mailto` syntax and how it influences apps and is controlled by the default file associations offered by software: `www.ianr.unl.edu/internet/mailto.html`.

All browsers allow you to access a range of file formats (for example, txt) directly within the browser window if a link to the file is provided. Some browsers may try to launch another application from within the browser window, if users have the supported product already installed and available. Consider something like iTunes pseudo protocol, which lets certain links open the application (and automatically navigate to the intended page). Offering alternatives for when these products aren't installed is critical to avoid dead links.

When it comes to offering extended functionality (beyond the installed defaults), browsers have become a complicated creature to account for. Because users can quite easily find and install extensions, plug-ins, or other features—which can affect the daily operation of a browser (positively or negatively)—the assembly of a toolbars and unessential components that a user can accumulate will degrade a site's performance over time. While most of these products aren't likely to cause much damage, some can affect defaults dramatically.

When you test for compatibility, be sure to factor in common alternative behaviors for things like keyboard shortcuts, file associations, and site or browser interoperability. For example, with something like screen resolutions, a few common configurations will enjoy the majority of usage, but it's also true that users with certain products installed may alter the defaults, potentially without the user being aware it's happening. Therefore, if a feature like JavaScript can be turned off by third-party plug-ins (and it can), avoid depending on it.

Best practices

> Verify that "out of the box" defaults in OSs won't affect usability.

> Make a list of popular configurations and extend support to these.

> As browsers function differently, don't demand users override settings.

> Keep linking to pdf or doc files, but consider that the results may vary.

> Use mailto and other pseudo links, but always offer an alternative.

Typefaces

The typefaces you pick can affect the consistency and stability of your layout. Because a large majority of sites are comprised of text-based content, it's important that the fonts you choose match what a user is likely to have installed. If the typefaces used can't be found in the OS's collection, aren't installed with software the user has, or are served via a service like Typekit, the output can vary drastically. With typeface support being heavily fragmented and anti-aliasing (Figure 10-4) varying between platforms, fonts are worth considering.

FIGURE 10-4: If font availability wasn't enough, font-smoothing technologies can affect the aesthetic too!

The following lists show members of this software's family tree and issues they can encounter:

Relatives:

> ClearType (Windows)

> CoreText (Mac)

> CoolType (Adobe)

> FreeType (Linux)

Considerations:

> Non-rasterization

> Typeface formats

> Websafe stacking

Practical solutions

A critical aspect of typography that many of us fail to account for in our designs is the lack of rasterization (or *anti-aliasing*) available to the user. Some typefaces are dependent upon being optimized for LCD screens and their kin but aren't necessarily any worse off if the already-included capabilities aren't taken advantage of, and others fall into the category of useless without the technology being enabled. Windows XP is a classic case showing what happens when the feature isn't forced into being used (and users will feel its effects).

The problem with working around the anti-aliasing issue is that you can't magically force users to turn on the feature. Moreover, different operating systems can use different sub-pixel rendering methods, so typefaces will not look the same on Windows and a Mac. On

Windows, Safari actually has its own built-in rasterizer, which just adds fuel to the fire! Your choices are to either dodge fonts that depend on the feature, or test on each OS (and Safari in Windows) with anti-aliasing technologies turned on and off to ensure readability.

When it comes to using typefaces in anything content related, the choices are many. This diversity is especially visible in browsers where designs can be based around fonts, but the recognition of typeface availability falls to the OS by default. Among the different formats you can choose from, the choices (which can, in certain cases, be embedded) include TrueType (TTF) and OpenType (OTF). But for compatibility, you'll also need to cater to the more openly supported WOFF, the IE-only EOT, and even SVG-based fonts . . . yikes!

Reference Many services are available to help you determine and select the best font stack, and some can help you find licensed typefaces for the Web. One of the best CSS3 @font-face generators can be found here: `www.fontsquirrel.com/ fontface/generator`.

Supporting all of these necessary components is a pain in the neck, and ensuring that your fonts fall back as you intend and degrade gracefully can be tricky. However, the simplest option is to use a stack builder with websafe typefaces, an already-established typography provider (which offers fonts that are ready for embedding on the Web), or a solution that's already gained support. Using established sites such as Fontdeck and Typekit guarantees that you'll have the required license to use a font for the purpose of online embedding.

If you've been building sites for a while, you have probably come across the font-family CSS property. This property allows you to provide a prioritized list of fonts that you would like to see your content in on users' machines. The great thing about this property is that it accurately matches the whole adaptive-design way of thinking: You design for the best, and plan for the worst. Because visitors' operating systems determine what typefaces can be used (based on the collection they have installed on their machines), the browser will go forth and use the font that becomes available first from the list you provide in your code.

To build a websafe and compatible font stack, you'll need to first throw away any beliefs you may hold about your visitors seeing text the same way you do. It's a simple fact that users can uninstall or disable fonts from their computers (or not have them installed in the first place). Therefore, even popular fonts may not appear for a small group of your users. Offering some similar fallbacks is the solution. Have one font that you'd like to see, one alternative, one similar common font, one backup font, and the font family they belong to.

Best practices

> Safari for Windows has its own font smoother; test to ensure readability.

> Avoid rasterizer-dependent typefaces until Windows XP is no longer used.

> Be sure to embed each Web typeface format; doing so increases support.

> Employ Web typography services to avoid embedding licensing issues.

> Build a solid font stack with plenty of typeface options and a font family.

Colors

Although some devices and hardware are more capable of viewing color than others, OSs are inherently linked to showing colors on-screen. With the capability to switch between color depths and brightness levels and to calibrate using preinstalled software, the OS remains firmly in control when it comes to enhancing or reducing the accuracy and range of colors displaying (Figure 10-5). Understanding this level of customizability helps you to utilize the now-deprecated system of CSS color properties, controlled by the operating system.

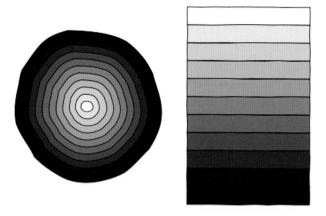

FIGURE 10-5: Even monochrome palettes come in a variety of shades, which software can control.

The following lists show members of this software's family tree and some issues they can encounter:

Relatives:

> Really-safe palette

> Websafe palette

> WebSmart palette

Considerations:

> Swatches and palettes

> Calibration and control

> CSS 2.1 system colors

Practical solutions

In terms of color, as showcased within monitors and OSs, early devices limited the palette and swatches that could be used, which made designing more colorful sites rather difficult. However, we've gone through various iterations of what's defined as a websafe palette as technologies have evolved, and for compatibility, some designers still consider restricting color use worthwhile. Though while not many old color-limited devices are still being used today, some new devices still aren't that color savvy.

Working around the issues of color compatibility in sites can be challenging. If a visitor suffers from color blindness, for example, that person may be unable to see all colors or shades of an existing one (or more). A key principle for color use is to have every color contrast greatly against its environment (strong differences between the foreground and background, for instance) and test your work in a color blindness filter. Also, start with a basic palette and restrict the number of colors used to avoid flooding the user's senses.

Operating systems provide a great deal of control over how visuals look on-screen, but if you're the pixel-pushing type, you know that screens are notoriously bad at representing colors accurately. You can still spend thousands on a quality television set only to find out it doesn't have the settings required to make colors match real life as effectively as you'd like. This issue is very common online, and only enthusiasts who are willing to test and make the changes will resolve such issues by calibrating their screens.

Note

When providing compatibility with older devices, visual burn-in can play its part in stability goals. This type of issue isn't so common these days, but if a visitor has an old display attached, it may distort visuals (emphasizing the need for color clarity).

To check color accuracy, you must calibrate your device against a standardized test image. Some OSs come with software built in (third-party products can also do the job); others may offer nothing to help. To ensure the site remains effective when calibration settings are incorrect, you must provide a sufficient amount of contrast to pages, check your work by cranking the screen's brightness up and down, and avoid very tiny text. As displays get better at being precalibrated in the future, such issues will be easily noticeable on pages.

You need to consider one final color-related compatibility matter: system colors. System colors are a range of old CSS color values that have been around since the dawn of the language but are now being deprecated in CSS3. Unlike other color values in the CSS specification, this unique series of keywords allows you to demand that a browser styles your site's content as it would a control or a section of your operating system's current theme, like the color of the title bar, the default text colors, or even an inactive window.

Arguably, because this is a deprecated piece of code, many designers probably won't be using it, even though it could potentially be useful in ensuring that your theme matches the user's actual desktop environment. Because it's one of the few CSS variables that draws all its power from the OS, rather than the browser's renderer, it is still worthy of mention as a rather unique way to cater to individual devices. Though, as users can change themes, the value can alter on a user-by-user basis and cause conflicts, so it's probably best to avoid it.

Best practices

> Use strong contrasts in your scheme to reduce color deficiency situations.

> Be smart with colors and try keeping color noise levels to a minimum.

> Recalibrate your device's color to see how your site will look on-screen.

> Push your site's visuals to their limits by testing in high and low brightness.

> Avoid using system colors in CSS because of their uncontrollable nature.

Security

The security precautions you take are some of the most overlooked aspects of interacting with the Web. Security software comes in many forms, such as the applications that keep our children safe (and our PCs free of malware); the systems that interject and prevent pages loading for reasons provided by tools like antivirus or antimalware guards; search providers (Figure 10-6); and form-filling software that helps users increase productivity. The consequences can mean getting blacklisted by browsers, or user data being hacked.

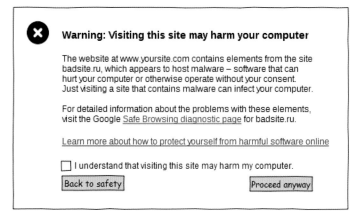

FIGURE 10-6: Browsers like Google Chrome will block infected sites before users can even load them.

The following lists show members of this software's family tree and issues they can encounter:

Relatives:

> Security scanners

> Safe-surfer filters

> Information manager

> HOSTS IP mapper

Considerations:

> Safe browsing reports

> Standardized form labels

> OS Level IP blockages

Practical solutions

One of the worst things that can happen to your site is to have it suddenly go offline. An even worse situation occurs if your site is listed as dangerous for users by a security app. As you can imagine, this will have long-term consequences for a brand and the longevity of its site (hence, the future-proofing link). Many browsers these days possess some level of quality control in that they find sites that could be infected with malware, blocking access to them entirely. In addition, most Internet security apps will block sites within a browser!

Prevention is better than cure when it comes to security issues on the Web. Test your site for vulnerabilities and to ensure that your site's administrative features are protected by a complex range of passwords. Also, ensure that the software you use like CMSs forums or tools with server-side write-privileges, are up-to-date (reducing the exploitation potential), and regularly moderate input to your site so that you don't get put in the infection sandbox by the likes of Google. Security is a big issue, and stable sites must remain on top of it.

Many people use form-filling software to speed up common actions online. They may also use a built-in form-filling solution provided by a browser vendor or a separate product with added functionality or stronger security. Not only can these tools help visitors recall their passwords more easily (which is actually better for security reasons because they're less likely to pick a weak one), but they also reduce the frequency of mistakes when filling in those critical forms on your site as data entry becomes more automated and predictable.

Reference

A good method for checking whether visitors can use secure form-filling tools (or if they need to keep reentering data) is to test your forms with existing products. Beyond testing in the browser's built-in form fillers, it may be worth trying this: `www.roboform.com/`.

One of the best ways to accommodate such needs in your site and increase productivity is to use sensible naming conventions for input forms. Because form-filling tools primarily work by remembering data entry for specific input widgets (by name), they rely entirely upon the form to ask for the right data type (as previously entered), and thereby determine what should be entered by default. For example, If you want a name, use the ID "name," for e-mail use "e-mail," and for address use "address"; it generally is that simple, really.

One final security trick that the OS has in store for us (which affects us on a security basis) is the hosts file. Although its primary objective is relating to mapping the IP addresses of hosted sites to domains, some security products will add certain records into a host file in order to redirect the user or to prevent the site from being opened (leading it into a dead end). Although this occurs on the client's OS over which you have no control, it does provide a good lesson about how to treat connectivity issues regarding site unavailability.

If you get a message telling you that your site isn't available or has suffered downtime, you might try to load it yourself only to find that it works for you and seems to be free of any errors. Initially, this may seem like good news; however, the fact a user is having problems may mean that more users are having similar issues (they just haven't come forward). If you do get a message like this, investigate possibilities such as IP banning, DNS issues, or a HOSTS incident as a result of some software product. Otherwise, you've lost a visitor.

Best practices

> Tighten your own security practices to reduce the exploitation of sites.

> Resolve issues immediately if the site is flagged by a security vendor.

> Follow existing form-naming conventions to help automated input tools.

> Don't cripple text-pasting as password managers depend on the feature.

> If users have connectivity issues, appropriately investigate each case.

Details on Design Software

Common pitfalls with CMSs, visual editors, snippets, and wizards

DESIGNERS MAY DISAGREE, but users and their environments aren't always the cause of problems with interfaces. Occasionally, designers create the problem themselves. The issue might result from something as simple as a software product you use to construct a layout, causing you to inadvertently create a non-flexible design, which isn't future-friendly. In this chapter, you'll explore the potential pitfalls of visual editors, content management systems (CMS), and other code-generating products (like script frameworks).

What You Code is What You Get

If I had to hold one piece of software accountable for much of the mess many sites are in, it would likely be the visual web editor. Some products are more code-oriented and produce decent results, but the majority of them produce code that would strike fear into the heart of the *Flying Spaghetti Monster*. Back in the early days of the WYSIWYG (what you see is what you get) editor, Microsoft FrontPage was well known as a contributor to poorly generated source code. While these tools have gotten better, generated code issues remain.

Code generators can have a profound effect on your site. Sometimes, they manage to interject code that adds more fluff than features; other times, they may provide something that doesn't work across browsers. Coding by hand is considered beneficial as you remain in control of the output, but doing so isn't always a viable option as building your own CMS isn't straightforward or cost-effective, especially when programs like WordPress do a fair job (though each product will differ in terms of flexibility and standards adoption).

Tip   If you're going to use the automatically generated components of any service, product, or framework, be sure that you understand how the underlying code works. By blindly accepting outputted code, you leave your site vulnerable to a range of instability issues.

Many CMS solutions come with mobile-friendly plug-ins (while others don't), syndication feeds (which are useful for supported devices), and a good level of interactivity with little redundancy. The code can also usually be tweaked to take advantage of many extra tools. Even the modern WYSIWYG editor can offer some pretty neat scripting framework hooks that allow you to make your work increasingly flexible for a variety of mediums. Be aware that the limitations of such features can seriously affect how optimized your code will be.

Content management systems can work very well, and if used correctly, they can help you avoid common problems within interfaces. If you don't use these tools correctly, results of unmaintained output can yield explosive results (namely layouts can break and variables can be affected). CMSs tend to base a layout's visual effect on one set of conditions and rely on the techniques used by the manufacturers of the product (think of the default theme used by a CMS). Avoid sticking with default themes to cater to your audience effectively.

As the complexities of the Web increase, the use of tools like CMS engines will become increasingly common for the backbone of all projects as they offer a standardized solution to being proficient in every technique and direction the Web seems to get pulled in. That's not to say handcrafted sites will disappear, but we must be wary of the blind acceptance of these referencing tools as they create an additional layer between the browser and the user (which could become a barrier). Outdated, broken, or poorly built programs could also trigger issues.

The FrontPage WYSIWYG

How a site is constructed will determine just how likely it is to be stable upon many different platforms. In this example we'll use the case of a site that was built using a WYSIWYG editor called Microsoft FrontPage. Within the Web design industry, this product gained notoriety for its poor code quality output, and while arguably better programs have superseded it, legacy software is still in regular use. In this case, a novice site designer put together something via the drag-and-drop visual interface, and paid little attention to the code that was being output.

Unfortunately this has proven to be a huge mistake. Because the program is unable to determine the right tag for the right job (as context is something only humans understand without some assistance), the source code ends up littered with redundant code and tags that shouldn't be in use (it's worth noting here that while modern products like Dreamweaver are better at getting the code right, they aren't excluded from overusing DIV or container elements). As the site that's been constructed uses a fixed-width grid, this also makes the site's users suffer.

The code our novice designer outputs sends shockwaves to users. They complain that the layout doesn't work properly outside of Internet Explorer (as the preview pane only uses that, novices could easily miss testing outside of it with other browsers). Additionally, the fixed-width layout looks hideous on a handheld device, as everything is forced to scale outward to keep the full page in view. The redundant code isn't helping matters as it uses up more of the mobile user's bandwidth and slows the speed of page loading. If only the designer had kept to the code editor instead!

CMSs

Content management systems have been popular for many years; however, even though CMS products have greatly improved over those created during the 1990s, if not handled correctly, these products, just like WYSIWYG editors, can have a negative effect on the longevity of code. Some CMSs (see Figure 11-1) are very customizable, enabling you to edit an entire codebase and providing the extensibility for plenty of plug-in features (with a low impact on users), while others that rely on third-party hosting can limit a website's options.

FIGURE 11-1: WordPress is the leader of CMS products in terms of popularity, and is worth considering.

The following lists show members of this software's family tree and some issues they can encounter.

Relatives:

> WordPress

> Drupal

> Joomla!

> ExpressionEngine

> MODx

Considerations:

> Configuration potential

> Semantics generation

> Upgrade frequency

Practical solutions

One issue that many CMS products can introduce into a design's compatibility and overall flexibility is how easily the products can be configured and customized. Some tools, such as the ever-popular WordPress, allow the use of stylistic changes and extensions that could revamp an interface to the extent it bears no resemblance to the default installation. Other CMSs only offer only a few settings and have a more limited range of choices, but though they're cross-browser compatible, they may not be as flexible as you'd want them to be.

Choosing the right CMS is an important step. Doing so not only allows you to understand the limitations of what you're working with, but also you can see how well the platform is supported. Also, having a good, open community that develops for the platform means that you can find more support if something breaks, better-quality extensions, and potentially a wider range of themes and flexible templates. So, to increase the chances of your site being stable, do your research and be sure that what you're using is right for the site's needs.

It's fair to say that CMSs like WordPress are getting increasingly better at dealing with browser discrepancies, but many still output far more code than is needed mostly because they aren't able to determine the right tag for the right job without human intervention. Unfortunately, some of these tools can also create code that won't validate, that uses in-page styling, and that embeds scripts and styles within pages. This situation will improve as CMSs mature in the future, so pick a product that seems to have some longevity in it.

 Standards-compliant, accessible, well-forged CMS products exist. Consider the forum software Vanilla as a case in point. Unlike comparable products, this one is forward thinking in its emphasis on quality code. Get Vanilla here:
Reference http://vanillaforums.org/.

If you look inside a CMS and really tweak its code output, you can make your sites more semantically valid and accessible, which improves the sites' performance as a result. Optimizing your CMS's performance requires work, but it's worth the effort if you can reduce any bandwidth waste, usability flaws, or bugs that can negatively affect an experience. In the future, browsers will likely become less forgiving of poorly constructed code, and users will be less forgiving of frustrating usability issues (as they become more Web aware).

Having a great foundation for a site is all well and good, but life isn't this simple. You might have a CMS with masses of extensions, yet it may not be deemed fit if the core package isn't kept up-to-date by the manufacturer. With security being a major concern and with the emphasis placed on keeping up with the latest innovations, staying current makes sense (though beware that upon upgrading, files will be overwritten). Ensure that the CMS you choose is regularly updated, and that data can easily be migrated to another platform if needed.

Dealing with updates is difficult because they can vary considerably, but whatever you do, avoid CMS products that haven't been updated in a year. If you find a CMS product that has major milestone builds mapped out and if there are nightly builds along with a good community developing the product further, you've found an ideal candidate. You could use something updated less frequently if it's open source and you can make the improvements yourself, but this can be time-consuming, so it just makes sense to use what already exists.

Best practices

> Always go for a downloadable CMS in preference to a hosted solution.

> Research your options carefully before committing to a particular CMS.

> Go for a product that is easy to customize and that has an active community.

> Check the product's output for bloated, error-packed, low-quality code.

> Avoid tools that aren't maintained or those that aren't used as much as others.

Visual Editors (WYSIWYG)

WYSIWYG (what you see is what you get) editors (such as the one shown in Figure 11-2) enable beginners and competent coders to construct sites without using an ounce of code. Because of their lack of dependability in terms of quality output, many of these tools fail to offer the same level of quality and stability that hand-coding offers. Nevertheless, their popularity and ubiquity justifies considering them. Depending on the output quality and the preview renderer used, these editors can negatively affect the flexibility and durability of any site for your visitors.

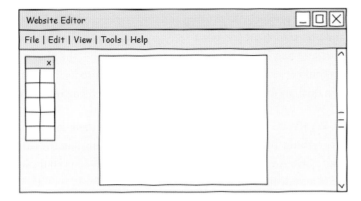

<small>FIGURE 11-2:</small> Visual editors focus on getting everything fixed in position, rather than flexibility.

The following lists show members of this software's family tree and some issues they can encounter.

Relatives:

> Dreamweaver

> iWeb

> FrontPage

> ExpressionWeb

> NetObjects Fusion

Considerations:

> Syntax redundancy

> Cross compatibility

> Restrictive features

Practical solutions

Although CMSs tend to produce some bloated markup, they at least are tested at the base configuration level to ensure high-level cross-browser support. WYSIWYG editors, on the other hand, aren't in this category because there's no base configuration to begin with. Some simpler products of this type may require users to employ a series of templates to overcome such issues, but if you want a highly personalized site that meets the needs of an audience, limitations won't cut it. Overcoming redundancy is a major issue in these tools.

When it comes to these editors, you really have only two ways to reduce redundancy in your code. First, you can dump the product you're using and find something that does the same job but in a more standards-compliant and bloat-free way. Other than that, it's up to you to avoid all visual editors and hand-code everything. On the one hand, the poor output from WYSIWYG editors could be excused for their behavior if you're producing a rapid prototype to get an idea for a final product, but for production sites, they're unacceptable!

In addition to the fact that WYSIWYG editors produce a lot of bloat in their code out of their attempts to squeeze everything into its rightful place, you need to consider the cross-compatibility factor. Building a layout with something like Adobe Photoshop is equivalent to using a WYSIWYG editor (the code it outputs is unlikely to be semantically sound). The best practice here is to export Photoshop (or equivalent application) creations into a series of cropped, web-ready images (for embedding), and code the structure by hand.

Note   WYSIWYG products can be very flexible when used as a general code editor, but as Dreamweaver and its competitors tend to be priced much higher than a simple non-visual code editor like Notepad++, Coda, or TextMate, justifying their use is hard to do.

Sites that are dragged and dropped into existence suffer unwieldy code that demands a level of compatibility for a pixel-perfect environment (which doesn't exist). This is why, when you export code from a non-coding environment, you must do some post-production work on the graphics or layout to ensure everything remains flexible. To address this issue, turn the fixed dimensions into relative ones (using percentage, not pixel widths), ensure your graphics scale or skew appropriately, and test in various browsers (not a preview pane).

As you can see, I'm not exactly a fan of WYSIWYG editors, but if you stick to the code window rather than the tempting visual editor, you can make even the most evil of editors do the job properly (even Microsoft FrontPage). One problem with visual editors with no coding window is that you can't be sure of how code will turn out until it's published or exported, which is often bad news for more temperamental browsers. Also, because many of these tools may not have been equipped with the latest features, many sites are limited.

Avoiding the limitations of previously built tools is part of what helps you stay on the cutting edge and gives you the best chance of ensuring you have a site that will work for as many users as possible. If you're already an established designer, the need to avoid these products is probably something you already know all too well. However, for many who are designing for the first time, the easy option proves all too tempting, and the wish to be future-proofed against the many battles a site faces is quickly lost in the cloud of code.

Best practices

> Avoid the visual window and stick to coding by hand to avoid a nasty mess.

> Do post-production work on layouts exported directly from Photoshop.

> Avoid testing cross-browser compatibility only in a layout's preview pane.

> Always use a good-quality CMS rather than a bad-quality visual editor.

> Never allow your code to go unchecked; maintain whatever you construct.

Snippets

Love them or hate them, code snippets (Figure 11-3) have been increasing Web designers' productivity for many a year. However, the ability to produce generic cut-and-paste scripts has created a legacy of poor coding, and ugly libraries have littered and proliferated the Web. Although you must understand what the code within snippets does before using it, it's possible that an innocuous script with noble intentions can conflict with existing code in a layout, affecting your work as a result. You need to avoid bad or temperamental code.

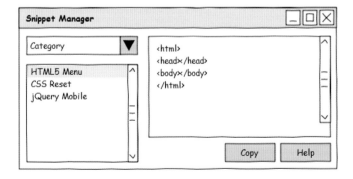

FIGURE 11-3: Code snippet managers can help designers retain reusable code they know works.

The following lists show members of this software's family tree and some issues they can encounter.

Relatives: **Considerations:**

> Cut-and-paste scripts   > Quality control levels

> Developer libraries   > Conflicting variables

                                     > Repurposing limitations

Practical solutions

A simple Google search will bring forth a heap of results if you're looking for some code snippets to help you implement something quickly, and beyond this, a massive array of frameworks and developer libraries also exist. A number of high-quality examples can be found on the Web within articles, tutorials, and solutions to questions posed by other users, but there are also many questionable snippets that unfortunately weren't created to a very high standard. So, you need to form some kind of quality control to weed out ugly code.

One of the best ways to resolve quality-control issues is to know and understand what your code does. If you do take advantage of an existing solution, be sure to examine the code, come to grips with how it operates, test it in a number of situations, and don't be afraid to reject it. Frequently, you don't really need an entire prebuilt snippet to get what you need. If you understand the mechanism and have an idea about how you need to use it, you'll be able to produce something clean and agile based upon it, which is better for your users.

One of the dangers of using code snippets is that the styles and behavior they output may conflict with existing material on your page. If the snippet has HTML that shares an ID with something on one of your pages, conflicts may occur. If the snippet has some general stylistic properties that target an entire element or document, your existing styles will be overwritten by browsers. Additionally, using JavaScript-based behavior that clashes with a code snippet's demands could potentially break the entire site and its core functionality.

Tip

The importance of the software layer is undeniable, but the decisions of an author and the intended or unintended consequences of his work on an interface are without question. Designers can make mistakes (just like browsers), so be careful in your code.

Hopefully, most snippets you'll encounter were built to ensure that such problems would not happen. But problems can occur, especially because plenty of ugly scripts are left over from the 1990s that could stomp around your site like Godzilla! Overcoming conflicts in your code requires understanding what you're putting in the site. To resolve issues with a snippet, you'll either need to edit the code to ensure that everything plays well together, or (in the case of future-proofing) ensure that the code you inject works well across browsers.

One of the great things about code snippets is that they allow developers to repurpose code regularly to avoid having to reenter the same data to get the required effect each and every time. Established designers often build a vast collection of snippets they produce and reuse regularly, which can speed up production times. Unfortunately, aside from conflicts, which can arise, the usefulness of snippets is bound by the need for every site to be unique (this means that situations may require you to keep editing or adapting the code for each use).

It makes sense to use code snippets if you're regularly trying to create a certain piece of functionality such as a drop-down menu or a social networking panel that will look and work identically across each implementation. You must, however, organize code so that it provides you with the hooks necessary to customize and style that object to an individual site's needs. Every site will have its own visitors, and each visitor will have unique demands on your interfaces; never fall into the trap of a one-size-fits-all mentality.

Best practices

> Examine the contents of each snippet to identify harmful source code.

> Try to improve the quality or agility of every code snippet you include.

> Remove code from within a framework if it's not being used in the site.

> Be on the lookout for conflicts and resolve them all before publication.

> Continuously revisit your code to ensure it works with future standards.

Wizards

Although WYSIWYG editors have been making their mark on the Web, software wizards (Figure 11-4) that create code based on preconfigured routines remain a favorite of many designers who want to achieve a commonly used effect (with best-practice requirements taken care of). Found both in software packages and on sites (often hosted solutions), these tools output the code required to put a wizard results into action. Although wizards can suffer code quality issues like other editors, they generally achieve a reasonable result.

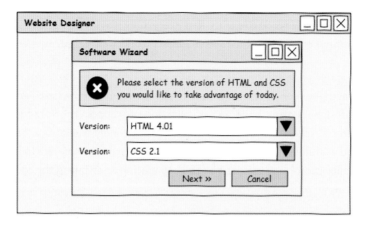

FIGURE 11-4: Wizards can achieve specific coding goals by customizing a well-made solution.

The following lists show members of this software's family tree and some issues they can encounter.

Relatives:

> Code generators

> Template builders

Considerations:

> Service maintenance

> Limited applications

> Agility and efficiency

Practical solutions

In this modern age of complex scripting, styling, and compatibility, tools offering a quick-and-easy method of generating code have become increasingly popular. From animation generators for CSS to specific JavaScript implementations, you can get an idea about what's commonly used by those who've refined the processes. If you compare these kinds of tools to other tools that authors use, you'll see that code generators mark a merging of the WYSIWYG editor (with its lack of coding) and a snippet (with its tightly regulated output). In the future, this trend of common, customized scripts will continue.

Moreover, wizards tend to help you achieve one set goal (such as a font stack or patterned background) that won't affect the rest of a layout and will really be just one combination of a popular feature or technique from a site (like a slide show builder). However, you do need to be aware of how well the wizard is maintained. Perhaps the code it outputs is no longer needed, or maybe something else needs to be added; weaknesses or bugs within generated code will be reflected in your site's visuals (so keep your knowledge of coding updated).

Although most code wizards can do one thing well (because they rigidly control the basics of outputted code and just make minor adjustments as required), they tend to be capable of that one task alone. Although some wizards can do multiple things, the more complex a wizard becomes, the more likely the quality of the code it outputs will suffer. By focusing on generating one particular function (for example, an opacity script), the wizard allows you to embed what's needed, where it's needed within your existing code structure.

Reference Many code wizards for designers exist. You can find a few that are worth trying at the following websites: `http://css3generator.com`, `www.css3.me`, `www.css3maker.com`, `www.phpform.org`, `www.codestyle.org/servlets/FontStack`, and `http://animatable.com`.

The limitations of a wizard's functionality can be a real strength as it reduces the chances of tweak-resulting errors. To ensure your code retains its compatibility with the generated material of the wizard, carefully read the instructions provided with the tool and fill out any required boxes or forms as accurately as possible. Although the author of the tool may have taken a wide range of circumstances into account, if you fail to accommodate any special requirements the code may have, you may end up making something fail or break.

The great thing about wizards is that they work like code snippets, providing previously built code that can be used at a moment's notice with the added benefit of being easier to customize if you're not that comfortable with code. One of the downsides with anything pregenerated, however, including a wizard, is that it might provide style or functionality limitations based on its offerings. Wizards can't make assumptions about what your code contains because they don't analyze your code. They do their job independently of it.

Keeping your code agile and responsive can be tricky if you constantly use third-party code that was generated at the source. Although wizards are cleaner and more agile than libraries, frameworks and WYSIWYG editors (as you only need to copy, paste the output), you'll need to ensure the code a wizard outputs doesn't conflict with anything you've used previously in styles or scripts. Perhaps you already use a CSS reset, or perhaps you already have that jQuery reference; if so, you don't need to make the same declaration twice.

Best practices

> Stay on top of the latest techniques to avoid poorly aging code generators.

> Determine where a wizard's capabilities end; then match any restrictions.

> Only use wizards for their primary purpose; it's the safest-possible option.

> If the code a wizard outputs repeats already in-use code, reuse what exists.

> To make old code easy to retire, group it together for ease of maintenance.

Befriend the Web Browser

Considering desktop, mobile, proxy and alternative renderers

COMPATIBILITY ON THE WEB can be affected by numerous variables, but in times of trouble you tend to go with what you know. If history has taught Web designers anything, it's that the browser is often the root cause of most unexpected visual problems. In this chapter, you'll explore the code-rendering engines that power these mission-critical applications, the variations among browsers optimized for various platforms (such as the desktop and handheld market), and rules of thumb to become as bulletproof as you can.

Windows to the Web

One common feature that causes, and has always caused, designers a mixture of wonder and frustration in equal amounts is the browser. When considering how flexible or future-proofed your layout is, you'll need to consider the numerous browsers as a top priority. We are required to not only test our sites upon the legacy products, which have long since been retired (to ensure compatibility), but to ensure that our work doesn't break in the latest and greatest iterations of these powerful tools (which may require adjusting your code to cope).

Within each browser, you'll find a rendering engine, which acts like the motor in a car that drives the browser to take all of the code within a site and make something useful out of it (based on the instructions set by the markup and scripts). Every designer must be aware of the individual rendering engines, because as surprising as it may be, the browser's own software isn't the only factor that affects how your sites render. It's the engines themselves that present what you've designed (and determines code compatibility). So, this variable is doubly critical.

Note
Browsers often come with tools like stylesheet overrides, zooming, text resizing, and the capability to alter a site's encoding. These pieces of functionality are independent on the rendering engine, but they can affect how a site is viewed (so consider trying them on your site to see how your work may be affected if such a feature were used).

When websites first came on the scene, browsers could only render HTML. Subsequent advances in CSS have enabled vendors to be increasingly competitive in their support for the latest standards; even to this day, the competition among the big brands is still as intense as before. However, these days, many producers of browsers recognize the importance of standards and have high regard for using correct code for their renderers, as empowering designers into using what they support encourages browser users get a good experience.

Many browsers share a rendering engine (or a variation of one engine, known as a fork) and, in some cases, a few can actually use more than one of them, which makes testing in certain browsers rather pointless, as a shared rendering engine means the same output will result. Though while some browsers may share a rendering engine, they could use their own JavaScript interpreter or an older version of an engine, so it's worth ensuring that no differences in the output will exist before excluding them from your site testing workflow.

When dealing with browsers, consider their age; what engine (and version) they use; how the interface or tools built into the browser may affect content visibility; whether it's a text, graphical, or unique environment; and whether it's oriented toward handheld devices. These types of consideration demand a lot of testing (and emulation) to ensure that both your site and the entire family tree of browser genealogy work in the latest and greatest ways. Compatibility with standards will determine the code you can use in such browsers.

Designing for old and new browsers

Examples of how a web browser may affect your site are very easy to come by. For example, consider a user who browses to your site using a browser that causes designers around the world to suffer nightmares: Internet Explorer 6. Perhaps you have a lovely and well-crafted site that uses the latest web standards, has some interesting, innovative features, and is built to a really high standard. Too bad, because as you're probably aware, Internet Explorer 6 has been lingering around like a zombie for far too many years, and its capabilities are quite limited.

In another browsing session, one of your loyal visitors upgrades his browser to the latest version of Mozilla Firefox. With the latest build he is able to take advantage of standards that previously had little to no support within the browser and in this case, as you utilized that code with the necessary fallback for users on products like IE 6, the Firefox user finds that his experience is improved as a result of his browser gaining support for the technology you've had in place. Perhaps it's only a minor improvement, but it's one that this user may notice.

In an ideal world you would be rid of an old renderer like IE 6 and provide every user with an equal aesthetic. However, the IE 6 user is trapped into using the product by the organization he or she works for. With no upgrade policy in sight and a need for IE 6 for an intranet, your user is probably going to be stuck with it for a while. When using new technologies, ensure a fallback for old browsers exists (alongside using the lovely new code for where it's supported). Make sure it works with rigorous testing, and use tools like conditional comments if necessary.

Trident

When it comes to browser compatibility, Trident is the most notorious of them all. If you weren't aware or hadn't guessed its origin already, it's the rendering engine behind the troublesome product, Microsoft Internet Explorer (known as *IE,* see Figure 12-1). Though this notorious browser has improved in recent years and supports a range of standards, it's integration into Windows OS and upgrade policies have resulted in increased legacy needs, proprietary code, and unwelcome, well-publicized surprise defects in its rendering engine.

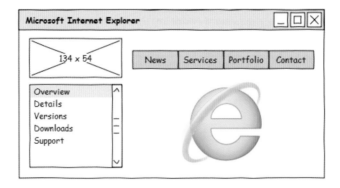

FIGURE 12-1: Internet Explorer is recognizable for its blue "E" icon, and being the default Windows browser.

The following lists show members of this software's family tree and some issues they can encounter.

Relatives:

> Internet Explorer

> Avant Browser

> MSN Explorer

> Maxthon

> Sleipnir

Considerations:

> Upgrade policy and cycles

> Inconsistent standards

> Proprietary innovations

Practical solutions

Trident's first issue regarding rendering inconsistencies relates to how Microsoft handles upgrades. In addition to upgrades being voluntary (which is troublesome for a product bundled or embedded within Windows by default), individual versions have sustained a staying power unlike any browser in history. IE 6, for example, is still in use and is 10 years old! This situation is made worse as users of older versions of Windows may not even be able to install new versions of IE because of Microsoft's lifecycle support policies.

To combat the issues of older versions of Windows being forced into old versions of Internet Explorer, you're going to need to maintain support for older versions of this product unlike you would for something like Chrome, Opera, and Firefox that actively encourage upgrades. Check your analytics package or some independently verified and reliable global statistics for usage details and try to maintain support for versions of the browser that continue to have more than 1 percent of the combined usage total of your site.

Unfortunately, individual versions of Trident are so different in standards support that you might think each one is an entirely different browser. Although most other vendors give regular intermediary updates that fix bugs and offer new standards support over the apps lifecycle, Internet Explorer just offers "major-version-releases" (beyond betas and RCs). Additionally, older versions of Internet Explorer (6 and 7) are notorious for not supporting standards and being exceptionally buggy; even their compatibility modes differ slightly!

Reference

Conditional code is useful for offering future-proofed support for degrading IE versions. Although targeting browsers is generally frowned upon, this solution is generally deemed to be the exception to the rule (because of the issues surrounding old versions of the product), as described on Wikipedia: http://en.wikipedia.org/wiki/Conditional_comment.

Working around the issues that occur in old versions of IE may require unhealthy hacks or some conditional comments. Out of the two, the latter is better, though Internet Explorer 10 will not continue the tradition of offering them. You also will come to dislike Internet Explorer 6's "hasLayout" and *quirks mode* glitches if you choose to support it. To combat the real inconsistencies in this browser, test your site against each version independently and apply fixes (hacks and filters), fallbacks, or script and CSS replacements as necessary.

Nevertheless, Internet Explorer was responsible for introducing several useful features that are now standards in browsers and W3C specifications alike. Although these innovations don't let Microsoft off the hook regarding its lackluster attitude toward the standards that did (and still do) exist, they have made compatibility for future standards less problematic in situations like CSS3-embedded fonts, the overflow (x/y) property, AJAX, and opacity (via proprietary code), which means that some current coding techniques can be used now.

It makes sense to take advantage of any innovations made by Internet Explorer during the early years of the Web, but you need to be careful if you take advantage of proprietary code that is required to achieve the effect within the browser. Examples that spring to mind include VML (which would need an SVG alternative for non-Internet Explorer browsers), ActiveX, VBScript, and other proprietary code including CSS expressions (which are now deprecated). If you can follow the standard, do to avoid such features.

Best practices

> Users may be trapped into old versions of IE; avoid ignoring them entirely.

> Set a threshold for continued browser support for older versions still in use.

> Use conditional comments and code compilation rather than outright hacks.

> Test each IE version independently and degrade the interface as necessary.

> Avoid proprietary code unless alternative solutions cannot be implemented.

Gecko

When Internet Explorer defeated Netscape during the browser wars, no one would have imagined that the offspring of Internet Explorer's nemesis would be the one to press it into a corner. Gecko, the descendant of Netscape, is among the most popular renderers to date and is found in Mozilla Firefox (Figure 12-2) and a range of other similar clients. Highly extendible and open source, Gecko has become a cross-compatible giant with support in most OSs. It boasts good standards support and is prominent on many mobile devices.

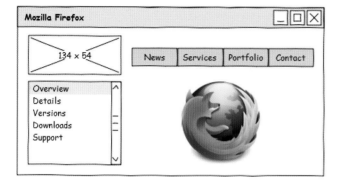

FIGURE 12-2: Firefox is one of the most customizable products because of the thousands of add-ins that exist.

The following lists show members of this software's family tree and some issues they can encounter.

Relatives:

> Mozilla Firefox

> SeaMonkey

> Netscape 6+

> Camino\

> Epiphany

Considerations:

> Debugging environment

> Plug-and-play capabilities

> Descendant family tree

Practical solutions

Unlike Internet Explorer, Gecko, which is the basis of Firefox, is very good in adhering to the latest, greatest web standards. Although it's perhaps not as frequent with its updates as Google Chrome (which feels like it gains major version upgrades every month or two), Firefox does offer one of the greatest compatibility-testing features that a designer can hope for: its extensibility for add-ins. To showcase the benefits it has, download extensions like Firebug or the Accessibility toolbar. They can help you identify issues in your code.

One rule that many designers follow to this day: If a site looks and works well in Firefox, it shouldn't visibly break under the same conditions in any of the other browsers (except Internet Explorer), as they all tend to render pretty equally in general. Firefox's debugging environment gives it a real advantage in identifying and resolving behavior or functionality quirks in a site, and the scale of other browsers using the same renderer places it in a good position to kill two (or more) birds with one stone. As a test-bed, Gecko is a great choice.

One of the key features of a future-proof site is that it can handle any sudden changes in the environment based on the unique choices made by users and the devices they use to browse. Gecko is deeply extensible, with each add-in able to "plug and play" into your sites and read, manipulate, and affect your code. It gives you a good point of reference to build a site and ensures a compatible layout that can utilize add-ins. Whether a user wants a screen reader, style reformatter, microformat extractor, or something else, Firefox has a tool for it.

Note   If visitors have extensions installed, they may not have the latest version of either the add-in or the browser. Luckily, browsers like Firefox automatically disable extensions, which are known to be incompatible in a product version before the user completes a product upgrade. This will reduce the impact of outdated, broken extensions on sites.

This chapter doesn't examine the extent to which each of these tools can affect a site's code, but it's imperative that you test sites in environments where extensions are both enabled and disabled. You may find that something functions differently on your version of Firefox than on someone else's because of a particular add-in running behind the scenes or working itself into the interface. This isn't to say that a test-bed (workflow for testing) should always have an "out of the box" install, but it shouldn't be out of the question.

The Gecko rendering engine isn't entirely free from version-based complications. Because a number of developers have created their own browsers based on the Firefox rendering engine, people using tools that haven't had frequent updates will have an older version of Gecko installed (or Mozilla, the old Netscape renderer), which could subsequently affect the compatibility of sites. There is also the possibility that a user may avoid recommended updates and put his compatibility with your site into question (as updates may fix issues).

Problems with "dead" projects in the Gecko family tree aren't as troublesome as they are with Internet Explorer, simply because there are fewer users of these forked projects. Try to support at least one prior version of Firefox just for safety's sake; also, you may want to test against each of Firefox's major milestone builds. Standards support within Gecko is pretty high, so you'll probably encounter only a few minor quirks. Be sure to test the use of mobile Firefox, Fennec, and Minimo to be sure your site can support handheld devices.

Best practices

> Download extensions like Firebug to help you identify glitches in your code.

> Test using browsers with extensions enabled, and then all of them disabled.

> Have freshly installed browsers to avoid extension-based tampering.

> Stick to testing the current version (desktop and mobile) for compliance.

> More hardcore designers should test back in each major milestone version.

WebKit

Just as Firefox and its renderer Gecko showed that it's possible to build standards-savvy layouts without being trapped into version numbers, the true rockstar of the rendering age has to be WebKit. Not only has it made its mark in the industry by being included within two of the top five browsers in use today (Figure 12-3), its rapid development cycles and speedy rendering makes it a solid environment to browse the Web. With the highest level of handheld device support it's a real workhorse and a critical renderer to support.

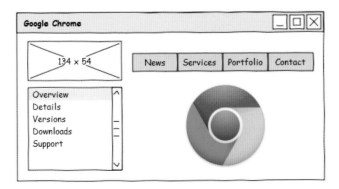

FIGURE 12-3: Google Chrome (whose icon is pictured) and Apple Safari share this popular WebKit renderer.

The following lists show members of this software's family tree and some issues they can encounter.

Relatives:	Considerations:
> Google Chrome	> Flash compatibility
> Apple Safari	> Porting and updating
> iCab	> Defaulted ubiquity
> OmniWeb	
> Chromium	

Practical solutions

One of the biggest clashes of compatibility (and one of the most debated design subjects to date) is Apple's refusal to support Flash in iOS. Ironically, while Safari for iOS doesn't allow Flash to be embedded, another popular browser, Google Chrome, actually embeds Flash within its browser, keeping it up-to-date without any user actions required. That makes it both the most- and least-supportive Flash browser online!

We already know that despite Flash being a non-ubiquitous proprietary technology, it has its uses, especially when displaying rich multimedia. However, it's worth taking the time to consider whether Flash could be used to enhance sites over an already-constructed base formed of HTML, CSS, and JavaScript (in preference to depending upon it). That is, if you feel the technology could bring something useful to a site that can't otherwise be achieved by using more open standards. If you do decide to use Flash, *always* have an equal fallback.

Finally, you should pay some attention to the ubiquity that WebKit seems to have sustained among a wide range of devices. Although Trident is stuck inside Microsoft's own desktop and mobile platforms, and Gecko is still trying to find its footing in the handheld sphere, the WebKit rendering engine has ended up getting fired onto a whole range of platforms, including iOS, Android, Nokia, Palm, Symbian, and even the Amazon Kindle, making it a dominant, successful force that you should cater to if you want to keep your users happy.

Reference Although WebKit has the highest market penetration levels (cross-platform), unlike other rendering engines, a range of differences that could affect a site's visuals exist (so beware that WebKit isn't always WebKit): `www.quirksmode.org/webkit.html`.

Ensuring compatibility with browsers isn't the easiest job, because unlike desktop versions of the product, device manufacturers tend to customize their copy of the rendering engine to give their users some suitable tweaks for the environment. While this is fine in theory, it can mean that you may see code breaking in a user's handheld environment. The only way to test and ensure cross-compatibility is to get your hands on as many handheld browsers (and devices) as possible, checking that your handheld visuals do in fact work correctly.

One of the most notable things about WebKit is how amazingly rapid the release cycle has been. If you consider that Google Chrome recently reached version 14 but is only 3 years old; whereas Internet Explorer, which has been around for decades, is only reaching version 10. The pace at which WebKit has pushed into the latest, greatest standards is staggering. Also, WebKit was forked from a renderer called KTHML that powers the browser Konqueror, and this factor could have implications.

Although rapid releases seem like an issue waiting to happen, Chrome silently installs fresh versions as they become stable, reducing the impact on users. In the vast majority of cases, users will have the most recent version. Regarding other WebKit browsers, such as Safari, it isn't upgraded as regularly, and the Windows installer is often bundled with other products. So dialup users may find the update process time-consuming. But, this savvy renderer is pretty forgiving and also standards compliant, so don't be afraid to experiment.

Best practices

> Use Flash, but be sure it has a viable fallback for iOS-like situations.

> Check your site on Konqueror (Linux) because it uses a forked renderer.

> WebKit renders for numerous handheld browsers; test on a range of them.

> Chrome and Safari both have minor differences, so test with them equally.

> Some renderers aren't as fortunate as WebKit; do take pity on them!

Presto

Though not as well known as the engines discussed previously, the renderer Presto powers one of the longest-running browser applications and has managed to cling onto its spot as one of the five "most-used" browsers on the Web. Just like Internet Explorer, it makes use of a proprietary rendering engine. In its early days, Presto was a "shareware" browser, which ultimately cost it in terms of popularity. Now a freeware product, it contains a vast array of features and good standards support; nevertheless, Presto remains eclipsed by its kinsmen.

The following lists show members of this software's family tree and some issues they can encounter.

Relatives:

> Opera Browser

> Nintendo Browser

Considerations:

> Browser connectivity

> Markets-share potential

> Proprietary problems

Practical solutions

The first issue you need to account for with the Presto renderer is its unique approach to connectivity and integration. Not only does it support plug-ins within the Opera browser (see Figure 12-4), it also supports extensions, widgets, and panels (for its speed dial tool), all from within the same interface. This variety of different modes of integration makes the browser easily one of the most durable in terms of features, and unlike other browsers, it comes prepackaged with a wide range of tools, to the extent that you may not need to install anything else.

With Opera, compatibility is a lesser problem than it is even with tools like Chrome and Firefox; the browser takes a Swiss army knife approach (by providing multiple functions built into the interface). Support for torrent downloads, RSS feeds, e-mail, newsgroups, IRC, and more come right out of the box; with its extensibility, you can really have some fun pushing the boundaries and integrating code with the browser. If you do choose to use any features that can be unlocked, just be sure to check that they work for users.

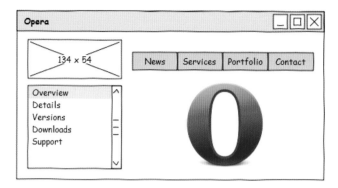

FIGURE 12-4: Opera is a small, all-inclusive, feature-rich browser that deserves more credit than it gets.

As a relatively unknown desktop browser, Opera doesn't have the numbers in its favor, though as a designer, this means that in stark contrast to Internet Explorer, Opera gives you a pretty easy time in testing. It's one browser that has kept on top of the latest standards, with a fast rendering engine and good, all-around features, and users are readily willing to upgrade versions. Like any rendering engine, it does have issues and things may render incorrectly, but if you debug the code, determine the issue, and resolve it, you'll be fine.

Note   Presto comes with a range of alternative Opera implementations for various platforms, including cellphones, game consoles, tablets, and more. Interestingly, it's the second most-popular handheld browser going (beaten only by the reigning kingpin, WebKit).

To maximize the Presto experience, make sure your Web site is as usable and accessible as possible because unlike other browsers, the range of tools included in this application suite for accessibility-dependent users is pretty extensive. It has predefined templates for high-contrast styles (overriding your CSS), a very accurate voice controller (and built-in screen reader), and it even comes with a built-in proxy browsing mode that speeds up sites for the bandwidth-impaired. If users want to take advantage of these tools they should be able to.

One advantage that proprietary solutions such as Presto and Trident have over their open-source competitors is that they're less likely to be forked into many different browsers, each with their own compatibility quirks and defects that are not as quickly resolved if manufacturers neglect their users. Because everything is closed from public contribution, only Opera gets the say in what the Presto browser supports; though compared to

Internet Explorer, it's been supporting standards and speed, not proprietary tools and unfixed bugs!

When considering compatibility, some argue that keeping a browser proprietary reduces the potential for hackers to find exploits to target, but that it also puts the responsibility of fixing dangerous bugs firmly in the hands of vendors. With Opera, the lower desktop-user ratio means your users should be safer from Opera exploits, but as Internet Explorer shows us, a few lines of code can cause a crash (on purpose or by accident), which isn't at all considered a good sign of stability, and needs to be dealt with by designers directly.

Best practices

> Test in Opera's out-of-the-box experience because it's quite extensive.

> Ensure reduced feature browsers aren't left with broken functionality.

> Bugs and security exploits may take a while to fix; check for known issues.

> If your site crashes or lags a browser, find and resolve the offending code.

> Try your site with Opera's various accessibility aids to see if they work.

Mobile

Even though the big four rendering engines account for 99 percent of all desktop traffic, there are (of course) a range of dedicated renderers that have been produced solely to give handheld users a basic level of standards support. See Figure 12-5. Many smartphones stick with a mobile-oriented variation of an existing desktop renderer, and a number of these devices have dropped their proprietary rendering solutions in favor of more established browser engines, but as legacy support is integral to ensuring compatibility, you cannot overlook such tools.

The following lists show members of this software's family tree and some issues they can encounter.

Relatives: **Considerations:**

> Blazer   > Deprecated renderers

> NetFront   > Reductionist aesthetics

> OpenWave   > Stealthy user agents

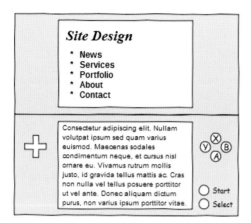

FIGURE 12-5: Handheld browsers allow gadgets like the Nintendo DS to access your sites and services.

Practical solutions

Many rendering engines have already come and gone in the mobile arena, being replaced with ported desktop solutions, which is great for compatibility fans. Yet, the need to ensure that your sites work on the widest range of devices forces you to still consider testing on those rendering engines that have been largely deprecated but could be in use by thousands or millions of featurephone users. Three examples of renderers that fall into the category of lost but not forgotten include Lumi, Mango, and Fugu, and, no, they're not mushrooms.

Dealing with dropped rendering engines forces you to confront the fact that flaws and bugs in the products aren't going to be fixed. Standards support among these three in particular offer fairly good support for HTML (version 4 and mobile editions, not the newest version 5), patchy support for CSS (it's a game of trial and error), and mixed support for scripting. Your best bet is to ensure your CSS degrades to what you'd expect in Internet Explorer 5 (yes, I said IE 5!), avoid scripting, and try to keep each of your pages under 100K in size.

An interesting thing about less-capable browsers, such as those you'd find in less-capable devices like featurephones, is that they tend to break down a layout to avoid more common rendering defects such as the demand for multiple columns on a screen that's only capable of viewing one (and can only scroll in one direction). Although some handheld renderers like NetFront are slightly more of a bridge between the likes of WebKit and more limited tools like OpenWave, they all try to focus on a reduced aesthetic to maximize the usability.

Reference

The PSP uses the NetFront rendering engine, and there's an old but still very useful tutorial to designing around this hardware. To see how this device can be made compatible, read this guide: `www.brothercake.com/site/resources/reference/psp/`.

When dealing with featurephone browsers, NetFront really is the king of the jungle (in terms of standards support). Although the newest version of the browser/renderer combo uses WebKit, the classic NetFront renderer still exists, is supported, and offers most modern web standards to users who haven't got a smartphone device. If you are unlucky enough to be stuck with something else, be prepared for little to no CSS support, plain ole HTML, and little to no JavaScript. In such cases, test your site with scripts crippled and CSS off!

The final thing you need to consider regarding compatibility (and this applies to every one of the rendering engines, desktop and handheld alike) is the issue of fake HTTP user agent headers. If you've ever tried targeting a browser for style or behavior, you've probably encountered detection scripts or sniffers that try to figure out what users are browsing with and then attempt to serve them a tailor-made layout. Because of abusive practices of this in the past, browsers have tweaked their agents to make detection results highly inaccurate.

To avoid "designed for X browser" messages, which would refuse entry to a site if a user didn't have the right browser installed (which were popular during the browser wars), many clients like Opera allowed users to falsely identify themselves as another browser. This spoofing technique rendered identification attempts useless, and as many desktop and handheld browsers can still do this today, it's important to avoid using such techniques. Feature detection that examines what browsers can actually do is better than guessing.

Best practices

> Deprecated renderers are still common in featurephones; don't avoid them.

> Mobile browsers can't handle too much, so keep pages as light as possible.

> NetFront is standards savvy, but avoid burdening it with laggy effects.

> As a matter of principle, ensure the site works with CSS and JS turned off.

> Avoid using browser-detection scripts as many of these browsers fail them.

Proxy

As you analyze the effects of rendering engines on your interfaces, pay some attention to the tools often referred to as proxy browsers. Traditional rendering engines take the code that has been downloaded from a server and process it at the client side (thereby making all your wonderful pages look and feel the way they do). Proxy browsers, alternatively, in an attempt to save bandwidth for handheld users, process code at the server side and then serve users with a more optimized, compressed layout, which they proceed to download. See Figure 12-6.

FIGURE 12-6: Proxy browsers help cellphones access sites quickly, reducing bandwidth consumption.

The following lists show members of this software's family tree and some issues they can encounter.

Relatives:	Considerations:
> Opera Mini	> Small screen rendering
> UC Browser	> Event process delays
> Bolt Browser	> Compression artifacts
> Thunderhawk	
> SkyFire	

Practical solutions

Dealing with mobile browsers can become troublesome, but if you want a true guide to the extent of handheld compatibility (and the range of renderers that exists), you need to come to grips with proxy browsers and the manner in which they reduce bandwidth consumption for users with data caps. Proxy browsers can be used on featurephones, smartphones, and desktops alike, so they're pretty ubiquitous as a platform browser. However, you'll need to make a few compromises, and real differences in how these products handle code exist.

For example, if you use Opera Mini for compatibility, note that, unlike a more traditional browser, it deliberately tries to push everything into a single-column layout (if a handheld stylesheet isn't provided). By using this technique, the application helps avoid bidirectional scrolling and allows the user to make better use of the available viewport space. Other common features within proxy browsers include long lists being collapsed like content lists in Wikipedia, reducing the need for extra scrolling (but they'll expand upon clicking).

Many sites, even mobile ones, take advantage of scripting whenever possible, as there is no realistic replacement for its capabilities. Although proxy browsers may be fairly limited because everything has to go through a server, your client-side scripting is treated like a server-side script. Because the proxy browser renders code before performing the size-reducing compression, scripts run on the server end, and the results of that action are rendered on your device. As you can imagine, this process can complicate interactions.

Tip   Because of the need to break highly complex sites into easy-to-view components, more in-page objects like frames may be affected in dramatic ways in browsers. Test your work using a selection of proxy-browsing services to see how things will finally appear.

When utilizing scripts in your site, remember that "onclick" and other DOM events are performed at the server, and once each action is undertaken, it's sent back to the server for processing (similar to submitting forms via PHP), and any future clicks or responses will have to be dealt with separately. These events work on a "send and fetch" methodology, so avoid animation, timed events, or AJAX, because the stuff sent to a browser will be limited in seeing the results, not the interactive process. Scripted reactions should be instantaneous.

Media and images suffer the most compatibility issues in a proxy-browsing experience, mainly because of the amount of data the files consume and the techniques browsers use to resolve the situation. Proxy browsers won't support animation, sound, or video (even the blink tag and animated GIFs), limiting such features to avoid draining precious system resources. In any event, supported images will be heavily compressed, quality lowered, and the file downsized, which could make some images illegible as a result of the distortion.

I'm certainly not saying that you need to eliminate all images from your documents, but it's important to avoid using images purely to showcase text. CSS3 fonts have evolved enough to replace this method, and because proxy browsers can be affected by using such images, it makes sense to avoid them, offering a proper text description instead. Because other browsers can turn them off, images aren't considered reliable enough to be 100% future-proof. Check any image use in proxy browsers to determine readability.

Best practices

> Allow your content to responsively collapse into a simple linear list.

> Offer a handheld CSS media rule; some devices will still support them.

> Treat your JavaScript as a server-side script, as events aren't run locally.

> Stay as uncomplicated as possible; beyond scrolling, interaction is limited.

> Images will be heavily compressed; test their readability with pixilation.

Alternates

Traditional rendering engines have a huge effect on how accurate your layouts appear to individual users. However, just because things can be shown in a traditional way doesn't mean that unconventional alternatives can't be used or don't exist. Sporting a range of unique features like text-only browsing, 3D rendering of entire pages, or highly refined rendering capabilities, you need to consider that your users may see your sites through unfamiliar eyes in these unusual, but equally experience-immersive, Web browsers. See Figure 12-7.

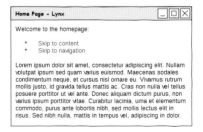

FIGURE 12-7: Lynx is the most popular alternative browser, and it only supports textual content!

The following lists show members of this software's family tree and some issues they can encounter.

Relatives:	**Considerations:**
> 3B	> Independent functionality
> Browse3D	> Barebones readability
> KidZui	> Means testing protocol
> Dillo	
> Lynx	

Practical solutions

You need to be aware that alternative browsers tend to go in an entirely different direction than many traditional browsers do. Consider something like a 3D web browser, which is a bit of a novelty but actually exists. It takes advantage of the more unusual virtual reality languages like VRML, X3D, and their kin to render sites similarly to a virtual world. This independent functionality is tricky in terms of compatibility because, until the industry decides to make the jump into that niche, browsers are unlikely to offer you much help.

The choice of alternative browsers is mostly about being compatible for users in unusual circumstances. It's not something that every single site will have to deal with, and it's not something worth testing for (or supporting) right out of the gate; that is, unless your own site's offerings match something related to that niche's capability. If, for example, you've built a site for young kids, then testing the site in KidZui and other child-friendly browsers should immediately be on your to-do list. Understanding your users' needs really matters.

Although many browsers have numerous options and features, some go to extraordinary lengths to keep things simple and clean and they subsequently lose sight of your interface. Although they aren't exceptionally popular outside cult niche circles and the web design community, text browsers like Lynx have been showing you how simple sites can be if you just remove the redundancy or anything unrelated to content. It's certainly an extreme style of browsing, but Lynx is worth investigating for its accessibility factor properties.

Reference

If you search Google, you'll be able to locate some previously compiled versions of Lynx for a number of different platforms. For you Windows users, I've done the hard work and located a stable, good quality build with an installer: http://csant.info/lynx.htm.

Lynx doesn't support images, CSS, scripts or anything apart from HTML and content. If you need to test your site's support and readability for older browsers that existed before and midway through the first browser war, Lynx is an essential application to have. The app runs with little overhead and can be very useful in severe bandwidth limitation cases (but no handheld version exists yet). Test your site with Lynx if you want to test keyboard-only browsing, the hierarchy of content, and to really push your site's compatibility to its limits.

Finally, with regard to alternative browsers, we must mention means testing. As designers, we tend to get so caught up in the ever-growing list of what we need to take care of that we rarely find the time to actually focus on what's really important for users, which is what matters the most as they are the critics who will deem our sites useful or useless. When you're getting ready to build a site, knowing what browsers to test against is critical to your workflow, so you need to do your research and find the top priorities before continuing.

When means testing browsers, the rule is to select a list of the ten highest-rated browsers that visitors use. You should pick specific rendering engines or specific rendering versions (just remember to focus on the rendering engine because you don't want to end up testing on the same thing 100 times over). The only exception is Internet Explorer because it hides a multitude of sins beneath its shiny wrapper (as we all know). Once you've written and prioritized the list, stick to it and support other browsers if and when you have the time.

Best practices

> Look for unusual browsing trends and support them if they gain momentum.

> Consider specialist browsers like child-friendly products if the site is for kids.

> Test sites in Lynx; it really helps to see the layout stripped to its minimum.

> Get an analytics app if you haven't already done so to track visitor trends.

> Prioritize your support; more users will utilize Internet Explorer than Lynx.

Providing Powerful Plug-Ins

Working with enhancements, extensions, and multimedia

PLUG-INS LIKE SILVERLIGHT, Java, and Flash continue to play an active role in the usefulness of many sites, and while it's true that HTML5 is replacing the need for many of these proprietary components, the Web wouldn't be the same without them. This chapter examines how browser plug-ins, extensions, and embeddable media players affect your compatibility chances; the issues surrounding being dependent upon third-party components; and the benefits and pitfalls such tools can provide an experience.

Plug-and-Play Interactivity

When aiming for compatibility, it's important to examine the wonderful but sometimes annoying plug-ins and extensions that add features and interactivity to your designs. You can use extensions to help alleviate and supplement the somewhat lackluster standards support that older browsers like Internet Explorer 6 offer, as well as provide useful functionality to users that may otherwise be impossible (such as video playback). Plug-ins are rather unique as they represent a variable that works between the browser, OS and user.

If you've been building sites for a while, I'm sure you're aware of the Web's most widely recognized, but lamented, proprietary plug-in technology: Adobe Flash. You're probably also aware of the incompatibilities between Apple's iOS platform and the Flash platform. Many plug-ins can suffer similar apathy levels regarding compatibility, so you'll need to deal with the fact that there's no guarantee users will have them installed or activated on their devices or systems, and that users will be required to keep such components up-to-date.

Note

Flash isn't the only plug-in having issues with vendor support. For example, you won't find support for Microsoft Silverlight on anything other than a cellphone powered by Microsoft's mobile platform; Shockwave is a general no-go area when it comes to levels of compatibility; and browser-based Java applet support is fragmented. In cases where a technology is used but isn't supported, offer a HTML or media download fallback.

You also need to be aware of the extensions (installable toolbars or components) that can be attached to user's browsers and affect your sites, as all the major browsers now support them. As with plug-ins, the impact of extensions depends greatly upon the level of ubiquity or popularity they've attained. As a variable that's become a central part of the browsing experience, extensions contain the capability to customize not only the browser, but affect (and in some cases override) how code and objects behave, interact, and appear on-screen too.

Because of the number of extensions that exist, you can't expect to be compatible with them all. It might be worth giving some of the more popular or influential extensions a test run before going public, but do so on a needs-only basis because the effect they have on your site can differ dramatically (some may just read page data, whereas others could write or override it). Among the extensibility that exists, Opera supports custom speed dials, IE 8x supports accelerators and hSlices, and all Web browsers support the OpenSearch protocol.

Another influential browser element to account for is the embedded media player. Back in the 1990s, you had to place video or audio players directly into pages using a plug-in such as QuickTime, Windows Media Player, or the RealOne Player. Because not everyone had the software installed, issues with compatibility and support for formats occurred on a very frequent basis. In due time, Flash came onto the scene bringing with it the ubiquity needed to stabilize and standardize media playback online. However, Flash's fall from grace has resulted in a push back to in-browser playback via HTML5, which could lead to trouble.

The issues of plug-ins

Imagine that a user is browsing to your site with Google Chrome. With this browser, she's particularly lucky because the Flash plug-in comes prepackaged, requiring no maintenance from the user. Her system is therefore ready to always play Flash-powered media. In addition, Chrome's interface is designed so that plug-ins will have a minimal impact on the browser's performance (meaning less lagging for you, as unresponsive plug-ins could be temporarily disabled). Unlike iOS users, she can happily utilize any Flash interactivity within your pages.

But with the sweet comes the sour, and with Chrome's scriptable extension capabilities comes the use of valuable real estate (to show their toolbars and sidebars). This may affect a site's rendering. Because many of Chrome's plug-ins will render within the browser's viewport, your user notices that styles have been overwritten by an extension (rather frustrating), and not only are your site's PDFs redirecting her to Google's Docs, but RSS feeds are redirecting her to Google Reader. Sites need to accommodate users like her who want to use such features.

Resolving extensions issues is complex, as we can neither rely upon them being available nor avoid the impact they can have upon our sites. While they often interact by taking control of your site and its code, the motives of users for using extensions are rarely bad. Users may be trying to make the content extra-readable, strip out some useful metadata, block adverts (a popular option with ads as intrusive as they are), or attempt to gain other meaningful ways to improve their experience. Essentially, all you can do is resolve quirks by trial and error.

Enhancements

Because they can be embedded within any page, plug-in components allow you to do more with the space you have available. A few of these tools are ubiquitous enough to be trusted in production sites, but the user must have the required plug-in installed and enabled (see Figure 13-1); their browser must support any proprietary file formats that the plug-in uses. Compatibility becomes an all-or-nothing affair as the embedded data will either work flawlessly or not at all, so using any plug-in (such as Microsoft Silverlight) is a risk.

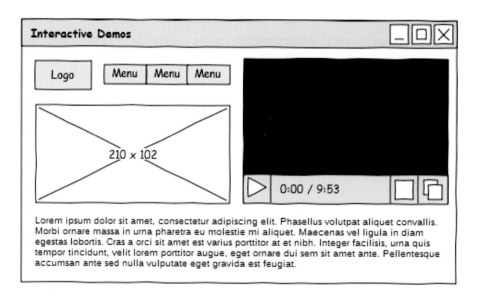

FIGURE 13-1: Embedding a Flash movie into a site is commonplace, but it requires users install the plug-in.

The following lists show members of this software's family tree and some issues they can encounter.

Relatives:

> Adobe Flash

> Microsoft Silverlight

> Oracle Java

> Microsoft ActiveX

> Adobe Shockwave

Considerations:

> Self-contained rendering

> Moving to open standards

> Unique interaction usability

Practical solutions

When it comes to compatibility, plug-ins such as Flash and Silverlight, if installed, tend to be extremely stable with regard to rendering. Because these potentially useful objects are embedded directly within the page, the browser has little control over what happens once the file is loaded. By embedding Flash into the page, the plug-in remains responsible for its own rendering, and no matter what platform you use, that content will display identically. While stable rendering is great for consistency, there are some finer points to consider.

One of the key points regarding these plug-ins' dedication to self-rendering is that support isn't exactly a given. Ensuring compatibility has to be done on a basis of usage statistics, platform support, and the general availability or usefulness of the tool itself. Apart from an iOS, Flash maintains fairly high levels of support, which makes it worthy of use when it's appropriate. As for its competitors, Silverlight has a lower adoption rate and is supported by fewer devices, and Java applets, although quite ubiquitous, have limited browser support.

Since the days of Flash and of Apple's lack of unconditional support for its iOS devices, the design community has pressed for more open and accessible standards. In recent years, we've seen a sharp rise in cross-browser support for HTML5 and CSS3 and an increased awareness about what can be achieved with JavaScript. This move toward adopting new, non-proprietary standards does have its benefits for the Web's future, but because these tools aren't self-contained, we return to the issues of compatibility within web browsers.

Note

Because Flash and other plug-in products aren't rendered by the browser (the browser handles the embedding process, but the rendering is done entirely by the plug-in), you have to consider that each instance of Flash uses more of a visitor's system resources. It might be better to try to keep the number of plug-in instances to a minimum.

When using Flash's more open replacements, you need to consider browser support, and you need to identify what can be used within each renderer. Then you are in a position to offer appropriate and equivalent functionality. With all of this in mind, note that you don't want to dump Flash entirely. When it comes to broadcasting and streaming media, Flash is, for now, the best solution going. However, if you're looking for some nifty effects to make content fly around the page, CSS3 animations and transitions are better solutions.

Technologies like Flash were originally invented to create experiences that, at the time, couldn't be built using technologies such as HTML, CSS, and JavaScript. Although users of plug-ins like Flash have the tendency to design feature-heavy layouts in order to get some really unique interactions going, I suggest using constraint with that kind of thing. Flash is capable of creating pretty much any type of design you might want to build, but going over the top with unconventional styling could reduce the usability of your website.

Avoid building unnecessarily complex Flash designs and ensure that all Flash usage has a suitable fallback. While Flash may seem like a harmless way of giving users something to talk about, visitors expect the Web to look and behave in a certain way, and as much as shock value or beautiful graphics may naturally want to deviate from this, browsing the site will become more difficult. Also, try to keep the size of Flash files low by reducing the amount of media or images you use; no one wants to wait ten minutes for a splash screen!

Best practices

> Don't worry about code support, as plug-ins render themselves.

> Avoid using plug-ins that currently have minimal adoption rates.

> Use Flash when open standards aren't supported.

> If stable alternatives do exist, use them for a more accessible site.

> Avoid unconventional navigation menus that degrade usability.

Extensions

Most desktop browsers offer some form of extensibility, and with this power comes the potential for your interfaces to be manipulated. Your sites rely upon rendering engines to ensure that everything loads in the correct position, but toolbars, sidebars (Figure 13-2), and other components can extend a site's functionality (beyond the browser's capabilities). Some of these extensions will influence a site's code or layout; others extract data for their own ends. However, these tools can also enhance the compatibility of certain functionality.

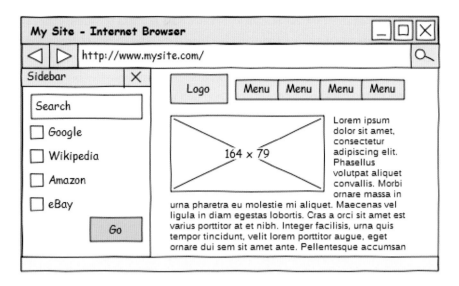

FIGURE 13-2: You can't just rely on screen resolutions; sidebars can absorb valuable real estate.

The following lists show members of this software's family tree and some issues they can encounter.

Relatives:

> Toolbars

> Sidebars

Considerations:

> Viewport reductionism

> Scope for interoperability

> JavaScript bookmarklets

Practical solutions

Extensions allow you to do a lot of cool things with a browser, but with the installation of these tools come the demands for their own little plot of screen real estate in order to help the user and continue to function. Because some extensions may require more space than others, and some can be much more invasive to the browsing experience than others, be considerate of users who've got these useful tools bolted into their browsers, whether by choice or as part of a package or preinstalled configuration. The point is to be flexible.

Sometimes, extensions like browser toolbars and sidebars will consume physical space on the screen, which reduces the available viewport space for users to consume your content within. Toolbars are usually more forgiving because they tend to be relatively thin and just increase the need for vertical scrolling. Sidebars, on the other hand, introduce horizontal scrolling and can break fixed-width layouts. To check how flexible your site is, enable a range of toolbars and sidebars and then determine whether your site responds appropriately.

Although many plug-in tools can be docile creatures that keep to themselves, a number of extensions can literally interact with a page. They can do useful things with the content of a site, or they could seek code conventions or underlying features of a page and act upon it, for example, by using microformats or increasing the page's inherent accessibility. Extensions can also change functionality on a page to suit themselves. Stylesheet swappers or extensions that make phone numbers into clickable links are classic examples of this.

Tip

Toolbars and sidebars can be stretched and skewed like a browser window. There are no guarantees, therefore, that extensions users have installed will match an easy-to-determine set of dimensions you can measure against. Never assume the size of any windows, and use a flexible layout to allow for temporary fluctuations in viewport size.

Because of the sheer number of extensions that are available for browsers, don't assume that you can make your site work and render flawlessly for every single product. Chrome's StumbleUpon extension, for example, has given me trouble in the past because of the way in which it interacts with CSS. You should find out which extensions visitors regularly use or request, and try your work out within them. Who knows, if you find a particular extension that could bring added usefulness to your visitors, you could promote it on your website!

Also, you may want to check out bookmarklets. Bookmarklets are clickable and actionable pieces of JavaScript that are built to perform a particular function. They are formed of a URL that is comprised entirely of JavaScript (using the `javascript:` pseudo-protocol). For handheld devices that don't support browser extensions, these tools can prove quite useful. If the browser supports JavaScript, this functionality can be saved within the comfort of a user's bookmarks menu, and it also carries the inherent benefit of not stealing screen space!

Code can be inserted directly into your pages by extensions and users can then take advantage of these tools more easily, or it could simply be used to offer an easier way to view a page (via CSS or JavaScript). The only time you should use JavaScript in a URL is when you want to provide a bookmarklet for your site. Links should perform a clear action, so if scripting is turned off, all attempts to use script-powered links would fail.

Best practices

> Ensure that your site works in a cramped, extension-rich environment.

> Design around the available viewport space, not around screen resolutions.

> Test popular add-ins and those associated with services your visitors use.

> Browsers handle extensions differently; test them on a case-by-case basis.

> Treat bookmarklets as extensions for less-capable browsers or devices.

Multimedia

The embedding of video and audio in sites has increased over recent years. In the past, you could get away with using a built-in media player provided either by the operating system, users (by choice), or the devices they used; times have changed. With a wide range of formats to cater to, it's no longer acceptable to rely on ActiveX components that place high demands upon users. With plug-ins like Flash, compatibility issues have forced designers to seek alternatives, looking to HTML5 and feature-rich, third-party services (Figure 13-3).

The following lists show members of this software's family tree and some issues they can encounter.

Relatives:

> Apple QuickTime

> HTML5 Elements

> Real Player

> Windows Media Player

Considerations:

> Prepackaged players

> Embedding support

> Buffering and formats

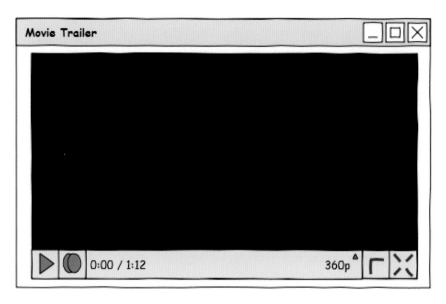

FIGURE 13-3: Compatibility issues have forced designers to seek third-party alternatives to Flash.

Practical solutions

Multimedia remains one of the most popular types of embedded content, so it's important to understand how certain devices handle your media. At times, you may find that using HTML5 video or audio will launch the default prepackaged player; other times, multimedia plays inside a Flash browser object. Understanding how browsers treat media is important because there's no point in offering multimedia that won't be visible on a specific user's platform because of how it's being served.

When preparing media for the Web, it's worth having a mixture of output sources, from Flash (for older browsers) to HTML5 (for newer browsers). It may also be worth offering download links in a range of formats (for everyone else). Some devices may come with a built-in media player that'll take over the media-streaming responsibilities from browsers and play the file in a lovely, full-screen environment. While full-screen playback is useful on handheld devices, devices with larger screens can afford not to achieve this by default.

Before Flash was available, a great deal of disparity existed among multimedia formats on the Web. Because a video playback standard wasn't in place, and Flash lacked the support it has now, people used ActiveX objects (and alternatives provided for the other browsers, such as Netscape) to embed the media players users had installed on their devices inside the browser. This approach caused a great deal of confusion because there was no way to know which player users were likely to have installed and if it could handle the media.

Note

There are far too many formats to list in this book. Some are better at compression than others, some have more or less widespread recognition, and some allow raw output at the highest quality. As a general best practice though, you should look to sites that deal in multimedia regularly (like news sites or podcasters) to find common practices.

Today, it's much harder to find such embedding practices online, but they unfortunately still occur. Some sites require users to have Windows Media Player, some demand Apple's QuickTime, some demand Real Player, and a few demand rarer formats such as DivX and XViD. Because all of these applications and their plug-ins can be uninstalled or disabled, you should never resort to using these products over browser-native players (if possible). Users can remove file associations, the plug-ins, or apps, resulting in an unplayable video.

Finally, you need to know what happens after you have that multimedia embedded and listed on the page, as well as the importance of format diversity. We already know that media can cause accessibility hurdles, like the interruption of screen readers (the voice is drowned out by the content). However, media that automatically downloads or buffers without the user clicking Play isn't good either. If a user has no intention of watching the video, you've just wasted loads of his bandwidth and slowed his browsing experience.

To overcome issues of bandwidth waste and reduced speed, avoid triggering the download or buffering of videos when a page is being rendered. If users only want to read the text that appears on-screen, you're draining bandwidth that could cost them a fortune if they're on a restrictive data plan. Also, offer a range of popular media formats for downloading or streaming at various quality levels. Offer MP3 for audio (varying compression) and MOV, MPEG (H.264), WMV, and WebM (VP8) for video in HD, SD, and various display sizes.

Best practices

> If a device launches videos in a separate app, don't try to block the action.

> Some devices cannot stream media, so downloads are a helpful alternative.

> Always use Flash or HTML5, in preference to media player embedding.

> Make sure that your media buffers and downloads only if users click Play.

> Offer a variety of formats and sizes so users can pick what works for them.

Alternative Content Applications

Designing for reformatters, apps, accessibility tools, and more

SOFTWARE AFFECTS SITES in ways that can go beyond even the browser. Tools like RSS readers and accessibility aids are classic examples. Users consume your content in ever-more unique and interesting ways, such as reading it within purpose-built offline clients and with browsers embedded in apps, so if you maintain a level of support for such useful implementations, you'll increase your content's exposure (potentially increasing your audience, too). This chapter examines these influential applications.

Browsing Without a Browser

A web designer's biggest consideration when dealing with users' non-browser software is compatibility. Users install, remove, disable, and configure software, and they can select the product of their choice to undertake the task. What's more, users rarely upgrade their software on a consistent basis. The power of the OS, browser, apps, and plug-ins may help your work really stand out, but they ultimately affect how your work is utilized and have the potential to affect the total readership of your site.

Because they can read content when, how, and wherever they want, users are more frequently turning to products like reformatters to access content. These products can reformat and standardize entire articles by removing objects that aren't critical. For example, Instapaper is a popular reformatter that strips extra formatting from a page but saves content deemed important. When a user bookmarks a e-zine article to Instapaper, the banner graphic might be eliminated from the article, but the text of the article will still appear. At first, you may be concerned that users aren't clicking your site frequently as a result (opting for a selective viewing experience), but in this age of flexible design, you want to do your best to support the products that users prefer.

Note   Some users may use your site through a web-enabled third-party application rather than through a common browser within an OS. These third-party applications can load sites without opening the browser. In these cases, your users' ability to interact with your site may be restricted because bookmarks or features such as zooming may not be available in the app's built-in menus.

Syndication clients (such as RSS and Atom readers) and reformatters (such as Safari's Reading List feature) will turn a site's content into a tangible, browsable offline piece of writing that refreshes when new content appears. Apps can "mine" a site's code for useful data, or utilize APIs; widgets can be embedded within pages to syndicate useful content such as Facebook comments; and accessibility tools (such as screen readers) and augmented reality tools can extend a site's functionality and its value to users of such software.

Because of the availability and number of tools that can connect to your sites and take advantage of your content, you want to avoid becoming too dependent on features or functionality that's provided within browsers. Some applications may load a site using the browser's default rendering engine, without actually opening the browser or offering tools you'd expect, such as page zooming. Other applications may connect to the site, download pages in the background, and then use the information to offer readers a unique experience.

Be extra flexible when designing for users with disabilities so that you can accommodate their needs. Many assistive tools exist, such as screen magnifiers that work independently of a browser but offer functionality that allows users to use the product of their choice. Products like these will affect how content is accessed and consumed, and creating an accessible site is critical to future-proof design. With so many users needing tools to help them browse, it's important to support them as best you can.

Designing an accessible website

Consider the perspective of a visually impaired user who requires the use of screen-reading software in order to browse the Web. Because the user has little to no vision and cannot take advantage of a display, the aesthetic appeal of your content is of little to no value to him. When the user enters your site, his screen reader kicks into action. This tool examines your site's content and reads it aloud using speech synthesizer software. Your user listens to the content of the site through the speakers.

The user will have a positive experience if your site's content is clean, free of typos, and condensed to the extent that it doesn't resemble a novel.

Keep in mind, too, that users of screen readers are affected by anything that interferes with their ability to hear what's being said, such as automatically playing media.

You also must consider your site's layout. Although making a layout accessible doesn't require a great deal of work, you need to remember that you can't simply redirect accessibility aids to a separate speech optimized layout. Unlike a smartphone, which has notable variables (for example, a fixed-dimension screen), a screen reader sits on top of a normal browser (or within it) and processes the content with no traceable effect on rendering inside the browser itself. If you include well-defined links, alternative text for images, and well-structured content, the site is a joy to use, however.

It's also worth noting that for budding businesses, ensuring that your website is accessible is a legal requirement in many countries.

Reformatters

Ten years ago, you wouldn't have thought about letting users reformat your carefully built design or download it into a purpose-built app. You certainly wouldn't have encouraged viewing your site outside a browser. However, both of these things are now considered best practices. From syndication feeds (shown in Figure 14-1) that allow meaningful alerts to your latest posts to the content-acquisition tools that let users store and organize articles they'd like to read later, visitors are pushing the Web's responsiveness to the limit.

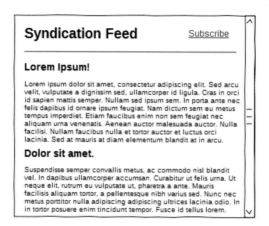

FIGURE 14-1: Many web browsers include RSS and Atom feed readers, but dedicated apps exist, too.

The following lists show members of this software's family tree and some issues they can encounter.

Relatives:	**Considerations:**
> RSS and Atom feeds	> Client availability
> Instapaper	> Structure handling
> Safari's Reading List	> Restreaming issues

Practical solutions

Reformatting software provides one of the few web-based interactions that can take place both within and outside a browser. You can find podcatchers for audio and video feeds like iTunes, and a wealth of RSS syndicators exist for every platform imaginable (some are built into browsers or the OS). These tools are restricted in how they portray content, which makes it easier to ensure consistency because content feeds are themed around the UI.

One of the major problems designers contend with in all syndication clients is whether the user will have access to such a product. It's fine to throw a feed at a user and tell her to subscribe, but not all browsers have a built-in client (Google Chrome, for example). The best way to ensure that users without a feed reader can view and use your content is to use a third-party service like FeedBurner, which allows the feed to be turned into and visualized as regular HTML. This feature allows regular web browsers to see the content.

When you use a reformatter application like Instapaper, the first thing you realize is that software developers have become adept at stripping unnecessary features from a page, showing only what's useful to readers. To use Instapaper, for example, visitors are able to use a JavaScript bookmarklet to save the formatted content to their server so that they can view and manage it later. With this in mind, make sure that these useful, popular clients can handle your content easily.

Reference   Apple offers an excellent guide to building a feed, especially for working it around the needs of the iTunes library. If you want to get your media into iTunes and open a new avenue for visitors to enjoy your content, especially if you're a podcaster trying to get into their directory, read the following: `http://www.apple.com/itunes/podcasts/specs.html.`

First, be sure that your content is formatted with semantic HTML because these products won't be able to handle content embedded in a Flash file. Next, don't depend on CSS to dictate how content appears within the page because these products ignore CSS styling and positioned content may be affected. Finally, keep adverts and navigation in their rightful place. Sure, having advertisements on the page is fine, but if you smear them everywhere, the site will have readability issues. A clean, logical, and carefully thought-out design is the order of the day here.

"Read it later" products like Instapaper function kind of like a proxy browser. By passing the data through a third-party service, your site's content is reformatted and presented to match the best reading style the app can afford — that is to say, minus all the unnecessary bits you usually find in a site. As with proxy tools, because the content is dealt with at the server, you cannot depend on scripts to generate content on-the-fly because it won't be shown within the page. Hidden content will become visible, but AJAX will not.

JavaScript can be a powerful tool, but it can also be a pain in the neck when web designers wrongly assume users have the technology available and usable. Although the major browsers (such as Firefox) can happily work away with some lovely, functional script (unless it's disabled), plenty of reformatting tools that ignore scripts entirely will be affected by dependency upon it. If you just want to progressively disclose data, use a stylistic method of altering visibility. Don't use intrusive scripts to load data remotely.

Best practices

> Offer both an RSS and an Atom feed to support clients' applications.

> Utilize tools like FeedBurner to ensure that Chrome users can read feeds.

> Make sure your HTML is appropriately marked up for consistency.

> Don't try to smear adverts everywhere; these tools will block them.

> Avoid depending on scripts or images to render important content.

Apps and Widgets

Browsers aren't the only applications that can have web connectivity. Many applications (a greater number than the total number of browsers) offer built-in browser windows. These browser windows can connect to sites and parse content, offering a reduced feature set and overriding CSS or JavaScript preferences to ensure that the look and feel of your site matches users' expectations. These browser windows are also highly ubiquitous on a number of platforms. Widgets built into the browser offering added functionality (see Figure 14-2) are also very popular online.

The following lists show members of this software's family tree and some issues they can encounter.

Relatives:

> In-app browsers

> Web-app widgets

> Desktop widgets

Considerations:

> Recognized data parsing

> Vendor-reduced feature set

> Pixel-precision engineering

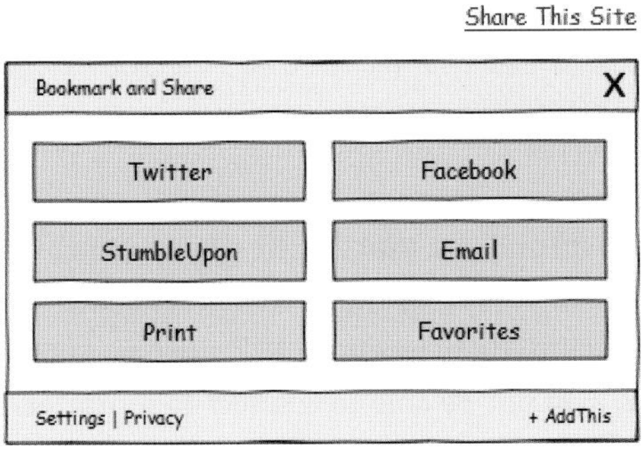

Share This Site

Bookmark and Share	**X**
Twitter	Facebook
StumbleUpon	Email
Print	Favorites
Settings | Privacy	+ AddThis

FIGURE 14-2: Just as applications can use content, widgets can offer functionality through third parties.

Practical solutions

Widgets are selectively designed micro-applications that you can embed within a browser. They take a site's content and proceed to turn it into useful web functionality. Some widgets require that APIs or specially produced code is used to connect and grab the required data, whereas some older and perhaps less-stable variations use a method known as *data parsing*. When a widget parses data, it grabs an entire file, uses its knowledge of the site's structure to chop out what's unnecessary, and does something to the interface with what's left over.

Deciding whether to support data-parsing widgets isn't easy. Not all of these products are "good natured." These tools can be built to leech content, stealing and republishing what you provide. However, because every barrier put in their way seems to fail, swimming against the tide makes little sense. To help data parsers carry out their job, just don't change a site's structure regularly. As for apps, you can't prevent them taking credit for your work because they embed a browser window.

Because third-party applications can integrate rendering engines and small-scale browsers, traveling around a site can become complex, especially if the user is left with little other choice than to stick to the options available within a site (as opposed to the tools you would hope to find within the browsing product). Things like the ability to print a page or zooming might be missed, but other functionality that's missing could prove to be restrictive.

Note Browsers within apps often have a good amount of viewport space available because they usually come with fewer built-in features than standard browsers. They may also come with spoofed user-agent strings that will further confuse misguided attempts at web browser sniffing.

If a user makes a purchase on your site and you provide the option to print a receipt, you must be sure that the user can download or access the document at a later date in order to print it. (You might consider sending it to them by e-mail.) Not all browsers have the capability to print, and certain devices may not be able to connect to a printer. Also, be sure that each page of the site has a clearly accessible global navigation system, and avoid forcing pop-ups on visitors because some third-party apps may omit features like navigation buttons and multi-tabbed pages.

Widgets are recognized as having unusual UIs. Nevertheless, you must allow these third-party tools to retain the look and feel they require. The worst thing that can happen is that when visiting your site, the widget is forced to deal with unruly behavior that interrupts an experience. This variable is a rather unique one for sites to deal with (as seen in iGoogle), but it's one that can happily coexist with designs. Just make sure you put safety measures in place so that these useful pieces of code are allowed to work without code conflicting with them.

If users want to take advantage of desktop or web-based widgets that you or a third party has built, let them. Grabbing useful bits of data on demand allows these helpful tools to keep up-to-date with important events on your site. Widgets can also be beneficial in the attempt to bring the best bits of your site to a user's desktop, such as those found in Yahoo! Widgets and Apple's Dashboard. Use microformats and code conventions to better define what data is relevant, and avoid blocking or redirecting unknown user-agents from the site.

Best practices

> Don't constantly change a site's structure; it may confuse apps or widgets.

> Maintain conventions in your layout to assist common data parsing tools.

> Avoid replicating browser-native features; show how to use them instead.

> Don't rely on browser-specific features; they may not always be available.

> Ensure that your site won't break when being restyled for specific needs of users.

Accessibility Aids

Accessibility aids present themselves as "middlemen" between disabled users and the software they choose to employ. By accommodating users' needs (because of either inhibition or a disability), these products can affect your layouts in various ways. From on-screen keyboards that'll absorb real estate to screen readers (Figure 14-3) that focus users' attention on just a small cluster of pixels at one time, these tools repurpose layouts and interfaces by offering extended forms of on-screen input and output.

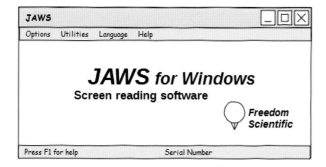

FIGURE 14-3: Screen readers like Jaws are terrific at helping visually impaired individuals use a PC.

The following lists show members of this software's family tree and some issues they can encounter.

Relatives:

> Screen readers

> Screen magnifiers

> Page zooming

> Real-time text

> Speech agents

Considerations:

> Aesthetic overriding

> In-app accessibility

> Accessibility testing

Practical solutions

One of the great things about CSS is that it's incredibly versatile. You can use media queries to provide a whole range of differently formatted CSS-powered layouts based purely on the amount of physical space within the viewport. Beyond this, custom stylesheet switching or stylistic overriding techniques can help you offer specific browsers or environments a layout that matches the requirements of an interface. With this level of power, you need to remain considerate of those choosing to overwrite your best efforts to increase content readability.

The accessibility tools built into browsers may allow content to be reformatted into a high-contrast layout that is suitable for visually impaired users. External tools may help focus a user's vision on a portion of the screen via screen magnification. To ensure compatibility, never block the zooming functionality on platforms like iOS (setting no to the viewport user-scalable meta tag), design so that scripts won't interfere with important stylistic changes, and offer a high-contrast alternative stylesheet with an on-page style switcher.

Although it's great that accessibility aids exist, the truth is that if you follow a few standard practices like the WCAG guidelines, you can decrease the need for users to invest in expensive tools or depend on browser features. Making a site accessible doesn't have to require a lot of extra work if you go into the process with the right mindset. Ensuring compatibility for accessibility aids is critical because many individuals do suffer from disabilities or impairments that can affect how they view and use your site.

Reference   You can find plenty of free tools that allow you to see how a site copes under the control of third-party assistive tools. Be sure to test the features offered natively in each device, OS, and browser. Also test any commonly used tools. The free screen reader at this site is an ideal place to start: `http://www.nvda-project.org/`.

If you can avoid using very small font sizes and fixed-width pixel units in your content and layout, users won't need to zoom to magnify the screen as much. If you avoid unnecessary data entry, the need for speech-to-text products will lessen. Providing large click regions will make a big difference in usability, both for people using handheld devices and touch screens and for individuals who have their viewport split into two screens in order to increase readability.

When users are forced to take advantage of assistive tools, their interactions with sites are often restricted. If they use an on-screen magnifier or zooming utility, their visible space is limited to the section that has been zoomed or scaled. Additionally, if visitors must use an on-screen keyboard for data entry, more than likely at least part of the window will be obscured while they type. As a designer, aim for accessibility from the offset, and check that the use of these tools doesn't break your layout.

Some platforms have access to a wider variety of assistive tools than others, and although you can't make the most of all of them, talk to your visitors to find out which features they depend on, especially when it comes to supporting accessibility. Encouraging your challenged community to speak out about problems they encounter will help you better understand what you can do, which may then be your justification for continually improving your site.

Best practices

> Avoid preventing in-page zooming; doing so can seriously impair readability.

> Some browsers allow alternative stylesheets; offer a high-contrast one.

> Make the site accessible to reduce the burden and need for the software.

> Test your site with a variety of built-in and popular assistive tools.

> Consider adding features that increase accessibility to help boost users' productivity.

Augmented Reality

The real world and the Web are becoming increasingly interconnected. With computer sensory input hardware (for example, a webcam, display, or GPS chip), browsers can provide us with a modified look at the world as we otherwise see it. With potential connectivity options for sightseeing, gaming, collaboration, entertainment (see Figure 14-4), and more, this futuristic technology could change how we use the Web, how we interact with sites, and even how we interact with each other.

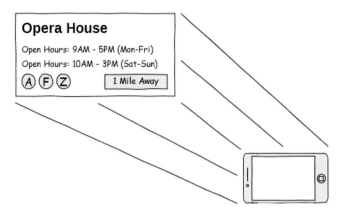

FIGURE 14-4: You can view a building with a smartphone to get useful details about it!

The following lists show members of this software's family tree and some issues they can encounter.

Relatives:

> Mediated reality

> Virtual reality

Considerations:

> Social engineering potential

> Physical service enhancement

> Virtual-on-virtual layering

Practical solutions

If you're the proud owner of a social networking site or even a site that engages in social networking, the idea of being able to enhance an experience based on real-world events is a cool prospect. Although support for the technology is currently in a niche category, a lot can be said for the long-term future of augmented reality. Be sure to treat such features as optional because the technology isn't appropriate in all situations, and misusing it might be considered intrusive.

Never demand that visitors hand over their location information or try to use their webcam without permission; such behavior will just lead to privacy concerns. If you offer augmented reality services, use an opt-in model rather than an opt-out scheme. This way, users control who can see or use the sensitive data they provide without interrupting their regular browsing experience. If all goes well, users will recognize the value of using the augmented reality features you're offering, and will use them regularly.

Linking a virtual object to the real world is just another peculiar example of how things have changed since the Web's inception. If you're a provider of real-world goods and services or use real-world facets (for example, locations) to give information to your users, the technology may be useful. Whether you're Wikipedia offering pop-up details about objects and places or a dating site that wants to give its members an augmented profile for real-world meetings, you must weigh the benefits of using this technology against ethical and safety concerns.

Reference   You can embed augmented reality functionality in business cards, merchandise, books, or any physical product to connect the real and digital world or to offer users helpful advice. The following tutorial provided by *Web Designer Magazine* is just the tip of the iceberg: `http://www.webdesignermag.co.uk/tutorials/get-started-with-ar/`.

Although it's hard to imagine that augmented reality could do people harm in the real world, such features can cause distractions with serious consequences. For example, imagine that you provide an augmented reality video, and then imagine a user taking advantage of it while walking along a street. With this scenario in mind, it's clear that your design must not obscure the entire screen — otherwise, the user might lose sight of traffic and become involved in an accident. You may think such concerns aren't serious, but people have been led astray by their SatNav, so who knows where augmented reality could lead them! Such technology may be seen as hazardous in the future because of the issue of texting while driving.

As it stands now, the routine use of augmented reality is rather slim for the average designer. However, this technology does have some cool tricks up its sleeve that could give it some credibility, as well as the prospect for feature support. For example, if you were to build a site for a museum or art gallery, you would be able to connect useful information about the exhibits to the devices that visitors carry in their pockets. Imagine being able to walk past a painting, find its history, and at the same time, order a poster of it from the gift shop.

Much of this probably sounds rather sci-fi, and for the moment it is, but as hardware gets better and the software is released, you may see this technology used more frequently on sites. To ensure compatibility with these kinds of features, don't be afraid to download or build an augmented reality tool and see what it can do. As with designing a site, your imagination is the limit, and if you can provide a startup with something that takes the Web into the real world, users will have more to interact with.

Best practices

> Support for this tool is in its infancy, so don't have unrealistic expectations.

> Don't force augmented reality on users; allow them to maintain control in the journey.

> Reality contains a lot of distractions, so allow users to pause their progress.

> Keep augmented interactions simple and avoid blocking the vision of users.

> Try some augmented reality in your business to enhance existing offerings.

The Consequences of Code

HTML, CSS, JavaScript, WML, and more

NOTHING IS MORE central to your site's compatibility than the code that governs the objects that exist upon a page. Code is the lifeblood of a site; without it, browsers, software, hardware, and devices cannot see your work. Browsers interpret code and render the pages, but your code's diversity and prevalence make it worth considering on an entirely separate level. In this chapter, you learn the importance of code and to identify the bleeding edge of languages that can help your site survive future browsers.

The Compatibility of Code

Without the underlying code "telling" browsers how to format and present your lovely, handcrafted layouts, there wouldn't be much of an Internet today. Moreover, surviving the advances of the Web means that you must ensure that the content, look, and feel of your sites survive and remain useful to users as languages evolve and expectations alter. This means you must make the most of the available development tools and identify where and when your work needs to undergo some maintenance.

The legacy of code is a long and interesting story, starting with the inception of HTML, the advancement of CSS, and the introduction of JavaScript as more than a cut-and-paste tool. With each browser shipped to the Web, these technologies have remained deeply ingrained in the renderer, leading to many innovations as the languages evolved, but also leading to compatibility issues such as the legacy of the browser wars. You may find yourself fighting the need to support both old and new code.

Tip

Sometimes you must account for two different implementations of a language to retain a solid level of cross-browser compatibility. If you want to use SVG in your pages, for example, you'll need to offer a VML alternative for old versions of Internet Explorer.

We won't go through the gory details regarding how the Web and its modern standards came to be — that is an entire book in itself. But it's important to realize that the evolution of the Web and its languages have occurred over many years, and through each new standard and advancement, designers have struggled to gain consistent code support among browser manufacturers. In recent years, this has become less difficult, but the legacy of bad behavior (and code) has led to many irritating compatibility quirks.

One of the major issues regarding code compatibility is support. Browsers must support a technology before you can use it, and code must be supported for users to get the benefits. First, you have to be sure that your code works on browsers, such as early versions of Internet Explorer, that can't properly handle modern eye candy. Then, you have to consider how browsers in the future will operate; what deprecated standards they may cease to support; and when you should employ the latest and greatest tools within production sites.

We're now in the age of a third browser war. With battles for dominance still raging, and with legacy tools such as featurephones still in common use, you must reinforce code with good fallbacks to degrade an experience to match user capabilities. Tools like progressive enhancement, graceful degradation, responsive design, and adaptive design can all help achieve this goal. The lack of standardized support for code in renderers is a bitter pill to swallow, however, as comprehensive browser testing and debugging become a necessity.

Disabled code issues

Imagine that a technically competent (if not slightly paranoid) visitor accesses your site using Firefox with the NoScript extension installed. (It's a popular extension, so there is a good chance that it, or something like it, may affect your site one day.) The visitor doesn't trust your brand yet because it's her first encounter and she's worried that intrusive scripting could negatively affect her experience on your site. Perhaps she has also come across too many anti–right-click scripts or irritating marquee effects that lead her to disable scripting by default.

As the visitor browses to the site with NoScript enabled, the tool does as it's told and turns off all script functionality within the page. JavaScript is enabled within the browser, but NoScript manages to give site-based permissions to help users make decisions about which sites they trust. Unfortunately, as is the case with many sites, you presumed that she would have scripting enabled. Because the scripts are embedded in areas they shouldn't be, the visitor can't browse the site because links became non-functional as a result of your coding methods.

This is a perfect example of why you cannot depend on any technology that can be turned off by visitors, even if the feature is something as readily used as JavaScript or CSS (both can be easily disabled by users). Create non-obtrusive scripts by separating HTML, CSS, and JavaScript code into separate files and layering behavior over styles and styles over structure. This ensures each language works independently and degrades gracefully. You can't demand that code be supported by users, so avoid making their dependency a prerequisite.

(x)HTML

HTML is the chief markup language used to create the structure (Figure 15-1) of web-pages. When it comes to ensuring code compatibility, no language has the same level of ubiquity as HTML (Hypertext Markup Language) and its strict brother, (x)HTML. As these fundamental languages cannot be disabled inside browsers, they're particularly dependable in design. Both languages have passed through several iterations. Although HTML compatibility issues exist, it remains the safest layer of the Web.

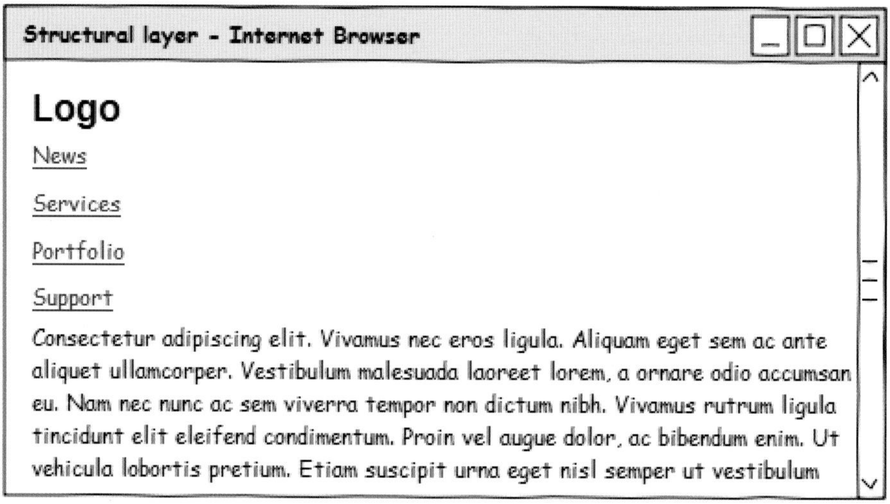

Structural layer - Internet Browser

Logo

News

Services

Portfolio

Support

Consectetur adipiscing elit. Vivamus nec eros ligula. Aliquam eget sem ac ante aliquet ullamcorper. Vestibulum malesuada laoreet lorem, a ornare odio accumsan eu. Nam nec nunc ac sem viverra tempor non dictum nibh. Vivamus rutrum ligula tincidunt elit eleifend condimentum. Proin vel augue dolor, ac bibendum enim. Ut vehicula lobortis pretium. Etiam suscipit urna eget nisl semper ut vestibulum

FIGURE 15-1: (x)HTML explains the semantic structure of your content, giving it contextual meaning.

The following lists show the HTML/(x)HTML family tree and some issues its members encounter:

Relatives:

> HTML 4.01

> HTML 5

> (x)HTML 1.0

> (x)HTML 1.1

Considerations:

> Degrading HTML5 elements

> The (x)HTML 1.1 conundrum

> Baseline rendering levels

Practical solutions

Although HTML as a language is well supported, we can't say the same about its youngest prodigy. Browsers predating HTML5 (which is still in development) can't be expected to support this new version because HTML5 simply didn't exist. HTML5 may offer a bunch of new toys to play with, but the code may encounter issues because not all elements are likely to be supported. This situation is especially prominent with the newest tags in the specification because older versions of IE refuse to render what they don't understand.

If you're going to use HTML5, be wary of what features you choose to implement. Using the HTML5 Doctype is fine because browsers don't show it on-screen (and legacy browsers can often interpret the code). However, more innovative features will likely require an elegant fallback, some potentially invasive scripting, or a healthy alternative to ensure that users can browse the site. This issue partially exists because of the way in which some versions of IE ignore what they don't like!

Before HTML5 became as popular as it is today, another specification called (x)HTML was in its prime. (x)HTML was a stricter language than HTML and was less forgiving of errors. (x)HTML currently is utilized in many CMS engines and websites, usually making use of version 1.0 of the specification. One version of the language, 1.1, has compatibility issues with the browser we keep complaining about: Internet Explorer (up to and including version 8.0). Thus, even though (x)HTML is still widely used, you're better off aiming for HTML5.

Reference The abolishment of table-based web design is a great example of how using well-formed code reduces redundancy, helps your content make sense, and aids accessibility and stability. The following site explains the justifications for why you shouldn't use table-based layouts: `http://www.hotdesign.com/seybold/everything.html`.

Because of its demand for a specific MIME type (application/(x)HTML+xml), (x)HTML's purpose was to give designers a greater level of interconnectivity with XML documents and several XML-based specifications. However, as Internet Explorer didn't adopt the strict MIME type, it fell into disrepute, and few people utilized the potential it offered. Therefore, if you must use (x)HTML for compatibility reasons, stick to version 1.0 with the classic text/html MIME type or use (x)HTML5. Otherwise, just use HTML 4.01.

You need to be sure that your code is semantic (uses the right tag for the right job) because the meaning you give to your site's structure determines how search engines will make sense of it. Try to keep your code's structure free of bloat because that enables you to more easily target elements for style or behavior. If your code is correctly written, you can usually dodge bullets thrown by browsers and reduce the chances of quirks occurring as you use CSS. In addition, if you build something that's agile and beautiful, you'll be proud of it.

You can help with semantics and also unearth your occasional mistakes (such as forgetting to close a tag that potentially affects your site's style) by running your code through the validator provided by the W3C. When you're sure that your code is accurate and well formed, see if you can reduce any redundancy that may have built up as you coded. Perhaps you don't need all those DIV or SPAN tags. Also, turn off scripting and styles so you can see how browsers render your layout by default in case these items of functionality become unavailable.

Best practices

> If you do use HTML5 elements with JavaScript crutches, offer a fallback.

> Replicate unsupported functionality with feature detection, but let it degrade.

> Avoid using (x)HTML 1.1 and the now-abandoned (x)HTML 2.0 in your sites.

> Be sure that the default styles that browsers apply won't negatively affect the layout.

> Ensure that you use the proper element for the job and validate your code.

CSS

Cascading Style Sheets (CSS) is the primary language used to visually organize a design (Figure 15-2). CSS has had a rocky time in terms of compatibility, and it suffers a range of issues relating to inconsistencies in standards adoption and rendering within old browsers. You must be careful if you want to ensure that CSS renders accurately across browsers. The general role of CSS is to handle a layout's aesthetics. With discrepancies in support and its native capability to be overwritten or turned off, however, it can be a beast of a variable to control.

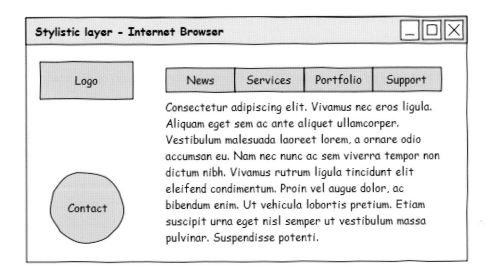

FIGURE 15-2: CSS allows you to visually control a site's layout, but only if browsers support the code!

The following lists show the CSS family tree and some of the issues its members encounter:

Relatives:

> CSS Level 1

> CSS Level 2

> CSS Level 3 (Modules)

Considerations:

> Stylistic interpretations

> Layering complexity

> Flexibility over fixations

Practical solutions

The unreliability of CSS results from several things. First, there's no guarantee that CSS will be available because it can be turned off. Another possibility is that when the language was implemented certain browsers didn't follow the specifications properly. In addition, you have the issue of stylistic interpretation, in which browsers may choose to actively implement something in a different manner. Additionally, browsers can behave rather oddly if quirks mode (rather than standards mode) is active. All these variables can lead to inconsistencies.

In each of these circumstances, you can do a few things to reduce a browser's influence over how your code is interpreted to try to ensure compatibility. Regarding how browsers interpret default styles, you could use a CSS reset mechanism to enforce one set of rules for all browsers. As for quirks mode, it's best to follow general browser recommendations to avoid it entirely by using a valid DTD, not using quirky tools such as the proprietary zoom property, and keeping in line with the W3C box model.

Unlike HTML, CSS is a relatively progressive language, which means that if something isn't supported it doesn't necessarily mean that the whole layout will collapse. In many circumstances, you can adapt the existing CSS 2.1 specification, using properties that have ubiquitous support and then layer on the extra functionality to take its place or to enhance existing code. An example of this includes the box shadow property that naturally degrades into not being visible if the property isn't supported (unless you offer a fallback).

Reference   A number of CSS properties have inconsistent or partial support within certain browsers. You can find several lists aimed at helping you substantiate where issues exist, such as this enormous guide: `http://westciv.com/wiki/CSS_Compatibility_Guide`.

Gracefully degrading CSS doesn't work for every situation. The CSS3 target selector, for example, allows you to restyle a page based on the fragment identifier in the address bar. If you click a link and the pseudo selector is supported, all the wonderful effects will happen on-page; if it's not supported, the link won't have much of an effect. In cases such as this, you need to provide a fallback so that the link still works in older browsers, just without the styling. Go further by adding support for the pseudo on top of an already-working link.

In addition to moving from a table-based design, the biggest evolution in the use of CSS is related to fixed-width layouts. When you had to deal only with desktop compatibility, a "960 grid" solution was acceptable. But when handheld devices came along, it became necessary to offer a range of sizes. With devices becoming ever more diverse, and the conditions for their use becoming ever more ambiguous, you must break away from a set way of thinking. As a result, the technique of using fixed-width layouts has become outdated and problematic.

To help assure compatibility and the flexibility of your site in the future, don't use print or PX unit measurements to define explicit layout boundaries. Using tools such as min/max width can be helpful in defining less-rigid designs because it removes the explicit nature of the units, in most situations. However, using percentage widths for a fluid or liquid layout and blending that with CSS media queries is much better than trying to treat your site like a shirt: offering a set range of sizes, and turning less conventional body shapes away from the store.

Best practices

> Unless you feel comfortable with cross-browser CSS, use a reset technique.

> Always use an (x)HTML Doctype in a page's header to avoid quirks mode.

> Ensure that your CSS will gracefully degrade if the code is not supported.

> Be responsible with your layouts; avoid code that's prone to browser issues.

> Use a mixture of sizing techniques to help your layouts scale to demands.

JavaScript

When HTML and CSS aren't enough to get the job done and you want to provide visitors with some garnishes to encourage interactivity (Figure 15-3), get out the client-side scripting language JavaScript. It allows you to provide unparalleled levels of interaction within your pages, making the language highly useful and powerful. Even though the ubiquity of scripting isn't as high with JavaScript as it is in CSS and HTML — because JavaScript can be crippled by users or by the browser, such as when it's turned off by default — it still remains extremely popular.

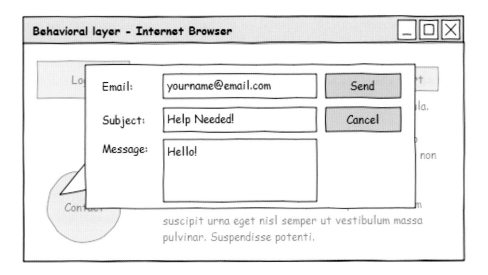

FIGURE 15-3: JavaScript lets you add exciting functionality, such as lightboxes, to your pages.

The following lists show the JavaScript family tree and some issues its members encounter:

Relatives:	**Considerations:**
> jQuery	> Obtrusive scripting
> JScript	> Negative interactions
	> Server-side safety

Practical solutions

Many sites these days depend on JavaScript. It's not really surprising considering the demands users place on sites for interactivity. But trying to browse some websites with scripting either unavailable or disabled can be unnerving. JavaScript can be turned off (as with CSS or images), and your request for scripting can be denied by the browser or user. In such cases, you must ensure that the entire site doesn't become unresponsive or crippled.

The goal for unobtrusive scripting requires designers to take certain actions. First, you must be sure that scripted behavior is taken out of the HTML page and put into separate JS files that can be referenced, cached, and reused where needed. Second, you need to do capability testing to ensure that the mechanism you want to use is supported; if it's not, a fallback is required. Avoid using event handlers within HTML, listen for each event in the JS functions, and act on them. This means avoiding JavaScript-powered URLs, too!

Among all the web languages, JavaScript has one of the most jaded histories (even more so than CSS). In its early years, it was perceived as a hackish tool to make pretty, but potentially unhelpful, things happen, such as the anti–right-click scripts I mentioned earlier. This behavior continued throughout the 1990s as designers used it to gain control over users in sort of a James Bond-style, super-villain way. They crippled the native behavior of browsers, reinvented existing functionality, and irritated their users frequently.

Note

Interestingly, to avoid the abuses of old and save users from script-inflicted damage, a number of popular web browsers automatically cripple functionality such as right-click prevention scripts. By reducing the impact of potentially hazardous scripting, browsers may increase the usability of sites automatically and help users out of potential pitfalls.

People didn't begin to catch on to the downside of such obtrusive behavior until the age of user-centered design. At this point, designers agreed that firing multiple pop-ups, disabling text selection, and blocking right-clicking were bad ideas. Damaging the browser Back button became a no-no, and hijacking the title or status bar with ticker tapes was deemed annoying and unprofessional. The lesson is to avoid doing these things and avoid employing scripts such as "print this page." Instead, encourage use of the browser's existing functionality.

Although client-side scripting can be disabled, server-side scripting cannot because the server processes everything before passing it onto users. Unfortunately, server-side scripting will not give you as many options for interaction with users, and it requires refreshes. Even so, server-side scripting may be a useful tool when you're attempting to give users a sensible fallback for scripts. Whether as an alternative to live-form validation, option selection, or memorizing user preferences in a session, you can keep things running without JavaScript.

To ensure compatibility in these instances, begin by offering a server-side alternative that can undertake the actions before continuing and provide the client-side version that detects any mistakes before the data is submitted. Then, if scripting works, JavaScript will notify users of issues immediately and no refresh will be needed; it will pass the checks at the server. However, if JavaScript is turned off, the script that passed the script-checked version will spot the issues and send the user back with details on how to resolve them.

Best practices

> Make scripts independent of the structure so they can be maintained.

> If scripting is turned off, don't just make the tool redundant; offer a fallback.

> Never cripple text selection or right-clicking; many users rely on these tools.

> Don't replicate browser functions because some of them won't support the action.

> Try offering a server-side fallback for interactive aids such as form validation.

WML

Although modern devices can cope with the browsing needs of users by using a blend of HTML, CSS, and JS, a less-fortunate array of legacy devices, such as featurephones, are stuck with older standards. Wireless Markup Language (WML) (Figure 15-4) is a structural language much like HTML, but WML must be coded independently of HTML. Although WML doesn't support complex styles or scripts, leading many designers to dislike it, it has gained high ubiquity levels (even now, as a deprecated standard) on featurephones, which cannot handle HTML. So don't ignore it.

My WML Website

Lorem ipsum dolor sit amet, consectetur adipiscing elit. Phasellus volutpat aliquet convallis. Morbi ornare massa in urna pharetra eu molestie mi aliquet. Maecenas vel ligula in diam egestas lobortis. Cras a orci sit amet est varius porttitor at et nibh. Integer facilisis, urna quis tempor tincidunt, velit lorem porttitor augue, eget ornare dui sem sit amet ante.

Site Map

FIGURE 15-4: Consider WML as a much-simplified version of HTML aimed at entry-level devices.

The following lists show the WML family tree and some issues of the language:

Relatives:	Considerations:
> WML 1.1	> Non-mobile support
> WML 1.2	> Card deck stacking
> WML 1.3	> Independent housing
> WML 2.0	

Practical solutions

Although HTML has fairly ubiquitous support across a wide variety of platforms, WML is entirely in the other camp. Because it's predominantly found and utilized in featurephones and devices with little processing power (or compatibility with the Web), users wanting the same experience they'd have on higher-end devices or a desktop environment must go out of their way to get what they want. Although support for WML on platforms such as Windows and Mac isn't impossible, achieving that support requires a heck of a lot of designer effort.

Users wanting to view WML pages on a desktop platform or designers looking to test the pages need to either download the Opera browser (which supports WML natively), an extension for Firefox (to handle WML), or get their hands on a special WML browser for their OS. A number of free ones exist, such as Klondike, if you look hard enough. To make your site fully compatible for non-WML devices (if you do support it), you'll also need to offer an HTML alternative. Although deprecated, WML does maintain a proportion of users.

Unlike HTML, WML has very few elements attached to it, which is why it is preferred by developers of many handheld devices. Because of its general simplicity and lack of fantastic features, it's fairly easy for your site to achieve compatibility with WML browsers and devices that can handle only WML. This ease of development, of course, comes at the cost of support for CSS, JavaScript, and other features we like to use but that aren't available.

Reference

WML isn't exactly a well-known language, so you'll probably need a good place to get started with the environment if you plan on supporting it for users of older devices that have no HTML support. The following site has tutorials that can help you learn the essentials of WML development: `http://www. developershome.com/wap/wml/`.

One of the cool things about WML is how it progressively discloses your content to users by using a *card deck stack*. Each page contains a series of cards (known as a deck), stacked in a logical order by the web designer. Some decks are used as index pages (page-long navigation menus), others contain purely content. Every card should be linked to from the index card (much like a sitemap). Cards that aren't linked to won't function, and users won't know about them. You should always break content into a deck of cards to reduce information overload on tiny screens.

WML is oriented toward handheld rather than desktop devices. Because of its separation from a traditional HTML site and its clearly defined objectives, you can safely promote the WML site as an independent website without feeling guilty that you couldn't make your main layout work for every user. Although there are exceptions to the rule, such as if you need to provide a Web application for specific devices, you should consider WML as the only case where it's necessary to build a separate dedicated site for a single audience.

Deciding whether to support WML-enabled users is a difficult decision; many more mobile phones and devices use browsers based on HTML than on WML. To ensure that your site is compatible with WML, however, if you see that audience as a worthwhile compatibility pursuit, you have to build the dedicated WML site and advertise it to featurephone users to ensure that they are aware of its existence. To help users find this separate site more easily, host it on a subdomain named *WAP*. WAP is the convention because WML sites uses the WAP protocol.

Best practices

> Check that your WML site works in a supporting browser (or a dedicated client).

> Ensure the WML site is served in coordination with a proper HTML layout.

> Break content into logical stacks and decks to avoid information overload.

> Be sure that every card is linked to from any index cards to avoid orphans.

> Offer a separate WML site from the HTML site; consider using a subdomain.

Metadata

Although HTML provides a great deal of contextual information about content on-screen, a number of code conventions, namely metadata and microformats, can add relevance and functionality to the content on your pages. Although the adoption rate of each one varies, these conventions can enhance a site's integration with services (Figure 15-5) or products that support these tools. Whereas metadata primarily focuses on explaining the relevance of entire pages (data about data), microformats enhance the semantic meaning of HTML.

FIGURE 15-5: Metadata and microformats can format data on the page into something more meaningful.

The following lists show this variable's family tree and some of the possible issues:

Relatives:

> Semantic metadata

> Microformats

> Syntax schemas

Considerations:

> Adoption requirements

> Active code maintenance

> Competing methodologies

Practical solutions

Making your metadata future-proof requires the same mentalities as a popularity contest employs. Only the metadata that designers employ will gain the recognition and adoption that "standardize" them. Although certain microformats and other metadata formats may not be supported by particular browsers, search engines, or social networks, they won't cause a site to break (if they are retired in the future), as they don't affect the physical structure or style of a page. The only negative effect they may have is wasting the user's bandwidth.

Using metadata whenever possible is an ideal way to future-proof your site (assuming that support will continue for the code). The semantic Web and the rise of products, users, and services interacting dynamically with your site's content justifies turbocharging the markup with these nifty, exploitable components of a site. If your content is ready for interactions of this nature, your site will be ready when a user or service supports and uses them natively or via extensions. If users don't have support for such features, it's not a problem.

As with all coding conventions, new metadata formats will come into action, taking over the responsibilities and jobs of older ones, and formats that used to be popular will fall into disuse. These older formats can add unnecessary clutter to your site. Because there are no specifications that explicitly prohibit the creation of new metadata standards (they all rely on conventions and popular usage), the scale of options at your disposal can be daunting. These tools give your content added contextual meaning, and that's good for everyone who visits your website.

Note

Semantic metadata can arrive in a variety of formats. You can choose among metatags, RDFa files, DCMI metadata, schemas, and microformats. Sounds like a lot? It is! Luckily though, they're all very easy to use if you understand both HTML and XML.

To ensure compatibility with the constantly evolving landscape of semantics and any new metadata conventions, you must be aware of the most popular options. The ones that have high levels of recognition in search engines are definitely worth supporting. The ones that work within browser toolbars or extensions are also worth a look. But whatever you do, note where you implement different microformats, schemas, or metadata; as time moves on and formats are deprecated, you'll want to clean up your source code as you go.

Although having these unique, extended methodologies to describe your content is a really exciting prospect, be aware that the semantic Web is suffering a bit of competition (akin to the browser wars). Although metadata has been around for a number of years, it's not as feature full as microformats. And although these cool, useful code extensions are increasingly popular throughout the Web, a number of search engines have a competing range of options that try to coax designers into altering their coding habits. Not exactly fun at all.

There's no telling where the winds will blow and what kind of metadata will wind up with the most support; however, you can focus on what such implementations bring to browsers and users, choosing the best from among them. For example, if designers utilize a third-party service or browser-based extension, the hCard code microformat can be then exported into a virtual business card that is compatible with many e-mail clients, address book products, and more. Tools like this could dramatically help your site's visitors.

Best practices

> Only use the metadata formats that best describe your pages' content.

> Microformats and metadata degrade gracefully; feel free to adopt them.

> Maintain your code regularly and flush out deprecated semantic formatting.

> Test your implementations with browser extensions to ensure they work.

> Competing formats for metadata exist; research your options carefully.

Non-Standard Code

Just as there are devices that maintain popularity, so are there languages and code that have more or less support in browsers. Being on the bleeding edge requires you to consider the less popular but more capable options when they are being used to test code within a new CSS standard, using a deprecated feature, or embracing a niche language requiring a plug-in to offer support. Ubiquity for such features has the potential to be low; however, be aware that many of these unconventional formats may be useful to certain niche audiences. See Figure 15-6.

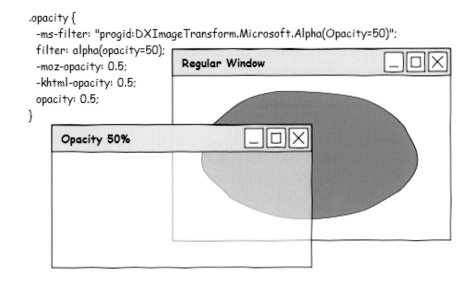

```
.opacity {
    -ms-filter: "progid:DXImageTransform.Microsoft.Alpha(Opacity=50)";
    filter: alpha(opacity=50);
    -moz-opacity: 0.5;
    -khtml-opacity: 0.5;
    opacity: 0.5;
}
```

FIGURE 15-6: Non-standard code is commonplace online; don't be afraid to experiment if it'll improve a layout.

The following lists show this variable's family tree and some of the possible issues:

Relatives:	**Considerations:**
> Vendor prefixes	> Multiformat rendering
> Deprecated code	> Maintaining retired code
> Niche functionality	> Competitive alternatives
> Proprietary code	

Practical Solutions

It's interesting that unsupported code is often attributed to certain rendering engines or browsers that are experimenting with new technologies. Consider, for example, vendor prefix code, which allows designers to play with bleeding edge goodies that haven't made the browser's final cut, but still have some rudimentary level of support. Although every major renderer and browser manufacturer is involved in offering some unsupported code as vendor prefixes, you should consider how using this code will affect the site's stability.

Although production sites need to be stable, allowing users to try great new technologies is a sensible step for designers to take to ensure a diverse, aesthetically rich experience — especially if you properly maintain your code. Returning to the example of vendor prefixes, because each renderer has its own prefix you may need to employ up to six different references to be sure each browser gets a piece of the experience. This may seem like a lot of work, but it enables you to prepare sites for when the code *is* finalized.

Compatibility with deprecated code could be described as a ticking time bomb, waiting to go off at the most inconvenient time. Many browsers do support deprecated code (often perceived as old and unnecessary code) to help designers through their transition to the use of the latest and greatest standards. However, the time will come when the switch will be flipped by browser vendors and old sites using proprietary or vendor-prefixed code will collapse into antiquity, leaving only old versions of browsers to support the outdated site.

Tip

Some proprietary features may actually offer quite widespread support and are worth considering. Take something like Amazon's OpenSearch protocol; most browsers on the desktop already support in-browser search enhancements and this useful format!

The best way to deal with deprecated code is to keep your site and code updated and use the most recent, finalized version of a language. Also, ensure you separate the structure, style, and behavior of a site to help with maintaining the code. Regarding compatibility in older browsers, very old renderers that don't recognize CSS will just show the HTML and offer little else. Although this isn't exactly elegant, you must offer a fair balance between support for old and new tools. So keep in mind that outdated browsers may still be in use.

When it comes to consistent support for different formats, the Web is full of surprises. If you want to use something like SVG, you must supply Internet Explorer with a VML alternative because early versions of the browser don't support SVG; they do support Microsoft's alternative format. There are other examples in the wild where proprietary or unique formats have been adopted over the Web standard, leaving you with a nasty trail of destruction to clean up. Although it's not an ideal scenario, proprietary code is everywhere.

When using HTML, you need to avoid certain proprietary tags by default, such as blink and marquee. CSS also has some proprietary features, such as CSS expressions, zoom, and scroll bar coloration, which you'll want to avoid as well. JavaScript has the IE-only conditional compilation that is essentially conditional comments for scripts (which might be useful). In addition, proprietary languages or unsupported code such as X3D and KML will demand software or a special plug-in to be installed; support these only if your users ask for it.

Best practices

> Vendor prefixes degrade gracefully; don't be afraid to play with them.

> Production sites can use bleeding edge code; just be sure to maintain it.

> After code becomes deprecated, upgrade it to the latest best practice.

> Maintain support for older code only if your users' browsers require it.

> Don't neglect users who depend upon formats with weak browser support.

Third-Party Dependency

Relying on resources, frameworks, and services

WEB PROFESSIONALS MUST sometimes depend on objects and technologies that they don't own or that their users may not have access to, and these external influences can take a toll on a site's compatibility aims. In this chapter, I highlight some of the critical third-party issues that play a role in the degradation of sites and their functionality, and you'll examine the dependency designers have on external resources, frameworks, formats, and services. This interconnected and constantly moving environment makes stability an ongoing chore.

The Weakest Link

The ever-expanding list of third-party assets found on many sites can include frameworks, hyperlinks, files in proprietary formats, media embedding (from sites like YouTube), and even entire services (integrated as part of social networks using APIs). Such tools give your site a relationship with other sites and their beneficial services, but force a dependency on the support they provide. Because of this, a worry exists that links may die or services you use will fail or disappear, leaving you and your users with a sudden loss in site functionality.

The number of links resulting in "file not found" errors highlights the damaging effects of third-party dependency. Worse than broken links, there are cases where cloud storage sites like Amazon S3 crash, taking thousands of sites down with it. If you use social networks, be aware that downtime on these tools could also render parts of your sites unavailable if you rely upon their APIs. All things considered, dependency is a risky proposition as we place our trust in often-critical features in the hands of providers we have no control over.

Tip Some products, such as iTunes and instant-messaging apps, offer browser-based app launching. By using the provided pseudo-protocol (such as `skype:`), you can provide users a handy shortcut to launch the product and run the service or function offered.

In the past, you might have found people cross-linking pages or taking advantage of an embedded video from your site, but these days, you embed all sorts of things onto your pages, such as frameworks like jQuery hosted on third-party sites, Google services, font providers like Typekit, and social networks that stream content. Yet all it takes is a DNS error, server glitch, or an upgrade that changes the location of files and boom! There goes the neighborhood! So, with each crosslink comes an increased potential for errors.

In terms of future-proofing sites, remember that no matter how good something is it won't last forever. Sure, bigger brands like Google have the resources needed to greatly reduce the risk of offline time, but designers regularly utilize the offerings of small services, rarely thinking of the consequences of untested scalability and longevity issues, and this needs to change. If your aim is to maximize stability, address anything that can pose a long-term risk to your site's availability. If you can host code locally, do so; otherwise, use a fallback.

Often, third-party tools are inconsistent in the levels of compatibility they provide for older or less-capable browsers. You need to test regularly and resolve such complications. Also, if a service has imposed limitations, you'll need to research the best route available before tying yourself to the service, as you don't want to have to keep changing packages every few months. Most importantly, maintain your site regularly to reduce the chances of issues occurring and take immediate action to resolve or work around issues as they appear.

Missing page mysteries

A classic example of third-party dependency gone wrong is the case of the missing link. If you're anything like me, you've probably encountered the HTTP "404" (page not found) error many times before. So, it's likely that your visitors may experience the same fate. Imagine your site has some dead links, lying undiscovered and dormant. A user finds you on Google and enters your site; the link works and things are fine so far. However, when she scrolls down the page and clicks a link to find more information from a third-party site, the error occurs.

You may think it's unlikely that this situation will happen on your site. However, if over time you've built up hundreds or thousands of pages of content, some links in the archives may be missed, forgotten, or overlooked; in your visitor's case, this happens to be the link she needs. Shortened URLs are particularly prone to such errors because some of these links are set up on a temporary basis, as are redirections (if you fail to maintain them). Ensuring that your internal and external links continue to work helps the site withstand the test of time.

It's important to realize that errors can affect not only the sites you link to but also the sites that link to you. You should take steps to eliminate such errors by frequently checking your links for issues or asking your users to notify you upon spotting dead links to keep navigation as error free as possible. Not all visitors will start their journey from your home page. I highly recommend that you provide a sensible navigation scheme and site map, which connects all of the pages on your site together. If you don't, users may end up trapped in an orphan page.

Resources

The Web is interconnected by an increasing range of resources and pages that link to each other. Although it's easy to control the internal links that you host on your sites, most sites at some point reference files, pages, and sites located beyond your reach. Being able to link pages together has many benefits, and embedding such solutions provides stable features with minimum effort. However, when it comes to the compatibility and future-proofing nature of your sites, remember that such references can degrade (Figure 16-1) over time.

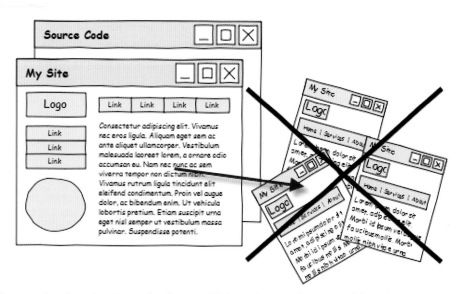

FIGURE 16-1: Over time, internal and external links can become disconnected from their source.

The below lists this variable's family tree and some issues they can encounter:

Relatives:

> External links

> Resource leeching

> CDN hosting

Considerations:

> Corrosion probability ratio

> Player-feature compatibility

> Error page enhancements

Practical solutions

The longevity of links has always been a problem on the Web. Because of the number of pages that have accumulated over the years, fragmentation is at an all-time high. For well-established sites with a good catalog of content, the chances of your sites suffering a form of link corrosion become an ever-greater threat as the number of pages you host increases. The more pages you have, the harder they are to constantly maintain and update (think of 100+ pages); as internal or external pages disappear over time, dead links begin to fester.

Although the risk of dead links occurring is high, many people fail to realize this, leaving long-forgotten pages to perish and archived links to go unchecked. Avoiding the problems of links corrosion is fairly straightforward if you have the right tools and know-how, even if you have a site with thousands of pages. Some free, high quality automated solutions such as Xenu Link Sleuth exist, and they can dig up problematic links. As your site ages, encourage users to notify you if they spot a dead URL; also occasionally check your links.

You also need to consider the issues that can occur with embeddable resources. We know all too well that our video and audio content is often at the mercy of the player that runs such content by default (or the prebuilt player we utilize). However, you need to examine the potential for any complications that result from linking to content that is hosted in a third-party service and cross-linked to your site. This particular behavior is popular among sites like YouTube because their built-in players remove the need for custom solutions.

Tip

Even custom solutions need a proper fallback mechanism. If you do cross-link to an image, ensure that it has some alternative text available, and if you link to a media file, ensure that a text transcript of the feature exists for accessibility tool-dependent users.

To reduce the issues that occur as a result of dependency on third-party resources, make sure your site's content (multimedia files like video and audio) is hosted on a service that's unlikely to experience downtime. Sites like YouTube or FlickR or Facebook aren't likely to suffer too much downtime that will break a player's capability to showcase media on your site (as they can afford the infrastructure). Also, pick a provider that offers a player that has enough features to meet the user's needs (such as subtitles, captions, or 3D support).

As a web designer, you also need to consider what happens when someone does stumble across a dead or misguided link (just in case someone spots something that you missed along the way). Sometimes these things will happen without you knowing about them, and if third-party sites try to link to a dead link in your content, they'll end up suffering the same "page not found" errors. When errors do occur, you'll need to provide users an error page that tries to help them out of the mess, and directs them wherever they need to go.

In dealing with dead links, first you need to redirect any pages that did exist (but now do not) to their replacement, if one exists. Third-party sites may link to pages or content that you've hosted in the past, so you need to redirect them to a page's new location, rather than force their users to start searching through your site's architecture from scratch. If users face an error message, don't leave them with the browser default, as it's not helpful. Customize the links to your Web site, and perhaps offer links to similar pages to the one they clicked.

Best practices

> Check your sites for dead links at least every three to six months.

> Maintain archive page references to avoid internal links rotting.

> Be sure that you use a reliable, stable third-party hosting provider.

> Make sure media players support specific tools your users need.

> Never rely on default error pages; instead, build a better solution.

Frameworks

The age of dynamic, increasingly interactive layouts has brought with it an era where many of the limitations of older browsers and devices have been addressed through the construction of agile, well-crafted scripting libraries, called *frameworks*. In some situations, these tools, often powered by CSS or JavaScript (see Figure 16-2), depending on their purpose, bring new levels of functionality to environments (mostly) ubiquitously, help address shortfalls in legacy support for such technologies, and give a standardized rule-of-thumb for design.

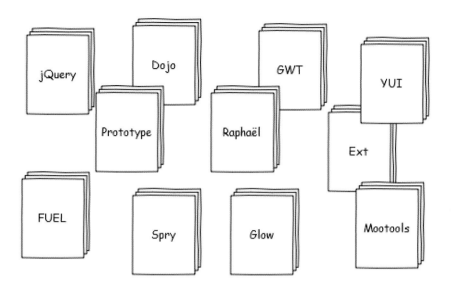

FIGURE 16-2: Many frameworks exist, and each has a defined purpose in helping web developers.

Here is this variable's family tree and some issues it can encounter:

Relatives:

> Source code library

> Component toolkit

Considerations:

> Potential for code redundancy

> Standardized implementations

> Cross-language enhancement

Practical solutions

Whether you're using a CSS or JavaScript framework, one of the most troubling things you must deal with is the amount of code that gets thrown into the layout; as it's much more than hand coding would require. Frequently, the use of JavaScript frameworks, in particular, tries to reinforce that code is agile and that it degrades gracefully, something hand coders may forget to do. However, the redundancy that can occur from features that aren't used (but are still included in the framework) can lead to severe bandwidth wastage.

In the case of JavaScript frameworks, the benefits outweigh the detriments, but it still pays to understand what you're using and to optimize what you have in order to be as succinct as possible. Some libraries of code can be 20K, 50K, or even more, and all of those bytes add up, even if they're being cached (which could add to a user's data bill or cap). The only solution is to determine if you can hand code a script to do the same job with less code. If the answer is yes, you'll want to consider hand coding, if you can ensure compatibility.

If you're a designer who's not comfortable with scripting, you are in luck. Frameworks come with a wide range of common tools, such as accordion scripts, drop-down menus, and animation effects, and they tend to undergo a great deal of testing before being put into the ever-increasing library of code. Although you want your implementation to be unique, frameworks often implement code in a way that retains the flexibility of customization, and matches that level of usefulness with an assured capability to ensure browser support.

Reference   jQuery is one of the most comprehensive frameworks going. If you take a look through its API reference, you'll see that jQuery and its UI brother can do some serious work. For a complete list of features and plug-ins, go to `http://docs.jquery.com/Main_Page`.

You'll need to check to see if your particular framework of choice adheres to best practices like non-obtrusive scripting and responsive design, or whether it's just a big, bundled mass of previously defined templates or code with certain effects. Frameworks can't do all of the hard work for you, but they can certainly make life easier and allow you to avoid some of the common bottlenecks and pitfalls JS can suffer. Frameworks are especially useful if you want a quick route into AJAX. Just ensure you know what the code does before using it!

Frameworks manage to integrate themselves into other languages like CSS, and they even attempt to resolve defects within certain browsers in regard to how code is rendered and supported. On the surface, frameworks may seem like an ideal solution to all of life's little woes. However, frameworks can be disabled, just as JavaScript can, which means that any good they might accomplish can be done away with in a matter of seconds. This limitation doesn't mean you should avoid frameworks, just don't think of them as a foolproof tool.

Frameworks can enable the use of HTML5 elements in old versions of Internet Explorer, and they can even give older browsers support for certain CSS3 features that would otherwise remain in the "give up" or "try again later" category. Because JavaScript can intercept and edit HTML and CSS, frameworks can exercise a lot of power over your interfaces. All of this is good; it lets you offer an alternative to broken standards and promises by vendors. But to be truly ubiquitous, account for how the site functions when JavaScript is disabled!

Best practices

> Determine if the JavaScript framework is worth the added bandwidth use.

> Remove all redundant code from CSS frameworks (if you utilize them).

> Check that your framework's core features are compatible across browsers.

> Never implement scripts submitted by others without vetting them for issues.

> Use scripting to supplement inadequate code support; also retain a fallback.

Services

Since the Web's inception, sites have demanded fairly similar features and components within their pages. With increasing services offering prebuilt stable solutions like forums, chat rooms, and social networking services (Figure 16-3), guaranteeing that your work will continue to function over time is difficult. As the tools you utilize are maintained by third-party operators who could update or abandon their own creations at any point, you need to be especially careful when implementing them, even if they're already widely used online.

Here is this variable's family tree and some issues it can encounter:

Relatives:

> Hosted applications

> Embedded services

Considerations:

> Long-term interconnectivity

> Server-side environment

> Migration and exportation

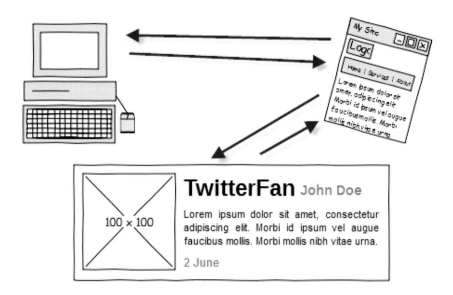

FIGURE 16-3: Prebuilt tools can be embedded in sites, but if they cease development, you're out of luck!

Practical solutions

Compatibility with third-party services requires considering the feasibility of embedding content from another site into your own. For example, if you embed a Twitter feed into your site, your layout needs the right amount of space to show what has been fetched by the site through the Twitter API. Although in ordinary situations, this issue shouldn't be a problem (because embedded content usually has standardized or flexible dimensions), you need to examine any of the API's restrictions to determine how and what you can display.

To be sure you're compatible with a third-party service (and aren't violating any of its license terms), read the developer's documentation before trying to embed a service into your site. Also, look at the site's history. If your research shows issues with malicious code getting through and search engines or antivirus products spot this (when you embed the service), your site could get blacklisted. The ability to embed content within a site is like a direct debit; you're placing a great deal of trust in the organization not to rob or hijack you.

Take the time to ponder what can occur with a connection between a service and your site, and don't be afraid to avoid embedding that service's tools if you feel uncomfortable.

If you host a service that someone else has developed (such as analytics software or forums), also take into account your hosting provider's limitations and whether it is capable of running the functionality or feature set you want to install on it. Not all hosting providers are born equal, and shared-hosting accounts in particular can have a lot of limitations built in.

Tip   If you're hosted on a Windows server, you may have a different range of server-side languages or database formats available than a Mac or Linux provider has. In addition, some hosts may not support certain languages like Ruby and Python. If you plan on making use of certain languages, ensure that your host supports what you require.

Compatibility between software products and a hosting provider can be problematic; in some cases, your host may only allow you to install or use services that have been pre-vetted (such as popular CMS products), known as quick installs. Check with your host to determine if any installation limitations exist and how they will affect your ability to install custom software tools. Limitations may mean that the site fails to function or the third-party product will collapse. Also, check to be sure your host supports the language or database you want to use.

No site or service lasts forever. Because services drop in popularity or go offline, your site must move with the times and not tie itself to the demands of a badly aging API or client (in the case of software). If a service you're connecting with goes offline, consider what will happen to that part of your site, and do you have a fallback? In addition, occasionally sites will experience downtime (or in Twitter's case, some more than others), so being able to handle temporary breakages between your site and a service becomes mission critical.

To preserve compatibility with the third-party services that house your data and connect it to your site from their network, make sure the feature you embed to connect the two has a legitimate fallback (even if it's just a link to a page). This fallback could be a helpful status message or something like a backup or mirror of the last recorded message (to put up as a placeholder). In addition, confirm that any service you use can export data, not just for the sake of having a sensible fallback, but also as a safety net in case their service closes down.

Best practices

> Read the manual to ensure that your implementation will work correctly.

> Beware of the potential for exploitation with third parties hosting your site.

> Check your host for limitations and support for packages you want to use.

> Remember to get a hosting package that meets the demands of your users.

> Services can (and do) disappear; maintain regular backups of hosted data.

Deliberations About Design

Planning architecture, content, layout, and iteration

PROVIDING A STABLE layout that meets the ever-growing, feature-rich demands of users, their devices, and browsers (while keeping compatibility in mind) is something many designers worry about. Because technologies evolve and sites increasingly need to provide user-centered experiences, visitors come to expect more from the layouts you offer. In this chapter, you'll see a few variables that can affect how your work ages over time. Although such variables won't make or break a site in a literal sense, the need to evolve remains.

The Art of Aging Gracefully

Designers are often surprised when I include a site's design in the future-proofing equation. Though the average design can last a lifetime and remain fairly usable, you shouldn't just stop improving your site because it currently looks okay and functions well enough. In the average site's lifespan, designs tend to and should be frequently improved, iterated upon, or refreshed over time. A number of justifiable reasons for this exist, including giving users a reason to keep returning, and to cope with any new demands of the tools we use to browse the Web.

Of course, modern standards and conventions for Web layouts are so much more advanced than they were in the 1990s. Those earlier layouts were often poorly coded and designed and you would be forgiven for cringing at how primitive, static, and unusable many of them were. Today's designers are in a better position to offer longer-term solutions than those from the "era of experimentation," partly because of the availability of better tools and agile frameworks, and also because of the focus designers now place upon usability.

Tip

Although it's not a necessity, following design trends and conventions can help reduce any barriers to entry for users. If a visitor recognizes objects on a page, they'll find it easier to locate important content. That said, don't be afraid to put a unique spin on any navigation system or tool you provide. Following trends doesn't mean don't innovate!

As the Web continues to evolve, increasing numbers of devices, hardware, software, and users are demanding access to your sites and services. In addition, the code you use and the standards you follow will be updated continually with useful and capable technologies. If you were to design a site only once, with no further changes, you'll still have to spend your days patching your site to ensure it continues to survive over time. If you're building a site to represent you, commit to a maintenance plan to achieve usability in the long term.

Whether it's your site's information architecture (the way you organize pages), content, or layout, you'll always need to make improvements. Perhaps you can remove features that have become redundant. Perhaps you can update your design to match the conventions users frequently expect to find while browsing the Web. Perhaps your audience has changed, as has their expectations of your service. Such considerations ultimately allow you to meet the long-term needs of an audience, which if you own or maintain sites, becomes critical.

Reviewing a design's previous versions lets you pinpoint areas that need improvement and address code that has become deprecated or outdated or that no longer matches an intended audience's needs. If you remain open to the possibility of redesigning or refining a layout, you may be motivated to do some research and reassess your audience, their requirements, and what you can do to keep them interested in your goods and services. Communication is critical in the future-proofing process, so don't be afraid to ask visitors for feedback.

Iteration and improvements

Consider a visitor who has been loyal to your brand for a number of years. She has become accustomed to your site's interface and features, and upon hearing that you're giving the site an overhaul, she's both excited and nervous about whether changes in content will match her individual tastes. As the updated site is launched, the user enters the site and sees plenty of objects in a familiar place (such as the logo and navigation system), but other parts of the site are dramatically changed. She pokes around the menus to see where her favorite tool resides, only to find that a feature she'd used regularly has been removed, with no alternative offered.

In this instance, you fail to research your audience correctly (or at all) and other visitors (like this one) begin to post complaints in the feedback form, asking for the features they know and love to return. Unfortunately, this isn't exactly an isolated incident. Sites all over the Web redesign without gaining appropriate feedback. If one of your competitors offers functionality that you fail to provide, your users may move to the competitor's site. When redesigning your site, remember the loyalty you have earned from your users.

Understanding when to alter or invoke a site's maintenance plan is as critical in design as the work itself. If users are forced to keep adapting to demanding changes in an environment, they may become impatient and look for an alternative that isn't changing its layout so frequently. Designers are often the guiltiest party in this regard because our aim is to give users the best experience possible. But we often overlook the benefits and utility of what's already working and produce throwaway reproductions instead. Users will thrive on what they can recognize.

Architecture

A site's *architecture* is comprised of the pages that interlink. Each site will contain links that connect internal pages to each other, hopefully in an organized and constructive manner. If optimized, visitors should be able to navigate with care and reach their final destination within just a few clicks. This architecture variable is usually based on offering consistency to aid the usefulness of content and uses the organization conventions often found within site maps, navigation menus, drop downs, or other link-oriented systems (Figure 17-1).

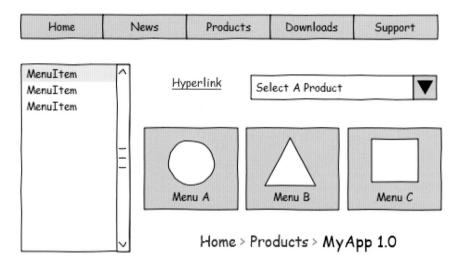

FIGURE 17-1: The architecture of a site depends on your ability to link pages together logically.

Here is this design feature's family tree and some issues it can encounter:

Relatives:

> Navigation menus

> Form redirection

> Site maps and indexes

> In-page shortcuts

Considerations:

> Self-contained layouts

> Human-readable site maps

> Navigation formatting

Practical solutions

One of the most popular design conventions today is the one-page layout. Often used in portfolios and online brochures, this layout provides a range of unique options for space utilization and for reducing the need for page refreshes. When examining the architecture of these sites, one thing becomes strikingly clear: As innovative as their interfaces may be, one-page layouts can still experience issues in ensuring that users find the content they're looking for, such as the use of navigation menus that fail to work if JS is disabled.

Navigation on any kind of site depends on clarity and accuracy. In addition to providing a link that is accurately referenced and labeled, be sure that users can actually tell what the links are and where they are. In an effort to improve your site's aesthetics, you may change font colors, remove underlines, change cursors, and more. But, for links to be compatible on a range of platforms, they must be identifiable (so be careful which styles you do alter) and clickable, thus they must function as expected. Otherwise, users will struggle to see content.

If there's ever a competition to find the most important and frequently used feature of any site (except content), the navigation menu will likely be the winner. However, because you have so many options regarding how to present your pages, compatibility issues can occur easily. You can do a number of things to avoid these issues, such as reducing the number of objects in each menu list, or categorizing menu items based on its relevancy. However, knowing which navigation menu type is appropriate or safe to use is extremely helpful too!

Note

Simple things can hurt a user in terms of menu compatibility. For example, powering menus with Flash is a big no-no if you want to ensure ubiquitous browsing; the same goes for using unlabeled icon menus (which can be confusing if images are disabled).

Now, I'd like to deal with disclosing navigation systems such as drop-down and breakout menus. The main concern with these is with touch devices, which may have significant problems utilizing hover events, so you need to substitute any mouseover events with an appropriate fallback that opens when users click a link, and that fades with a delay if they click outside of the menu. In cases where a drop-down menu is static, ensure that each link's click region is large enough accommodate touching and clicking on small screen devices.

When you future-proof your site, you also must consider the method you use to reference the pages of your site collectively. Most designers will already be aware of the importance of a file called a *site map* (an index of your pages that search engines can use to catch all of the important pages). One thing that very few people tend to do, however, is actually try to take the functionality of a site map and make it into something that humans can read, identify page relationships, and navigate (allowing people to find what they want faster).

To overcome this issue, the best practice is to have both an XML site map (to keep robots happy) and an HTML site map (to keep humans happy). While it could be argued that you really need only one or the other, having a specially customized human-readable version ensures that no document is left orphaned and users who cannot find what they're looking for have a universal signpost. If users are browsing on a device with limited interaction potential, a human site map allows scrolling a list of pages without typing search terms.

Best practices

> Links should look and behave differently to content that isn't actionable.

> If the links use a pseudo protocol such as `mailto`, inform users in the page.

> Offer XML site maps for search engines needing a speedy list of your links.

> Also provide an HTML alternative site map for humans needing direction.

> Make navigation menus degrade to match the device's core capabilities.

Content

If there's one feature your sites cannot do without, it's content. Content comes in all shapes and sizes (from text to images, audio to video; see Figure 17-2), and it must be designed so that visitors can consume it all. Content, on its own, has few requirements if supported by an appropriate structure and style, and embedded content (such as images and media) will function if it's implemented correctly. Consider the ways you can fetch and offer content, as it can suffer compatibility and readability issues based on the environment it's used in.

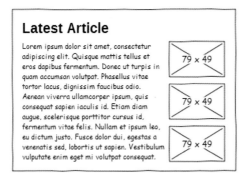

FIGURE 17-2: Content comes in all shapes and sizes, with images and text being the most common.

Here is this design feature's family tree and some issues it can encounter:

Relatives:

> Textual content

> Embedded images

> Audio and video

Considerations:

> Refreshing versus fetching

> Multipage breakdowns

> The format situation

Practical solutions

One major consideration in terms of content compatibility is the method you use to display it on-screen. Using tools like AJAX, you can omit the need to refresh a page and swap out content within your pages without thinking twice. However, as I'm sure you're aware, JavaScript isn't a sure thing, and with an unhealthy dependency on these technologies, you may find it challenging to ensure that even the fussiest of visitors can access content when the content is served dynamically rather than statically (as each page is downloaded).

If you choose to use AJAX as a method of swapping out content on demand, begin by providing users with a static, multipage, working site with no reliance upon scripting. If AJAX and scripting are available, simply override the link's behavior and have everything fetched from those separate pages (or database), as they're needed. This approach is the same as you use for form validation, and it's a time-honored fallback that users will find reassuring as it gives JavaScript-free browsers and users a chance to navigate your site.

The amount of content you include within a web site's pages is also a factor worthy of consideration. Many sites manage to control the level of content that users are exposed to in order to prevent information overload. Loading megabytes of text into a browser can result in all sorts of problems for devices that just aren't equipped to handle features such as smooth scrolling, and it will certainly affect keyboard users who'll need to press the Tab key incessantly, or those with slow connections (or restrictive and costly data allowances).

Reference For a complete guide to the various levels of support Web browsers have for specific formats (such as images and videos) and plug-in capabilities, check out the following Wikipedia article: `http://en.wikipedia.org/wiki/Comparison_of_web_browsers`.

The main way to solve this content navigation issue is to divide content into logical page sections (as occurs in WML decks) and show each block of content on a separate page or at a different point in time (many sites provide page numbers or other indicators, such as image galleries using lightboxes and thumbnails). Also, take into account that while some visitors will appreciate such a friendly approach, others with more capable devices and connections may want to avoid excessive clicking. Therefore, try to offer an "all in one page" option or a complete PDF copy for download in addition to the logical structuring.

Finally, consider different file formats and how well they're supported on the Web. Being able to embed an image in your site is all well and good, but if your users' browsers can't read the format, or if it's in an obscure format, which they neither have a program that can open it, nor any idea of what it does, they have no reason to download it! Although you can utilize some standardized formats, new ones are appearing regularly, and depending on the device a visitor uses, you may find the compatibility list for file formats rather restricted.

To maximize compatibility, only use formats supported by major browsers, such as JPEG, GIF, and PNG. Internet Explorer prior to 9.0 will have issues with alpha transparency in PNG files (9.0 itself isn't perfect), some handheld devices cannot cope with animated GIF files, and WML-only devices will likely just support WBMP (a monochrome format) or PNG if you're lucky. Avoid JPEG2000, APNG, TIFF, XBM, and BMP, though, because while they have limited support on individual browsers, all the others will ignore them.

Best practices

> Use JavaScript to override multipage, static layouts via AJAX functionality.

> Offer compiled and split copies of lengthy content to improve performance.

> Load individual files within image galleries only as thumbnails are clicked.

> Check that your images are in a Web-friendly, browser-supported format.

> If you have an exceptionally long document, consider using PDF instead.

Layout

Your design will underpin how a visitor sees and responds to your work. While layouts can vary greatly, many of them will share certain similarities (Figure 17-3). Picking the right number of columns, the right width and height for objects, and the right color scheme can affect a wide variety of variables. Help your users by lowering the learning curve and aim for as few barriers to entry as possible. Because each design you build should be unique, the level to which your work may degrade (as consumer use evolves) could differ greatly.

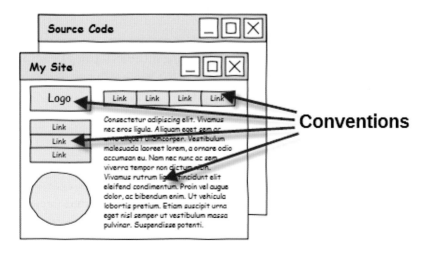

FIGURE 17-3: Each layout will follow and set conventions like the logo or navigation menu's position.

Here is this design feature's family tree and some issues it can encounter:

Relatives: **Considerations:**

> Conventions   > Cutting or bleeding edge

> Trends   > Web application UIs

> Patterns   > Unconventional layouts

Practical solutions

Chances are that at some point in time, you've wanted to put convention aside and use all the latest technology and tools to create a site so unique and interesting it'll blow your visitors minds. Unfortunately, one of the many things that hold you back is that compatibility with untested and untried techniques can be a real pain (to guarantee support). Although issues that cause sites to break in a browser can be worked around, getting these implementations to look or work as expected within various situations takes time, effort, and dedication.

To make your layouts work as effectively as possible, try several different versions of an implementation. In some situations, you might get away with just throwing something new into a layout, but providing substantial alterations to an interface or its functionality could annoy or confuse users that, in turn, could encourage them to seek out your competitors. If what you're doing can improve an existing situation (or help elevate issues on your site), go for it. But if the upgrade you build doesn't improve things, reconsider implementing it.

While traditional layouts are often associated with common conventions, visitors who visit on a specific platform will come to expect a different experience on others, based upon the environment they browse within. Each platform will have its own interface guidelines and recommendations built upon years of testing and usability tests, so it pays to examine these documents to see how you can give users a more natural browsing experience (rather than potentially making visitors feel like they've suddenly crash-landed on an alien planet).

Reference A couple of the resources listed on the following web page no longer work, but the ones that do work are exceptionally useful (and very comprehensive). These UI guidelines can help Web apps feel like they run natively (like a compiled app) by following device conventions: `http://www.mobilexweb.com/blog/ui-guidelines-mobile-tablet-design`.

Although Web apps don't require you to cater your work to a specific platform (unlike compiled apps), users will appreciate the effort. Whether the app is designed to work on desktops, or a handheld platform like iOS or Android, you should help the device offer the experience and visual theme that will match their expectations and requirements. In the case of traditional websites (rather than apps), or any device you can't or won't support (by way of a customized layout), offer a stable, flexibly designed default theme instead.

Unconventional layouts exist all over the Web, and this fabric of weird and wonderful designs increases our enjoyment of an online experience. However, there will always be people who go over the top and end up inhibiting the usability of a design, just for the sake of doing something different (which could anger users). Compatibility in design is about more than ensuring a site works on a series of platforms and with a series of variables; you need to consider the effect that unrecognizable layout conventions may have on visitors.

If you're using an unconventional layout (or a conventional one with some unconventional features), it's very important to undertake usability testing. By learning how real visitors interact with sites on the devices they own, and gaining empathy for the many variables they have to deal with themselves, you can gain an understanding of just how your site could appear or work for them. While you can spend time ensuring your layout works in emulators or browsers, ultimately it's your users who'll experience (or suffer) the results.

Best practices

> Investigate different ways to design a feature before sticking with one.

> Provide a global theme for app interfaces that aren't device oriented.

> Consider targeted designs if you want to offer a seamless experience.

> Good designs are invisible; try to make yours as efficient as possible.

> Conduct regular usability tests to avoid variable-based design pitfalls.

Iteration

Building a stable foundation is important for a site, but keeping up the good work is critical to its long-term success. As time goes by, sites naturally erode because of changes in users' expectations and requirements. Over a longer period, as web technologies and standards improve, older methodologies will become redundant, older tools will lose support, and web designers will have to catch up. Iteration (Figure 17-4) is the primary method used to ensure code withstands the test of time, but maintenance itself isn't an issue-free pursuit.

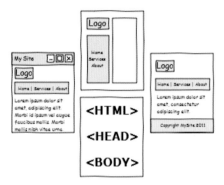

FIGURE 17-4: Iteration is a long-term process of continual improvement to overcome new obstacles.

Here is this design feature's family tree and some issues it can encounter:

Relatives:	**Considerations:**
> Major upgrades	> Legacy feature support
> Total reboots	> Uncovered bugs or issues
> Minor updates	> Reduction of usability

Practical solutions

Iteration gives designers the opportunity to seek out and remove any redundant or outdated functionality within sites you maintain (which is good for users and their bandwidth caps), but be careful about what you do choose to replace or remove. Although you may find that a particular navigation system is inferior to the updated rival you provide, some users may prefer to use what they know and love. An example of this is the BBC's iPlayer service: It removed its A-Z listing and then reintroduced it after scores of complaints.

Making the decision to improve a site by removing features that are no longer useful (or used) makes sense, but doing so could also cause a few upsets along the way, which may lead to visitors complaining. For every 100 users who are happy that you removed some obsolete feature, there'll often be a couple that want to stick with what they know and depend on it. If the old system has too few users to support it, remove it and make room for better tools, but if you don't have a good reason, keep the old stuff running.

Bugs on your sites and services are just as much of a pest in the digital world as they are in the natural world. When compatibility breaks down and a site cannot work in a particular situation or environment, it's your job to run around with a replacement part or some duct tape, patching things up and helping the site survive for as long as possible until a more permanent fix (or redesign) is provided. Regarding development: Nothing will ever be free of bugs because when complexity increases, unforeseen issues become more common.

Tip

Before trying to resolve issues in a site, check to see if other people have come up with some practical solutions for the problem. Of course, you shouldn't steal their ideas, but you may find that others have come up with a methodology you haven't considered.

Tools like responsive design can help you make your work more durable so that quirks are less likely to occur, but there'll always be a few situations that can act as the proverbial "straw that broke the camel's back." To help resolve errors more effectively, do usability testing at all levels of the build process and consider releasing your site or app in beta form so that your entire user base can try out the new look and give feedback. In addition, give users a place to report bugs (be it an e-mail form, forum, or some bug-tracking software).

Imagine that you build a totally new layout with a unique way of showing content and few recognizable objects from within the old scheme remain (so what you've produced has no resemblance to what stood before it). The layout and redesign may look nice, but does it actually help your users or improve upon what existed beforehand? Total redesigns can be fun, but they force you to retest everything you've produced as if it were a different site, which probably means you'll be checking against all of the book variables from scratch.

Redesigning isn't always the best solution. If you iterate and use the existing structure that you know works for a wide range of people, the impact of minor changes over time will be minimal (and the impact on HCI will be reduced), as will the shock to the user's system. Starting from scratch demands that your visitors learn how to use the interface again, and if you keep redesigning every few months (or less), users could struggle to adapt more frequently. When you redesign a site, consider providing tutorials to aid the transition.

Best practices

> Ensure that your visitors are happy with the removal of legacy functionality.

> Only update a component if your visitors agree it improves a situation.

> Let visitors notify you of any bugs or problems they encounter on your site.

> Avoid complete redesigns if iterations will work (to reduce learning curves).

> Use recognizable conventions to help users become familiar with your site.

Fun with Futuristic Features

Using visual effects, interactivity, and personalization

AS STANDARDS EVOLVE, new languages and the potential for new technologies become available in our sites. As a designer, you can use these tools to build fresh, exciting layouts. Also, as new frameworks appear, you gain access to functionality that otherwise might have been too time consuming to code by hand. Even with these benefits at your disposal, you must be aware of the upcoming technologies that potentially could be used seamlessly within your sites. This chapter discusses a few of these useful innovations.

The Tools of Tomorrow

As innovative and unique pieces of functionality present themselves (which could prove useful to our users), compatibility can become a bit of a chore. Nevertheless, with each new technology that arrives, awaiting our implementation and adoption, you gain new opportunities to create better-designed layouts filled with ever-immersive functionality. When the opportunity arrives to use such technologies and features, then certainly do your best to achieve this goal. Just ensure that whatever you do provide degrades well.

In this age of 3D cinema and interactive layouts, you are provided with opportunities to create simple flourishes that can charge your designs with emotion and depth unlike ever before. Subtle uses of animation and parallax effects can turn simple actions like scrolling or reading a page into creative features that users appreciate. Additionally, server-side scripting has revolutionized our perceptions of static pages and encouraged turning them into innovative mediums that are tweaked to users' needs, preferences, and environments.

Note   Numerous mobile apps allow you to change traditional 2D photographs into realistic 3D images (stereoscopic vision). As a result, the adoption of 3D-capable cameras is higher than many statistics may indicate (especially on the smartphone market). The results of these post-processing 3D effects can be seen on 3D TVs, laptops, and with 3D glasses.

High definition (HD) media is taking the Web by storm, and being able to view very high-quality content in a site is an exciting prospect. Three-dimensional (3D) media can utilize existing image and media formats, and because it has few barriers to entry, 3D media is moving closer to mainstream adoption online. Finally, you have virtual reality (VR). Although it has a slew of different languages and software trying to become the standard, VR does offer the 1980s vision of living in a *Tron* world, and has the potential to be popular.

As consumers adopt the latest, greatest technologies (like 3D), you can think about using it within your sites to provide a richer experience. High-definition equipment is affordable and many screens are already capable of viewing it. 3D may not be ubiquitous and requires use of special 3D glasses, but implementing the technology and the necessary fallbacks for both 3D and HD are achievable. As for virtual reality, the languages and software both exist and work, and projects like SecondLife are already taking advantage of this concept.

Using server-side scripting to make a layout visually unique isn't new (user profiles have existed for many years). However, designing your sites so that they can "flex" to match what your visitors use, how they use it, and what they want to see (or not see) could well shape how you handle compatibility in the future. As a designer, you spend a lot of time trying to assess what is important to individuals, so why not let them be the critics? You already have the technologies needed to craft behavior-rich interfaces; it's just a matter of being willing to take advantage of the technologies on both the client and server side.

Experimenting with 3D

Putting futuristic features like 3D into practice can have dramatic effects upon your users. Consider a visitor who has an up-to-date computer with a quality browser, who'll be an ideal candidate for the latest and greatest technologies. In this case, he has a high-quality Internet connection and a laptop computer with some horsepower behind it. This user enters your site and notices that you offer 3D versions of images in a photo gallery. Because he has a pair of disposable 3D glasses lying around, he selects the "View in 3D" option you provide, and reaps the benefits immediately. I'm not talking about science fiction; this is achievable right now!

Issues relating to compatibility with technologies like HD and 3D are closely linked to the capabilities of the device being used. If someone like your visitor has the glasses needed to view the images or media, it makes sense to offer such a unique experience. After all, many sites are currently experimenting with different forms of 3D to give an interface added depth. One problem that could arise might be if one of your visitor's friends gets a link to your site and finds that she doesn't have the tools she needs to view the stereoscopic 3D successfully.

Not everyone will receive the benefits of high definition video (just ask a lot of cellphone users coping with tiny screens), and it's certainly apparent that not everyone will have a pair of 3D glasses handy. However, the potential for using such technologies may justify offering them along with numerous other options. It's better to stay ahead of the curve, as new technologies such as 3D and HD are likely to be adopted by mainstream users in the future. Just be wary of how these technologies can affect less-capable users, and provide a fallback implementation.

Visual Effects

With new, exciting technologies being implemented into your entertainment devices, game consoles, and more, a range of attractive, functional visual effects have made their mark on websites (see Figure 18-1). This includes high-definition video (which can absorb loads of bandwidth), 3D imagery (as seen the movie *Avatar*), and the 1980s fad, *Virtual Reality* (that made everyone think they'd end up living online). As it stands, the technology behind each of these tools exists, the equipment exists, and they've seen some Internet support.

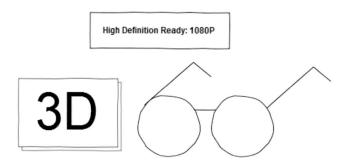

FIGURE 18-1: HD, 3D, and virtual reality exist; it's just up to you to decide whether to support them.

Here is this design feature's family tree and some issues it can encounter:

Relatives:

> High-definition (HD)

> Stereoscopic 3D

> Virtual reality (VR)

Considerations:

> Quality capability handling

> Overproduction engagement

> Technology sustainability

Practical solutions

When you consider using non-ubiquitous visual effects, first analyze how you can safely implement HD, 3D, or VR without creating errors for users. Remember some devices, for example, aren't capable of handling HD or 3D. The problems may in part be because of the age of the hardware in the user's device, or (in the case of 3D and VR) the need for additional hardware such as 3D glasses for users to see the effect. If you do utilize these technologies, fallbacks will therefore be required (such as low-definition media files and 2D imagery).

With high-definition video, sites like YouTube let users choose which video quality setting (such as 1080p) best meets their screen capabilities, so you should consider this. You could also provide a range of video sizes (set to different resolutions) so that visitors with small screens can avoid the overhead of downscaling larger-sized media (the same can be said for images). With 3D, however, the best approach is to offer two copies of the same image (one in 2D and one in 3D) and to let users select the one they want to use. With 3D, the default format for users should be 2D as it's the preferred method of viewing images.

Virtual reality environments can experience an issue that could well be deemed as *over-production*. Virtual Reality Modeling Language (VRML) and its successor X3D have made their mark in the engineering sector, but as far as the Web goes, it's never reached too far beyond the niche, enthusiast market. This is partly because it was used as a cheap gimmick in the past, and more often than not, the time and production effort it takes to produce a virtual world goes far and beyond the rather speedy delivery of a normal site.

Note   Some visitors (such as the visually impaired) may be unable to watch 3D images and others may experience side effects such as headaches when trying to watch them. So, don't just depend on the technology, but instead also offer an accessible 2D alternative.

If your site could benefit from virtual reality code, then by all means go ahead and use the formats that exist; you'll need to ask your visitors to install the extensions they'll require for the world to render from within the browser that supports such a plug-in. However, just like with Flash-based sites, you'll need to maintain a regular HTML-based site as the those users lacking the extensions required may still want to pay a visit to your site. If you do consider building the environment just to accommodate a few users, consider the value of doing so.

High-definition video, virtual reality, and 3D have been around for a long time, and they have all evolved over many iterations, with each step making them more realistic. As a result, people have become excited by these technologies and have begun to adopt them in various situations. Remember that as a new version of 3D or HD or VR becomes available, whether a language or format, you'll need to provide a compatible interface in order for your site to implement these cool innovations and your users to see the wonderful effects.

Because many of these technologies are evolving rapidly, it may be difficult to determine what is best for your site. Different brands of 3D-capable televisions may require different glasses and different formats for images and media files. For example, a stereoscopic red and blue pair of 3D glasses won't work on many televisions. As HD- and 3D-capable TVs enter the living room, web usage and ubiquity will increase. Avoid missing out on the fun by determining how useful they might be, based on the type of site that's being designed.

Best practices

> Always offer the 2D, standard definition, non-virtual page as the default.

> Let visitors choose the environment they want to use to view your site.

> Avoid going over the top by trying to use every existing technology.

> Offer support for different formats and implementations of a technology.

> There are a number of different VR formats; consider supporting several.

Interoperability

Being able to produce reactive sites (those redesigning themselves around the needs of the user, as shown in Figure 18-2) could have huge implications regarding how you can tackle the issue of being less generic. It's already being used, to a certain extent, by scripts that simulate missing browser features. Considering the potential of catering layouts to capable devices and functionality to capable tools allows us to better serve a widening and diverse range of users. As a result, it could potentially make interfaces work more seamlessly.

Here is this design feature's family tree and some issues it can encounter:

Relatives:

> Layout engineering

> Situational design

Considerations:

> Needs-based implementation

> Testing workflow increases

> Device-based limitations

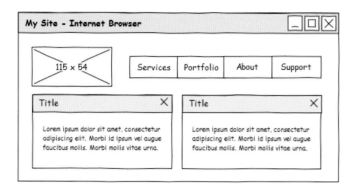

FIGURE 18-2: Reactive design is about tackling layout or variable issues before users see the page.

Practical solutions

When you use server-side and client-side scripting to make your layouts equip themselves to each individual user's situation, you must consider the added development time it'll take to account for each variable and circumstances (in preference to just offering a static site). Whether you want to use feature detection or a drag-and-drop layout that can automate some of the user's preferences while remaining customizable, you'll require extra coding, extra time, and need the required knowledge to achieve such a technical implementation.

When dealing with compatibility, you'll need to ensure that implementing something more interactive is in your user's best interest, as the added work involved may not always be cost effective, such as if you don't have a technologically diverse audience, or if you only have a small number of users to deal with. If you go down such a route, consider if an existing solution such as a CMS may offer the flexibility you require. If not, then you may want to begin by devising a framework that accounts for each variable you wish to target.

If you want to create a truly reactive layout that will flex to both the user's environment and the variables at work in their situation, you'll want to first identify the issue; next come up with a solution; and then finally go on to construct an implementation. An example of this could include the problem of IE6's lack of support for the CSS3 target pseudo selector, the solution being a way to emulate the effect that otherwise occurs naturally within CSS, and the implementation being the utilization of JavaScript's `location.hash` feature to detect the hash and activate the CSS!

Tip

Many content management systems (CMS) already offer tools that can automatically help users with their experiences. From scripting support for missing browser features to automatically formatting a layout for handheld devices, it all makes a difference to users. For example, WordPress can reformat its default layout to be mobile friendly.

Another example: Consider something like a "related articles" script; these clever, simple features, found in most blogs, expose other content within the site that matches keywords in the main body of the text on a given page. This is achieved using server-side scripting. To ensure the script works correctly and remains usable, implement each feature you want gradually and iteratively, getting feedback and bug reports from users. By removing issues from one section before working on the next, you reduce the chances of post-fix conflicts.

Although you can produce highly customizable layouts, you may find that some features are found only in certain devices and so fall into the category of non-essential secondary features. For example, sometimes it may not be productive to allow users to drag and drop a whole bunch of widgets around their screen (such as if they're browsing on a tiny screen with just a key-based input). When it becomes inappropriate for devices to take advantage of these assistive features, the interface should just do what's in the user's best interests.

Some devices support location awareness (GPS or RFID) or gesture support. The former feature could allow you to offer a geographically focused version of the site. The latter would allow you to create interfaces that can utilize simple movements (useful on touch screens). Ensure that your site asks users without localization awareness on their devices which version they'd prefer to use. Also consider users lacking gesture support on their devices, and offer links, buttons, and clickable regions that can carry out the same action.

Best practices

> Only implement automated features that users will be willing to accept.

> Determine the cost-effectiveness of automated fixes before building them.

> Engineer your layouts so that they work equally well in various situations.

> Always allow visitors to revert or undo an action made on their behalf.

> Don't remove a user's ability to make decisions over their choice of layout.

Personalization

Personalization makes it easier for a user to remain in control, as they can make decisions and set preferences over their experience. In addition, customizing an experience (Figure 18-3) allows you to memorize and carry user preferences forward as they browse on any other devices they own (or login on public machines). Sometimes, client-side scripting can help you avoid the need for logins, and other times you'll need to use server-side sessions to make the layout portable. The technology has a high ubiquity rate in CMSs, scripts, and online services, even though privacy issues over user data storage will be a future concern.

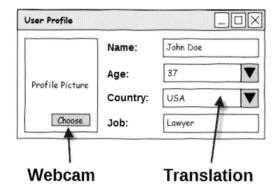

FIGURE 18-3: Many sites offer profiles; this level of customization is a classic sign of experience control.

Here is this design feature's family tree and some issues it can encounter:

Relatives:

> Cookie data

> Session IDs

> Local storage

Considerations:

> Portability and availability

> Accidental destruction

> Multi-user environments

Practical solutions

Customizing and personalizing sites are a vital part of your job as a designer. Because many people use the Web on the move, being able to pick up where they left off is very important. You also need to design your sites to be portable because users will not always remain in the same environment. For example, they may step away from their computer and continue browsing with their cellphone or another portable device, or alternatively, they may simply return to the computer they used previously, later on during the day.

To ensure a site remains portable and usable for the widest range of situations, you should first eliminate cookies and their kin from the equation. Files like cookies and local storage might help a user save and restore a session's data without having to authorize themselves with a user account, but with the privacy implications on shared devices and that the data is bound by the machine in which it's stored, the ability to synchronize a user's progress will be interrupted. It's therefore rather impractical for portability and longevity applications.

Another downside to cookies is that they can be accidentally or deliberately destroyed. If users clear their entire browsing history, the effort that went into building that cookie file will evaporate. When empowering your visitors to customize a layout, temporary storage is unlikely to be as useful to your users as solutions that can be associated with an identity and exported to whatever device they choose to use. However, local storage and cookies would be an appropriate choice for temporary session data, such as a progress meter.

Note

Cookies and offline storage can be an even bigger problem than you might initially expect. Because offline, local storage is a feature of HTML5, legacy browsers and devices won't support it. Browsers can also prevent cookies from being saved at all.

To design your site so that users can carry their experience with them, provide some tools such as member accounts, which use a database to store layout preferences for a visitor. Offer the ability to sign up as a voluntary feature, not a requirement, and allow users to keep a backup of their data. You might find that increasing the general portability of your site's experience will make users feel more comfortable, wherever they are. A benefit of server-side accounts (such as those used by Google) is that they are harder to accidentally erase.

Be careful when targeting customizable features at a particular individual because he or she might own several devices that use the same account. You will need to apply some best practices to server-side profiles to help ensure that visitors can pre-set and share preferences between devices (consider building functionality like Apple's authorization of devices in iTunes). Additionally, it might be helpful to notify users if they're logged into multiple places at once, and allow the quitting or timeout of sessions to avoid conflicts.

No two users are alike, and situations may occur where several people use the same device (like family-owned and shared computers). This has the potential to create privacy security risks for each user and it makes personalizing for individuals difficult. Each site that allows customization must let users sign out of their accounts; it also must allow them to protect their preferences with passwords, and must not restrict users to one account per machine. Consider how voting tools that track by IP unfairly block connection sharers from voting!

Best practices

> Only use cookies for unimportant preferences or device-explicit data.

> Use server-side sessions to remember a user's progress during a visit.

> Ensure that any user account services you provide remain voluntary.

> Remember that multiple users could have access to the same machine.

> Consider allowing users to set up unique profiles for different devices.

Dealing with the Robot Army

Considering search engines, social networks, verification, and more

ROBOTS, SCRIPTS, AND SPIDERS are important factors that determine how sites are discovered by users and will remain so in the future. This chapter helps you survive this ever-expanding group of non-human users that publicize your site via their own unique methodology. These fussy "individuals," which are less willing than your human users to compromise (often browsing with few features active), could determine your site's capability to become a success. Ultimately, these services and tools will play their part regarding how your site is used, so you must consider them as you design your site.

Of Machines and Men

To be future-proofed against the ever-changing tides of how users locate resources on the Web, your site needs the support of search engines and social networks. These robots work tirelessly day and night to keep your content indexed, spread your links to everyone with Internet access, and help your site receive the attention it deserves. Unlike many third-party functions packed within the walls of your source code, these services remain critical to your site's success and underpin the importance of fallbacks and a solid user experience.

Before there were so many pages on the Web, you primarily had to know an address in order to find a site. Obviously, if users weren't aware that the site even existed (no matter how useful it would be to them), it may as well not have. This quirk of fate is an important factor in the realization that your site's longevity remains not in your users' hands, or yours, but in the hands of third parties. While others burned out like a dying star, unused and glowing tragically as dead archives, successful sites were accessible to such tools.

Tip

Signing up on social networks and third-party services can increase activity on your site as it allows visitors to interact with any social, web-connected clients or apps installed upon their devices. Therefore, your site can become ingrained in their consciousness as they check their Twitter stream or check their RSS reader for updates you provide.

Visibility is at the heart of every successful site. If users can't find your site, your hard work is for nothing. Prior to Facebook and Google, directories that handpicked links to sites were popular. They provided fans of one site with cool discoveries that might be useful to them elsewhere online, and many sites continue this trend today. However, the birth of search engines like Google, the mighty giant that eclipsed them all, has turned the process of refining and helping users find sites and relevant content into an art form.

Although search engines like Google have remained strong through the years by reinventing their products as the Web has evolved, change is always on the horizon. Being compatible with search engines is as useful today as it was during the days of handpicked sites within META engines (which filtered results within the database). By being indexed by these digital detectives, your site has a greater chance to survive becoming an obsolete reference. Also, by offering active and frequently updated social-networking profiles with popular sites, you connect users to your brand, even when they aren't on your home page.

What goes on outside your site is as central to being responsive, flexible, and adaptive to users' needs and demands as the actual site is. Users expect to be able to follow brands for updates on Twitter, provide feedback via a Facebook group, and perhaps use a niche social network to help them bookmark your site easily. As you can imagine, these services have changed the landscape drastically, and, as a result, your site's durability will be measured by how well it keeps up with the Web's social trends, and how well your site uses them.

Visibility within Google

After launching your lovely new site onto the Web, one of the first visitors to check out what you've provided is the spider, which gets your site indexed for the first time. In this case, the spider is Googlebot, which is, of course, owned by the top-ranking search engine Google. Upon entering your home page it first goes to look at your source code to see what content exists on the page, and then by calculating the value of keywords used (and semantics you offer), it ranks you in its results accordingly.

The exact process the search engines undertake isn't known because they're highly guarded secrets to try to prevent people from gaming the system. However, it's generally accepted that spiders catalog and cache your sites and continue to play an important role in referrals. In this instance, the spider begins indexing your content; however, it immediately notices that your site is entirely built using Flash. This situation was common in the 1990s and somewhat today, and as search engines are limited to how far they can see into Flash files, indexing would likely be inhibited.

Luckily in this case, you realize that with the likes of iOS, not everyone has Flash installed and you follow the best practice of including a fallback. The spider sees this data all beautifully marked up in HTML, and it proceeds to use that information, plus any built-in semantics via microformats and metadata to add contextual value. Utilizing your site map and the `robots.txt` file, this spider is happy to browse through all of your pages. However, unlike a user, it pays little attention to visuals and only checks that code to detect keyword stuffing.

Search Engines

The great archivers of the Web, search engines and their robotic arms (generally referred to as *spiders*), navigate around your site's indexing content, categorizing it based on search terms that users frequently look up. While social networks are partially replacing the role of search engines by offering a more lively method of measuring trending popularity among sites, the classic search engine (Figure 19-1) remains a dominant force online. Spiders can read a range of file types, but content and context-rich material is what they favor the most.

FIGURE 19-1: Google remains the most popular search engine, and it also offers social networks too!

Here is this consumer's family tree and some issues it can encounter:

Relatives:

> Google

> Bing

> Yahoo!

> Baidu

> Ask

Considerations:

> Dynamic rank systems

> Regional fluctuations

> Webmaster aiding tools

Practical solutions

Making your site compatible with search engines isn't that difficult, but influencing them to give you a high ranking is another matter altogether. Trying to grab that elusive number-one spot in Google takes patience and the right mindset, not to mention that results can be affected by a site's location, language, and more. This book doesn't focus on SEO, but that doesn't mean we shouldn't highlight the importance of being ranked and how being listed in Google can affect your site's reach and its potential to survive against competitors.

When users try to find information in a search engine, they enter keywords that relate to what they're looking for. If your site appears in those results, it may receive visits. Search engines calculate rankings upon some top-secret variables, so you can't be 100% sure how the rankings are calculated. Nevertheless, as long as you have content for search engines to index, spiders will be willing to put the data to good use. To make a site more appropriate for indexing, avoid script-generated content, Flash files, or images with no alternative text.

Visibility in search engines is always a central goal in the web design process. Users rely on search engines to an incredible degree. So, if they can't find a site this way (in a purely theoretical sense, of course), to some users it's as though the site doesn't exist (sort of like the debate, "If a tree falls in a forest and no one is around to hear it, does it make a sound?"). One way to give your work a fair chance at being indexed is to use tools that direct spiders toward the pages that should or shouldn't be indexed; this is exactly what a site map does.

Reference Google offers some useful documentation detailing how to comply with its guidelines to improve a site's chances of being seen in search results. You can find details and its guide here: `www.google.com/support/webmasters/bin/answer.py?answer=35291`.

The most well-known files for making sites compatible with search engines are `robots.txt`, which restricts the indexing of certain pages, and `sitemap.xml`, which provides a complete index of the pages within your site (plenty of tutorials on how to make these files exist). You also can also request each search engine indexes your site (for free), which is a useful step to take with every site launch. Finally, if you're not already signed up, join and start using Google Webmaster Central, as it can help you manage a site and its Google listing.

Search engines can understand a great deal about a site and its purpose based on the URL, content, and technologies used in the site. Search engines also follow trends and measure popularity. This behavior helps search engines interpret users' interests and customize the search results, thereby personalizing them, which, in turn, can affect your site. By using a filter to narrow down the results, such as to just show pages written in English and made in the USA, a user can make all international content invisible, yours potentially included.

If you want your site to appeal to users in a certain country, you must find a way to get your site into its regional search results. For users whose language is other than English, provide your content in their language so that search engines can direct the content to the targeted users. Be sure that your content is written clearly and that it provides enough explanation to readers so they'll understand the purposes of your site and/or service. Oh, and to avoid getting banned, don't try anything sneaky or spammy like keyword stuffing!

Best practices

> Focus on the content's quality to ensure search engines "think" of you.

> Robots can't understand images and media; always use text alternatives.

> Use your content and features to direct the product to its audience.

> Never try to manipulate search engines; keep your pages organic.

> Take advantage of search-specific features such as `robots.txt` files.

Social Networks

Social networks such as Facebook and Twitter (Figure 19-2) offer a way to communicate with like-minded individuals. You can use social networks to expand the outreach of your site by providing updates of events occurring on your site. You also can also offer users a place to go in the event of your site going down because of a technical problem. Some social networks are more customizable than others, and some have stronger APIs for integration or extensibility. In terms of importance, though, they're way up there with search engines.

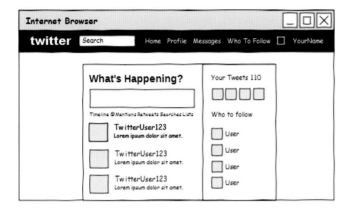

FIGURE 19-2: Social networks provide status updates, which can promote sites or influence users.

Here is this consumer's family tree and some issues it can encounter:

Relatives:	**Considerations:**
> Facebook	> General popularity ratio
> Twitter	> Integration possibilities
> Google+	> Niche service offerings
> LinkedIn	
> FlickR	

Practical solutions

Users increasingly expect that designers will adopt and regularly engage in social-networking activities. If your site isn't taking advantage of the latest online fad, you potentially risk inadvertently distancing your brand from users. Users have changed their use of the Web, and more than ever before, apps and tools connect to social networks, influencing when and how your site is accessed. For example, Twitter has software clients that can access streams, and if you let users know of updates to your site, activity may suddenly increase.

The main goal of the designer is to use whatever service is popular at any given time. Sites that still rely on MySpace and refuse to move to Facebook or Twitter, for example, won't be labeled as cool. Also, the features that users of these networks employ, such as the Like or Retweet buttons may not be able to work in your posts if the service suffers availability issues (like the Twitter fail whale), which in turn could cost you free marketing. It's this mutual dependency between you and third-party networks that's so dramatic and fragile.

Participating in social networking involves much more than simply having your site exist within the environment it provides (such as a Facebook wall). The quality of the content you provide must be of a high-enough quality to attract users to your site and to keep them coming back. The API-based functionality you embed within pages and connect to these social networks can help assure your site's compatibility outside its own domain. Even if some of these tools are more complex than others, users seem to enjoy social integration.

Reference   As a result of the social-networking revolution, a series of useful tools has appeared that offers the functionality you need to integrate your site with many different networks. These tools can help visitors easily bookmark the bits of your site they like. Two examples of this include AddThis, `http://www.addthis.com/`, and ShareThis, `http://sharethis.com/`.

Although users only need to read content to see Twitter streams, other social-networking sites have features that require more interaction; for example, users must click a button to submit a review for a site on StumbleUpon. For many sites, like Twitter, a user must have an account to *retweet* (share) other users' *tweets* (posts). These features add to an already-functioning interface, so the impact of such demands on users is minimal; they are free to do what they wish. However, supporting popular services is worth the effort for their users.

Beyond its popularity potential for integration into sites, social networking allows you to provide some niche features to an audience that will appreciate it. Although some sites, such as Facebook, provide ways to expand the reach of your content (such as answering customers' questions, giving details for events, and showing profiles), other sites exist for a central purpose, with other features built around that niche. For example, LinkedIn lets you build a visually standardized résumé that can easily be shared with potential employers.

To make the most of these services, investigate every nook and cranny of the features they provide, read the documentation such services offer, and then determine how you can go about bringing a bit of your site to the market that exists on these prepopulated gathering places. Sometimes, you'll be able to extend your site in only small ways; other times, you may find that they're major game-changers. What matters to users is that you're supporting the environments they want to connect with and that you're taking your site into the future.

Best practices

> Use the most popular networks, and deprecate those losing market share.

> Signing up for accounts is one thing, but you must use them regularly, too.

> Use social networks to supplement your sites, but don't force sign-ups.

> Consider using any social-networking tool that may benefit your visitors.

> Don't just stick to using a single social network; all have benefits.

Automated Tools

In addition to the search engines and social networks that comprise the majority of robotics on your site, other kinds of automated scripts and applications are available that can reach into your site and extend its functionality. Ranging from content reformatters to the more complex PayPal IPN scripts (Figure 19-3), these tools tend to work in the background, carrying out actions seamlessly, based on coded instructions provided by your site in some instances, and in others, provided by the tools' host, undertaking actions on behalf of users.

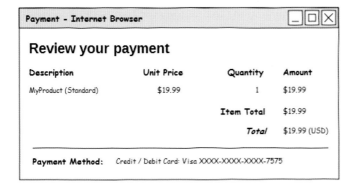

FIGURE 19-3: PayPal's IPN system allows sites to utilize payment information to process an order.

Here is this consumer's family tree and some issues it can encounter:

Relatives:	**Considerations:**
> Web applications	> Assumed coding structure
> Integral services	> API limitation considerations
> Automated scripts	> Human verification demands

Practical solutions

Server-side scripts don't interact with users but focus on getting a job done, yet we've all been affected by these scripts that are just doing their jobs without any recognition or appreciation. Whether you're allowing users to buy something from a store or to e-mail you a request for support, you can use these interpreted forms of interaction that demand no human intervention to give your site a more-involving experience. When these tools are being used, it's important to maintain them effectively or your site could become unstable.

For example, consider a PayPal IPN script that's been designed to generate a serial number upon confirmation of payment for a piece of software. It takes only one wrong incident to produce negative results; for example, if the IPN script is missing, if your site is down, or if you altered the script, which in turn causes previously processed payments to be ignored or handled incorrectly when queried. Getting code to be reliable is possible, but you also need to inform users when an error occurs, and ensure that they get support for the issue.

You also need to consider the API limitations that automated scripts can impose. It's a given that when you're using third-party tools from a service that you have no control over, the compatibility of your site's integration with that service is at the mercy of the provider's systems. If you must rely on other people, be prepared for any eventuality by monitoring sites for downtime (if you run a service) and being quick to respond to issues. Although there are plenty of reliable services out there, none can claim to be fully future-proof (and neither can we).

Reference To get an idea about how a status monitor lets users know about site maintenance that might affect the user's service, check out Skype's Heartbeat system status monitor at the following address. It really is a great example: `http://heartbeat.skype.com/`.

Provide a section or page on your site that notifies users about the site's status and about any issues or scheduled downtime with third-party services (such as when critical updates or maintenance is being undertaken). Also, try to provide an alternative service or try to keep as much of the site in action as possible, as visitors will avoid a service that's given them memorable negative experiences in the past; this is especially true for payment systems. Finally, if things do break down, provide ways for users to get immediate help.

Automated scripts can be helpful when used for the right reasons, but because of the level of abuse going on, spamming, content theft, and immoral acts are plaguing the Web and affecting user experiences worldwide. Although you can't really do much to future-proof your site against unwelcomed self-promoters and serial fraudsters, some attempts have been made to alleviate the situation through the use of CAPTCHAs, which ask users to verify that they're human. Unfortunately, those attempts haven't been very satisfactory.

CAPTCHAs are challenges for attempts to submit and access data. The CAPTCHA's goal is to ensure that a human and not another computer is making the request or response by requiring users solve a word, math, or picture puzzle. Although this seems like a clever idea, crackers tend to stay one step ahead by using OCR (optical character recognition), speech recognition, and spammers who are paid pennies to crack them. They make life harder for legitimate users, so they aren't worth considering as they do more harm than good.

Best practices

> If a social script breaks, ensure that users know how to report the issue.

> Check with the service producer if you require help with its API.

> Consider adding a system status page to notify users of potential issues.

> For critical system functions, be sure you have a fail-safe alternative.

> Do what you can to avoid spammers, but don't use CAPTCHAs.

Verification

Interestingly, when it comes to robotic interactions with sites, some tools are powered and regulated by people either verifying information or adding to collected materials. While these third-party tools (such as non-automated link directories, expert reviews, or child-safe parental filters; see Figure 19-4) are beyond the control of designers, they can influence users who come to depend on such quality-filtering tools. Designing a future-proofed site demands ensuring how the site appears on-screen and how other sites regard your content.

FIGURE 19-4: Parental filters can be included in browsers, operating systems, or within devices!

Here is this consumer's family tree and some issues it can encounter:

Relatives:	**Considerations:**
> Review sites	> Quality over quantity
> Directories	> Control and appeals
> Parental filters	> Software hardening

Practical solutions

Compatibility and the longevity of your site are closely linked to the availability of your site to individuals who aren't already aware of it. However, when thinking about services that can make or break a site's availability to an entire audience, surprisingly, few designers consider products like parental filters (such as those built into child-friendly browsers or operating systems) and other content-verification engines. It therefore makes sense to please these authorities if your users put any stock into what they say or block.

To keep your site from being blacklisted (thereby added to users' blocked sites filter list), you need to be careful about what you put on a site. For example, if age-inappropriate material is found your site could be labeled as a "for adults only" or "not safe for work" site. This, of course, isn't something you want to happen if you're trying to run a family-friendly site, so be sure to keep your site above suspicion. Methods of overcoming such situations involve avoiding bad language, alcohol, drug, or any age-inappropriate content.

When you receive a bad review, are blacklisted, or experience any kind of external factor that might influence or cause potential visitors to turn away from your site, try to deal with the situation as quickly and calmly as you can (avoiding drawing unwanted attention to yourself). If a site is blacklisted because of a security mistake, it may take time to resolve the false positive in security software; the same is also true for a site that's delisted from a search engine's index. Parental controls and review sites also require a tactful approach.

Note

People who use recommendation or review sites place a lot of trust in the experiences provided by third parties. What makes these tools so dangerous is they penetrate every search engine, browser, and device and can even influence a user's behavior! If a user reads a negative review of your site, it can sap your service for many years to come.

Your first call of action is to determine exactly why you ended up in the situation you're in. Although glitches can occur or a service may have mistakenly put your site in the penalty box, more often than not, it's the fault of the designer and can often be fixed by patching code exploits or removing bad code. If what occurred isn't your fault, appeal to the product's manufacturer for a resolution. Other than that, there's little else you can do, which can be very frustrating if a user's anti-malware guard cripples and blocks the site inappropriately.

Although this consumer-driven layer of the Web can throw all sorts of barriers at a site and its users, these influential services can affect popular browsers that are deemed "kiddie safe." Because Internet Explorer and third-party products contain filters that automatically scan for words or content that may be deemed unsuitable, sites containing the offending material could be blocked by the product or browser. Also, with malware detectors getting involved in the action, filtering is not something that you want to become associated with!

To help your site withstand filter products, you'll just have to conform to the rules they lay down, and hope that you don't become one of their casualties. If this doesn't sit well, just remember that sometimes the filters can become so dominating that an entire nation is banned from your site, so be thankful many of us aren't in that position. For example, just think about the great firewall of China or other traffic-shaping filters imposed by ISPs, and consider yourself lucky if you're not directly affected by them, as your users might be.

Best practices

> Avoid being blacklisted by steering clear of inappropriate subjects.

> If you are blacklisted, find out why and investigate how to resolve it.

> Don't sully the site's reputation by starting a war over bad reviews.

> Beware of word triggers that could make parental filters nervous.

> Make sites as trustworthy as possible to encourage user goodwill.

Factoring in the Human Element

Accommodating physical, intellectual, emotional, and social needs

THE END USER represents the one unique variable that no designer or developer can control. You may be able to produce beautiful code that works on a multitude of different devices, platforms, and browsers, but your site's users will ultimately determine the overall success or failure of a layout. In this chapter, I round out the book by noting the uniqueness of the individuals who interact with your site, humans being quite unpredictable creatures, and the importance of relating (generally) to a growing and ever-diversifying audience.

A Matter of Being Human

Before the days of accessibility, designers paid little attention to how individual factors and circumstances might affect users taking advantage of their sites. However, it's important to remember that users may be unable to use devices as you might anticipate, or perhaps they can't use certain pieces of hardware. The result is that usability can be hard to measure. Future-proof design demands a high regard for human-computer interactions (HCI) and an understanding of how users consume content, and the variables influencing their choices.

Users have unique ways of browsing sites. Accounting for this factor can be like trying to cater a site to billions of devices formed of the same basic structure but with a few unique characteristics thrown in. As people aren't machines, and don't act as such, you'll need to consider a wide range of variables that best show how certain types of users will identify with a site, instead of hoping that everyone will behave alike. For example, you could target audiences based on the variables of gender, age, and other demographics.

Note   The basics of human-computer interaction rarely change because human bodies have a limited set of input and output senses to relate with objects. This means that unless users evolve super powers, we know exactly what people have to work with but more importantly, what effects may be felt if their senses or a bodily function breaks down.

A number of variables relating to individual human abilities can affect how a visitor chooses to interact with your site. To help organize the wide range of accessibility issues that comprise this list, I've categorized everything in four distinct types of variables using a method known as the *PIES methodology* to deal with these issues. Put simply, you need to understand how *p*hysical, *i*ntellectual, *e*motional, and *s*ocial factors can limit, affect, or even cripple a user's ability to use a site, and what this means for your compatibility goals.

Beyond accessibility, at the business side of things, you must balance your "instincts" of what makes for a ubiquitous interface against the demands of your human clients (whom you'll battle against to implement many best practices) and the requirements of the site's users. Obviously, a human-centered approach is critical to the success of a Web site; your primary goal must be to please visitors in preference to search engines or the business you are doing the work for. If you can reach and maintain this healthy balance, good for you!

Ultimately, each site will have an audience, and its needs may well evolve over a period of time. What's important is that you continue to determine its needs and keep updating and maintaining the site accordingly (and if not you, the people who you designed for must carry out this role). Your unenviable job is to consider the "ifs and buts" of any situation and to weigh the pros and cons of approaches. Usability testing, accessibility audits, and statistics will certainly help, but you'll need to be vigilant to stay ahead of the competition!

Humanizing an interface

Consider if a visitor from France requires the very service you offer. He's in his mid-70s and could easily be classified as a "silver surfer." Enjoying his retirement, but with issues such as reduced vision and arthritis holding him back, he finds your site and begins exploring your offerings. He can speak, read, and write English, but it's not his native language. When he finds a term he doesn't understand, he's confused by the content. As French isn't offered on the site, he's forced to try to find the term elsewhere. Effectively, he's "lost in translation."

Culture and the study of ethnography and sociology can teach web designers a lot because individuals who browse your site rarely fit into one category. Although you can group users based on shared experiences, or things they have in common (such as nationality or age), don't stereotype them unless the statistics and data you have about your users support the need to address a common, shared issue. Designers often inadvertently imagine that a user's situation is similar to their own, which can lead to misconceptions about visitors' needs.

Medical conditions such as reduced vision can be aided by a browser. In your visitor's case, he could try to use the Text Size submenu in Internet Explorer. However, because your site uses pixel-based text sizing rather than EM units, the visitor finds that the options do nothing! Confused and frustrated, he turns to the browser's zoom facility that works well. Unfortunately, he must now scroll and pan the screen in order to see everything, and this constant movement doesn't help his arthritis. The moral of the story: Be considerate of a user's individual situation.

Physical Conditions

When it comes to accessibility and the successful navigation of a site, physical conditions tend to be the most intrusive factors. If sites don't match the needs of users with physical impairments, such as those with visual impairments (see Figure 20-1), the site could be in violation of disability laws worldwide. Websites must be designed to allow the disabled community to access content and services. Being accessible in such situations offers the benefit of a potentially larger visitor base, and it can increase your compatibility levels.

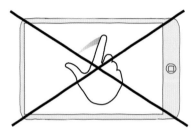

FIGURE 20-1: If a user can't see a touch screen, navigating one becomes difficult (though not impossible).

Here is this consumer's family tree and some issues it can encounter:

Relatives:	**Considerations:**
> Visual impairment	> Specialist interaction needs
> Auditory limitations	> Learning curve adjustment
> Motor functionality	> Fallback aid dependencies
> Speech impairment	
> Seizure disability	

Practical solutions

Depending on the tools provided by an environment, individuals with physical disabilities can encounter all sorts of direct complications when trying to access a site. Extreme visual impairments may be equal to that of using a monochrome screen (total color blindness) or working without a monitor. Deafness could be like working without speakers. Even motor impairments could restrict users to speech-only navigation. With these inhibiting factors being equal to a loss of hardware function, you must ensure accessibility needs are met.

Although the practice of ensuring accessibility in HCI is similar to dealing with devices that have practical limitations or the inability to do things in the same way many users are used to, the human factor of these often difficult conditions makes the need for solutions evermore critical. To ensure your site works for varying accessibility needs, the best thing you can do is get your site up-to-scratch with WCAG (the Web Content Accessibility Guidelines) and be accommodating to how such users would navigate and read your site.

Getting to know and love any interface takes users' time and energy, but coupled with a physical impairment, and if the features they need aren't provided, the process to achieve simple goals can appear to be an endless struggle. Although it's true that accessibility tools do a pretty amazing job (it's wonderful to think that severely disabled citizens can browse Wikipedia or Google at their leisure, without being inhibited), offering users some in-page assistive enhancements can make the task of browsing around a site both easier and faster.

Reference

Writing accessibility statements isn't that hard, but be sure to document the features you provide to help different devices. It's about being both proud of and practical in your work. As the following site shows, if you can write a jargon-free statement, your users will benefit: `http://juicystudio.com/article/writing-a-good-accessibility-statement.php`.

The most important thing a site can do to combat the issues that disabled users experience is to double up on everything. By this I mean that sites shouldn't just be interacted with via one browser or one input control or one type of accessibility aid or a single input or output medium. Broaden your scope to include a number of fallbacks and alternate mechanisms to give users a choice in content consumption. In addition, offer users pop-up tooltips and navigation aids like breadcrumb trails, calls to action, and a decent accessibility statement.

You know that things can go wrong rather quickly if someone's device doesn't match the specification you demand or their connection isn't as fast as you'd like. But for users with physical limitations in their interactions with computers, the need for a good fallback plan is even more critical because users can't replace the part of them that's broken or inhibited, and there's no simple way that many users can just struggle through the site and make the best of a poorly crafted situation. Being accessible, therefore, is central to compatibility.

Every site of any reasonable size or complexity should come with documentation or a user manual that's easy to follow and that describes everything a beginner needs to know to use the service on offer, whether it's an accessibility statement you provide or a getting-started guide with in-site functionality listed (consider a popular site and how useful its support pages are). Offer videos, tutorials, and readme files if you feel they'll aid users, but ensure that you offer help files and continually improve the quality of this material for your users.

Best practices

> Take any requests for accessibility changes from users seriously.

> Offer a statement of accessibility showing what the site supports.

> Reduce the learning curve by providing helpful aids within the site.

> If you provide a web application, ensure that it's well documented.

> Check that the site still functions if human senses aren't available.

Intellectual Challenges

Although physical disabilities account for a great number of variables that can influence a site's "user compatibility," the readability and navigability of information can also lead to issues about how the environment can be used. A user's ability to memorize important details and understand your content in order to make informed choices present a range of potential issues that affects HCI (shown in Figure 20-2). More importantly, the number of users affected by these issues is likely to be higher than those affected by physical disabilities.

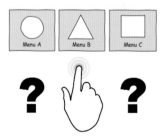

FIGURE 20-2: Complicated choices can affect a visitor's ability to select options with accuracy.

Here is this consumer's family tree and some issues it can encounter:

Relatives:	**Considerations:**
> Memory impairments	> Recollection of revisiting
> Learning difficulties	> Use of content linguistics
> Cognitive processing	> Choice or content fatigue

Practical solutions

There are a number of considerations to take into account when dealing with the human "intellectual" variable, but the one that seems to affect a great many people in a negative way is memory, and more specifically, how visitors manage to keep finding their way around the rat maze we refer to as a website. The importance of hierarchy and your site's information architecture cannot be understated, but the necessity of revisiting pages can lead to a few complications if you don't maintain the site or handle the situation correctly.

Being able to find your site among the many others that get stored in a browser's history index can be complicated. Although browsers deal with their history databases differently, if your site doesn't have a sensible title and a memorable domain name, more restrictive browsers may limit the chance of locating a site in the user's activity logs. (After all, can you quickly find a non-bookmarked site you visited months ago?) Useful titles will serve users well if they choose to add your site to their favorites list (or on a social bookmarking site).

Because sites are so dominated by language, your visitors' ability to comprehend what you write is important. Whether they're challenged by something like dyslexia, are still learning the language used on your site, or simply can't understand the jargon or buzzwords shown on-screen, you don't want to leave users without direction, understanding, or the ability to find what they're looking for. The issue of understanding your site's content, no matter how easy to see it may be, is referred to as *lingual incompatibility*, and it affects a lot of people.

Tip

Reductionism (known as the method of boiling down a site's contents into something more streamlined) is something I highly recommend with content. Because sites may have a limited amount of space to work with (in small viewport sizes) and scrolling for hours isn't much fun, saying what you mean and designing succinctly are worthwhile.

If you've ever tried talking to someone who doesn't understand the language you speak, you know that even with the latest equipment and the means to render a site, the content is useless to someone who can't read it. Ways to overcome such a problem include offering translations (or links to something like Google Translate), reducing the amount of fluff, buzzwords, or technical lingo that requires a background in the subject, and using things like explaining the meaning of abbreviations or acronyms (via title attributes in HTML).

In addition, too much content of any type on a site can be equally problematic. Besides the fact that older devices like featurephones may restrict the size of pages that will load (for the user's sake), as may a search engine or social network, because sites can use more than text within a page, at least consider offering more expressive (and condensed) content that could raise the interest levels of your visitors. If an image can say 1,000 words, what could a well-produced, informative 5-minute video say? Potentially, it could say quite a lot.

The ideal text-to-image-to-media ratio differs depending on the site and the needs of the content and target audience. Some people prefer to read everything in text; others may want a bit of media to help them absorb information (for example, if they're more visual than textual learners). But the important thing is to use content with care and to avoid presenting too much of it at any one time. If users suffer from information overload, they could end up with choice paralysis and this could impact their ability to browse the site!

Best practices

> To help jog a user's memory, provide signposts and directions throughout.

> Provide a proper title; it'll come in handy for when users search the site.

> Avoid using technical jargon or buzzwords that will confuse non-geeks.

> Match the text-to-image-to-media ratio to the type of site and audience.

> Avoid information overload; try limiting the number of objects per page.

Emotional Factors

The human emotion variable is rather interesting. Emotion gives designers the opportunity to encourage user interactions (Figure 20-3). Though this variable often gets less attention when we talk about it in terms of disabilities, emotion is deeply ingrained in psychological and sociological behavior, so it's important to consider the effect of emotional experiences upon our interfaces. If a user suffers from a disorder like anxiety attacks, the effects of the emotional variable and its side effects will likely influence any interactions with your site.

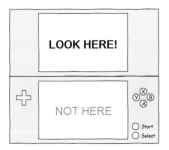

FIGURE 20-3: While we can influence actions with psychology, we must avoid being too manipulative.

Here is this consumer's family tree and some issues it can encounter:

Relatives:	Considerations:
> Emotional stability	> Attention prioritization
> Attention and focus	> Design lead perception
> Psychological state	> Addictive personalities

Practical solutions

When catering your designs to your visitors' needs, consider how to pull their eyes to the right sections of your pages at the right time. Be pragmatic in your design approaches and avoid doing anything to make users regret visiting your site. Seek attention subtly and with enough finesse that users will naturally accept the usefulness of the content. The goal you are trying to aim for is to have a site that influences users in all the right ways, rewards the loyalty and persistence of your visitors, and avoids causing undue stress or anxiety.

To ensure that your interface doesn't dramatically affect your site's usability, avoid using lightboxes or other centralized regions of attention on devices that have small screens (where the effect will be lost). Additionally, try to keep things that a user needs to see at the top of the page (think of the fold). Other than that, follow traditional design principles, such as enlarging text for dominance and using color to form psychological associations. The more subtly your interfaces flow, the more dramatic satisfaction levels may become.

Being compatible with a wide range of situations will often leave a site performing better in some areas than it does in others. Of course, although you'd rather enhance your work than design for the lowest common denominator (as you don't want the site to look like a cave painting), you have to put the brakes on occasionally to avoid landing in a situation that could harm users. Additionally, if users don't have a plug-in or scripting available, make the most of the situation, and try not to just offer them a bare-bones, ugly alternative.

Reference

Injecting humor into a website can make a negative experience bearable. If you stop supporting a variable or can't resolve a quirk, put a happy spin on it. Examples of 404 errors being given a lighthearted response can be seen here: `http://404lab.com`.

Here's a solution for dealing with the less-elegant fallbacks or alternatives you provide (like that watered-down layout for Internet Explorer 6 that made your beautiful jQuery-powered eye candy explode into an ash cloud): Don't just leave things looking basic or bland if you need to offer an alternative; be creative with this opportunity for a unique experience. Just because you'll occasionally have to degrade a site doesn't mean that the final experience can't look good. Don't make the mistake of just covering your behind and just bailing out.

The final aspect of emotional design that has big future-proofing potential is the concept of game mechanics. It is taken from the video game industry, and the ability to win points, prizes, badges, or recognition for your achievements when participating in a site has proven to be highly addictive. The downside of this addictive behavior is that it can cause your site's members to become overly competitive, adding tension and excitement (which could then lead to bad behavior). On the other hand, it can help build communities quickly.

Enriching your site with features that reward good behavior and useful contributions may seem like a funny way to go about ensuring that your site will last into the future. But with interactivity being high on the agenda, and attentions being so displaced online, you may want to take notice of these tools. Don't just think of them as being limited to things like forums. What if users got points or prizes for spotting bugs, suggesting a feature, being the first to enter your site on a new device, or something else? The possibilities are endless!

Best practices

> Make the most of the users' tools and direct their attention where it's needed.

> Don't use aggressive advertising tactics; they'll only increase stress levels.

> Use positive reinforcement to encourage interactivity and try to be friendly.

> Try to make interfaces a little more engaging; users appreciate the effort.

> Be aware of the side effects associated with reward-focused interactivity.

Social Expectations

When people get together, in addition to having their individual needs, they form group expectations and needs. Accounting for this behavior helps you gain broad appeal. By considering the effects of a group upon your site, you can account for more variables of human behavior, which could potentially affect how people use your site. Perhaps users want to offer you some insightful feedback (see Figure 20-4). Perhaps visitors are looking to discover like-minded users. All in all, communication is a variable of no insignificance.

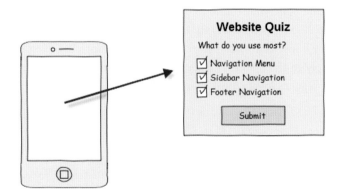

FIGURE 20-4: Visitors want to be heard, and they want to communicate. Keep the two-way channel open!

Here is this consumer's family tree and some issues it can encounter:

Relatives:	**Considerations:**
> Group dynamics	> Encouraging interaction
> Physical environment	> Antisocial behavior
> Community power	> Cross-cultural increases

Practical solutions

One primary route to ensuring that your site will withstand the test of time is to iterate and continue to improve upon what you offer, and the main way in which you can achieve this goal is, of course, through testing. Although it's perfectly fine to break open your big box of gadgets and emulators and test your work using everything you can find, your users can offer you a unique testing opportunity. They probably have a bunch of gadgets you don't have and they're in a position to let you know how well these devices function on the site.

To gain committed, friendly followers who'll help you improve your service, encourage interaction from the onset and build your community with a personal touch. Don't start off by creating a forum and hoping people will fly in all at once (if visitors see a dead forum from the outset, they'll just run away); start with smaller things like blog comments and remember to reply to them so that the conversation is not one-sided. After you're sure that you have a regular, loyal crowd, you can then think about moving onto grander projects.

Of course, in any community, there will always be users who'll try to cause trouble or push boundaries. Although you can be somewhat lenient and tolerant to a point (if you have that level of patience), deal with issues of a more serious nature immediately. If, for example, a user posts illegally copied content on the site, it would only take a DMCA (copyright) takedown notice to your host or Google to have your site suspended. At which point, compatibility issues will very likely be the very least of your problems.

Note　The great thing about encouraging social interaction is that it cultivates content for you. Consider the average web forum where you end up with hundreds or even thousands of posts giving advice, feedback, or support along with general interuser chatter.

You'll need to do your best to stay on top of things, as you'll be held responsible for the content that makes its way onto your site, making moderation mandatory. As the owner and/or designer of a site, you must ensure that the site's community is handled with care and you stay on its good side. Online communities that are allowed to get out of control can cause plenty of harm, but the ones that are cultivated correctly may become part of the site's extended family, serving you well in the future if you ever expand your offerings.

As time goes by, the users who frequent your site will change, and as new generations of budding members visit your site using the devices and tools that are popular at that time (each with new demands and expectations of your site), you should already have a solid backbone to begin extending your site's flexibility. This social interaction and commentary may attract other users, as you increase the site's flexibility. Who knows, maybe they'll add your site to their regular browsing list, and your site will continue to evolve around them.

Obviously, when you receive advice regarding changes or potentially useful updates from individual visitors, you must place their opinions and unique perspectives alongside those of your site's larger community of users. It's a bad idea to make changes at the whim of a single user's request, if that change could potentially have a negative effect on other users. By leveraging your community, your site, social networks, analytics, and the other useful variables at your disposal, you'll have a reason to keep aiming for a future-proof design.

Best practices

> Try to build a relaxed community early on to encourage repeat visitors.

> Get to know your audience; they're the ones who make your site popular.

> Deal with vandalism, spam, or harmful behavior quickly and appropriately.

> Reward your loyal visitors if possible, as they'll stand by you in the future.

> Keep referring to your visitors for improvements on a timely basis.

Index

6066 035